Teaching What You Don't Know

Therese Huston

Harvard University Press

Cambridge, Massachusetts, and London, England   2009

Library of Congress Cataloging-in-Publication Data

Huston, Therese.
Teaching what you don't know / Therese Huston.
    p.   cm.
Includes bibliographical references and index.
ISBN 978-0-674-03580-5 (alk. paper)
1. College teaching.   2. Effective teaching.
3. Learning.   I. Title.
LB2331.H875 2009
378.1′25—dc22   2009016140

Contents

Introduction

Zach is a tenure-track professor at a small liberal arts college. He exudes confidence. He is young and looks even younger with his curly hair and hip wire-rimmed glasses. Zach teaches chemistry and cares deeply about teaching it well, so he volunteered to teach a new course for freshmen to draw more students into the sciences. The challenge? The course is a stretch for him. It's called "The Chemistry and Biology of Fat." With an eye-catching title, the class has quickly filled and has a waitlist of hopeful students. But Zach doesn't know a whole semester's worth of material about fat. His expertise is in proteins, fat's more respected cousin. He has to learn about trans fats and saturated fats, olive oil and lard. As someone who once worked in a five-star restaurant, he finds the course great fun, but he's perpetually preparing for class: "When I'm lucky, I'm a few days ahead of my students. But some days, like today, I swear I'm just ten minutes ahead of them. That's not comfortable, goodness knows it's not comfortable, but somehow it's just enough."[1]

Then there's Andy, an adjunct instructor in education who is about to start his second year at a large state university. Andy had a fantastic first year—he earned high student evaluations in his seventy-student "Introduction to Education" course, and the department is advertising a tenure-track position in his specialty. But Andy had a terrible summer. The department chair asked him to teach the least popular course in the department, "Research Design and Statistics." No one wants to teach it. Students don't want to take it. Andy agreed to cover not one but two sections to be a team player, even though he's never used half the methods in the textbook. He hasn't said a word to the chair because he doesn't want to look incompetent or whiny (or worse yet, both). What does he do? Andy spends the summer with a stack of statistics textbooks, with *Statistics for Dummies* carefully hidden in the pile.

Zach and Andy aren't alone. College and university faculty members often find themselves having to teach what they don't know. They have to get up in front of their classes and explain something that they learned just last week, or two days ago, or, in the worst-case scenario, that same morning over a very hurried breakfast.

But stories like these can't be found in books on teaching, most of which begin with two premises: (1) to teach well, you need to have mastered the subject matter; and (2) that's still not enough. This is a well-intentioned scare tactic, but it's scary in the wrong ways. It's meant to jolt arrogant faculty members into paying attention to how good instructors teach and how all students learn, but it makes the rest of us question whether we really know what we're talking about.

Can you be a good teacher before you've mastered the subject matter? Or perhaps while you're mastering it? I believe the answer is yes. Plenty of faculty members teach outside of their expertise and do it well. In telling their stories, this book shows what we can learn from their successes, which are many, as well as from their failures, which are few but memorable.

Skeptics will concede that yes, newer faculty like Zach and Andy will find themselves teaching what they don't know, but they'll confidently contend that it's just a phase, a rite of passage. Eventually young professors will mature out of that stage. After all, one perk of the academic lifestyle is that we teach in our expertise for most of our careers.

Do we? Let's consider Susan, a finance department chair at a medium-sized comprehensive university. Susan worked at Prudential for almost a decade before becoming a professor. She's smart and she's devoted. The department has done well with her at the helm, but because of university budget cuts her requests for new tenure-track lines have been repeatedly turned down. To keep things running smoothly, Susan covers for her colleagues when they go on sabbatical or need time off, and she's taught everything from "Fundamentals of Real Estate" to "Global Economics," even though her specialty is retirement planning. "I am hardly a macro-person," Susan confides. "I'll teach it, but let's just say that the chairman of the Federal Reserve isn't calling me for advice." Susan never expected to be teaching new courses so late in her career. After complaining for a few moments, she leans forward in her chair, smiles, and says, "Once I stop learning a new textbook every year, who knows what might happen? I might just get some research done."

These three instructors face different problems, but they share a common challenge: they all have to stretch their expertise to teach their classes. Each of them is quick to admit how much they are learning in the process. Given a choice, however, they would prefer to be back in classes where they are confident of their knowledge and can take students' questions with ease.

Let's consider one more example, and a vexing problem. Cheryl is a very experienced teacher who recently became an adjunct dance instructor at a highly competitive drama school. Cheryl has been a professional dancer and choreographer for over thirty years and has enjoyed an international career on Broadway and the West End. She's a tall, lithe African-American woman whose posture makes you sit up straighter as you talk with her. In her early fifties, she was ready to pursue a less physically taxing career, so she turned to college teaching. Most of her students at the drama school were majoring in dance or musical theater, so teaching these talented students felt like choreographing a small off-Broadway production.

But as part of her university contract, Cheryl was also required to teach an "Introduction to Dance" class twice a year. It was a course for nonmajors who needed to fill a fine arts requirement, nicknamed "Ballet for Biologists" by some. Most of the students had never set foot in a dance studio, and many had never seen a live dance performance. Cheryl enjoyed their enthusiasm and their ability to laugh at themselves, but they were not the devoted dancers she was accustomed to teaching. She couldn't figure out how to give them feedback without sounding too harsh, and she had no patience for students who didn't practice between classes. "They didn't view 'dance' as homework," she says, with widened eyes and an exasperated flurry of her hands.

In this case, Cheryl was teaching something that she knew extremely well—dance. She was highly skilled in motivating a certain type of learner but frustrated and dumbfounded when asked to teach a very different kind of student, a more typical twenty-year-old who wasn't used to having a live drummer in class and who was not in it for the long haul. The challenge for Cheryl was not *what* she taught but *whom*.

These examples are just a few of many. College and university instructors across the country are regularly teaching beyond their skill set and beyond their comfort zone—teaching something they don't know or someone they don't know at different points in their careers. They are not absent-minded professors who forget the material from one year to the next; nor are they self-absorbed academics who ignore what's happening in their field. Most are good teachers, in many cases award-winning teachers. But for a variety of reasons, they need to teach themselves the material so that they can immediately turn around and teach it to someone else. Or they need to figure out how to close the gap between themselves and different kinds of students.

The idea that college and university faculty would teach a subject they haven't mastered will not sit comfortably with everyone in academia; nor will it sit comfortably with parents or students. Some might even claim that it's an oxymoron: by definition, we need to know something before we can teach it.

But let's be clear. It's not that faculty members are teaching courses they are completely unqualified to teach. For the most part, economists are not teaching Victorian literature; nor are voice coaches grading physics labs. (I say "for the most part" because you're about to meet a few people in this book who are completely out of their element.) The system is not arbitrary or random. Department chairs do not play a blindfolded game of pin the tail on the donkey when they do their course assignments. Departments still hire faculty with the best fit in mind, and they try to match each instructor's strengths with the needs of the curriculum.

What *is* happening is that instructors are teaching skills and content beyond their area of expertise, often in their own departments. For example, a biology instructor may be teaching a large, introductory course that covers everything from cells to evolution, from bread mold to macaque monkeys. Such a broad survey of the field requires the instructor to learn (or relearn) a variety of terms, update theories that are now outdated, and go looking for vivid examples. Given how rapidly some fields in biology are advancing, she may not have had exposure to some areas at all. Freshwater ecologists, for instance, don't necessarily know the latest research in primate genetics.

Instructors also find themselves teaching what they don't know in general education courses. An English instructor and specialist in Norse mythology may find that he has to teach an interdisciplinary writing course required of all first-year students, the quintessential "First-Year Writing Seminar." Students are promised an opportunity to work closely with a real professor in a small class on a thought-provoking topic. Evidently Norse mythology isn't thought-provoking enough, so our English professor is teaching a course on "Banned Books" instead. The website for the seminar features a picture of students with their desks turned into a circle and a bearded professor in a sweater vest listening intently. (You can almost feel everyone growing smarter.) But the course description doesn't mention that this professor spent the entire summer trying to become an authority on books he'd never read before. And the website doesn't reveal what he was thinking in that discussion circle as the photo was being taken, namely, "When *did* James Joyce write that? Oh, please don't ask me when he wrote that."

What's going on? Why are professors teaching beyond their expertise? Is this primarily an issue for new hires and junior faculty, or is it something that even mid-career and senior faculty face on a regular basis?

The problem is not that instructors are rushing into their academic positions unprepared. On the contrary, in most fields, to-day's junior faculty members spend more years in graduate school than many of their senior colleagues. For example, students in the physical sciences are taking 12 percent longer to complete their doctorates than their predecessors did twenty-five years ago, and graduates in education are taking 17 percent longer.[2] If graduate students are spending more time accumulating knowledge before they become faculty members, why are so many instructors still learning the material as they teach it?

That's one of the questions this book aims to answer. Who's teaching this way, why are they doing it, and how on earth can they do it well? Not to mention, do they still enjoy their jobs? As one professor aptly put it, "Those of us in academe, we're not terribly well paid. So if this isn't fun, if this isn't an adventure, then you really should think of doing something else."

As I researched this book, I approached roughly thirty-five college and university instructors and asked if they've ever taught outside their expertise. A handful were puzzled and said, "Never." A few famous faculty sent polite replies, thanking me for the invitation but saying that they teach only their favorite classes, on topics they know best. But most faculty jumped at the opportunity to talk. They started telling me their stories before I could switch on my digital recorder. Famous people. People who aren't yet famous. I quickly discovered that teaching what you don't know isn't the lonely plight of the newly hired Ph.D. but a common dilemma for faculty at all stages of their careers.

I also discovered that few educators talk about this side of teaching. Even fewer write about it. I decided it was time for that to change. Faculty need strategies for effectively teaching what they don't know, and this book digs through the research literature in education, cognitive science, and organizational be-havior to identify those strategies. Fantastic teaching *can* happen when you teach on the cusp of your comfort zone. It may not be the world's most comfortable teaching, but students can learn as much, if not more, than they can in classes where you're teach-ing from the core of your expertise.[3]

1 The Growing Challenge

Teaching what you don't know is an increasingly common reality for a majority of academics. The only instructors who may be exempt from the pressure to teach beyond their area of expertise are senior tenured faculty members at research universities and some part-time adjunct faculty. The first group spends most of their time doing research; tenured faculty at doctoral institutions with very high research productivity—particularly *senior* tenured faculty at these schools—often "buy out" their teaching requirements with grant money and teach very little. In fact, research shows that approximately 50 percent of professors at research-intensive universities teach less than four hours a week.[1] When they do teach, they often choose graduate or undergraduate seminars in their specialty. By definition, they are teaching what they know best.

The second group of faculty who enjoy the luxury of teaching in their specialty are adjuncts hired as part-time specialists, the "rock stars" of the department who are prized for their topical, real-world expertise. For example, a chief of police might offer a course in criminal justice. Likewise, a violinist for the local symphony might teach music lessons, or a former CEO might coach students on executive leadership skills. These experts are hired exclusively for their specialized knowledge and might teach only one or two courses a year.

Both groups do relatively little teaching. The remaining faculty—those who teach the bulk of undergraduate and graduate courses across the United States—are routinely asked to stretch their knowledge base in new or unfamiliar directions.

Why Teach What You Don't Know?

In researching this book, I formally interviewed twenty-eight faculty and administrators and discussed the general idea of "teaching what you don't know" with many more. As you hear their stories, you'll discover that faculty teach outside of their comfort zone for a variety of personal, professional, and even philosophical reasons. Nonetheless, I found that most people venture beyond their area of expertise because of (1) where they teach; (2) what they teach; or (3) the way higher education works. I've taken the liberty of adding a fourth reason: although no one mentioned it directly, mounting top-down pressures from administrators will most likely drive more faculty to teach this way in the near future.

Where You Teach

Not surprisingly, many faculty at smaller institutions teach outside their area of expertise on a regular basis. If you're in a four- or five-member department at a liberal arts college or comprehensive university, then you'll probably be picking up some courses in topics that you didn't study in graduate school. Mike Flynn, a linguistics professor at Carleton College, in Minnesota, was the sole instructor in his department for years. Of the twenty-five different courses he's taught, only five have been in his specialty. Like Susan, the finance professor, he has taught basically every course in the catalog, from "Language and the Brain" to "The Structure of Japanese." Mike explains, "Over the past twenty years, I've taught on average one new course a year, sometimes more than that. . . . It's not easy, but I've learned a ton."

What You Teach

As we've seen, some faculty teach in general education programs or cross-disciplinary seminars that push them outside of their knowledge base. Codrina Popescu is a good example. She's an assistant professor of chemistry at Ursinus College outside of Philadelphia and teaches chemistry most of the time. But she has also taught a first-year writing seminar called "The Common Intellectual Experience." She found herself teaching the Declaration of Independence and reading slave narratives, two topics never covered in her chemistry training.

But this isn't just an issue for faculty teaching cross-disciplinary courses or for faculty at small institutions. Most departments offer courses that are so broad that the instructor can't be an expert in every topic. Maybe it's a methods course, like the one that Andy, whom we met in the Introduction, agreed to teach, or a broad introductory survey course, such as the "Western Civilization" course that's a staple in most history departments. Dan Simons, a psychology professor at the University of Illinois at Urbana-Champaign, teaches the all-encompassing course "Introduction to Experimental Psychology." His expertise is in cognitive psychology and visual awareness, but when Dan teaches the introductory course, he covers everything from why people dream to why they make bad decisions, topics far outside his expertise. "In some ways, we're all faking it," he acknowledges. "There has to be a little overconfidence going into those kinds of classes."[2]

This isn't just how some *courses* work; I was surprised to learn that it's how some *disciplines* work. Take law, for example. Erin Buzuvis, as assistant professor of law at Western New England College, explained: "In law school, you're always teaching what you don't know. For starters, I teach 'Property.' The nuts and bolts of this course go back to feudalism, the theory and philosophy behind why this side of the yard is mine and why that side is yours. But you don't have to think about feudalism when you sit down with a client. Honestly, there's a huge chasm between what we teach and what we actually practiced."

Of course, some instructors teach outside their specialty out of sheer enjoyment. They could choose the well-worn, easy path, but they prefer to challenge themselves. John Bean, a professor of English at Seattle University and the author of *Engaging Ideas,* believes that teaching new material makes him more intellectually vibrant and more able to engage students in critical thinking. "I've never wanted to get comfortable with my lecture notes and just get more efficient at teaching the same thing," he admits as we talk in his office. "Very early on, I would notice I had colleagues that would always use the same texts in an 'Introduction to Literature' class. And it saved them a lot of time because they didn't have to reinvent it each year." John leans back in his chair and laughs. "But I've never done that! Each time I've taught a literature course I've wanted to have different readings. The teaching that I try to do is not simply the expert giving information to the novice; I'm teaching them how to make knowledge out of stuff that's confusing." He can model for his students how to wrestle with something confusing because he's still struggling with it himself.

The Way Higher Education Works

Some people teach what they don't know because that's the way the system works. It's certainly not the goal of higher education to funnel faculty into this situation, but three circumstances in particular lead to that unintended result.

First, for some faculty, a gap exists between the scope of their research and their teaching.[3] Scholarly research is typically narrow and specialized. A professor can dig deeper and deeper into the same topic for years, sometimes decades if the funding (and passion) lasts. By contrast, teaching topics change each day or every few days. And the best teachers try to think broadly about what their students already know. Does that background knowledge come from taking an introductory class, from reading Google news, or from having too many family dinners with racist Uncle Lou? The most talented instructors try to draw on that knowledge; they build on accurate pieces of information that students already know, and they transform the inaccurate pieces into something more informed and complex.[4] But anticipating all that background knowledge takes very broad thinking.

Let's imagine a professor of medicine specializing in genetic blood disorders who divides her time between teaching and research. In her lab, she is studying how to reprogram adult stem cells so that they behave like embryonic stem cells. She works with mice and receives a half million dollars each year to study sickle-cell anemia. The knowledge, resources, and facilities required to conduct this kind of research are highly specialized.

When this same professor is teaching a pathology course, she spends, at most, one class period on sickle-cell anemia. She might report on the hypothetical research study just described, but that would take maybe ten minutes of a ninety-minute class (maybe thirty minutes if she indulges herself). For the rest of class, she needs to brush up on other, general information that future physicians care about, such as how sickle-cell anemia can be diagnosed and, just as important, misdiagnosed. She has to be ready to answer wide-ranging questions, such as whether taking iron supplements helps combat the disease (that's controversial) or whether people with sickle-cell anemia are more likely to catch the flu (that's evidently true).[5] The knowledge she needs to answer a cutting-edge research question from a graduate student in her lab or from a colleague is relatively focused and predictable, but the knowledge she needs to answer questions from students in her class is broad and expansive.

And that's just a single class on anemia, the topic she knows better than any other. For the rest of the term, she'll be teaching about other diseases—topics that she knows less well but that probably matter much more than anemia to the ninety students in that lecture hall. After all, most students will treat more patients with heart disease and cancer than with sickle-cell anemia.[6]

What's worrisome to all those who care deeply about student learning and faculty sanity is that the divide between teaching and research will grow as academics experience more pressure to publish.[7] The trend at most institutions has been to up the research ante. Even instructors at community colleges, who have traditionally focused exclusively on teaching, are being pressured to develop research agendas.[8] If everyone in your field is doing more research and you have limited time and money for scholarship (and who doesn't?), you'll need to pursue more specialized research questions that are feasible, within reach, and publishable. As you create a specialized niche for yourself, you move further away from the broader topics you teach.[9]

But the problem doesn't stop there. This spiraling number of journals and articles yields a continuous flow of new information. I teach courses in cognitive neuroscience, and I struggle to keep up with the latest technology and findings. More research and more knowledge also mean longer textbooks. Even volume 1 of the *Norton Anthology of English Literature* grew 304 pages between the sixth and eighth editions.[10] This proliferation of information can be exciting, but what does it mean for our teaching?

Second, in some cases, new faculty and adjuncts are driven to teach outside their areas of expertise simply because of diminished job opportunities. The employment situation is like a bully lurking in the corner, threatening to beat you up if you don't give up your milk money and the classes you'd most like to teach.

When a faculty member first joins a new department, the chair typically assigns the set of courses that, at least on paper, overlaps with the department's needs and the instructor's area of expertise. Because the department's needs are broad and the instructor's expertise is narrow, new hires are often assigned to teach a few courses that are only remotely related to their specialty. A specialist in modern Japanese anime, for example, has to teach all the Asian art classes, even though she knows nothing about China's Ming dynasty. That's not to say that new hires are entirely surprised by their teaching assignments. But forewarned does not mean forearmed.

As we heard in Andy's story earlier, faculty in their first few years can be assigned to teach courses that their colleagues could teach but do not wish to teach. I hear this regularly about research methods and statistics courses. Even if no one says it out loud, the reasoning among established faculty seems to be, "I've carried the burden in the past, so now it's someone else's turn."[11]

So what are the prospects for future faculty? Overall, newly hired faculty members have fewer good choices today than their colleagues had five or ten years ago. True, the job market changes each year for most disciplines. Any given year could be a good hiring year for one discipline and a bad year for another.

But trust me, if you were to ask people in the market for an academic job, most would not say that they're swimming in a sea of options. The important question is not, "How *many* new faculty positions have been created?" but "What *kinds* of new positions are being created?" Colleges and universities are not making as many long-term commitments to new faculty as they once did. Ideal jobs, the kind most of us dreamed about when we first picked an academic career, are drying up.

The numbers provide a better picture of the problem. For starters, academic career options are decreasing because most new positions are part-time. Between 2003 and 2005, there were approximately 116,000 new faculty positions created, but 71,000 of these positions (or about 61 percent) were part-time.[12] This does still leave more than 40,000 full-time jobs, and that's a lot of new positions. But the number of tenure-track full-time jobs is dwindling. By 2003 most new full-time positions, a whopping 59 percent, were designated for adjuncts.[13]

So of those 116,000 new professors hired in two years, how many were actually tenure-track faculty? The number is very discouraging—only 18,000, or 16 percent of the total, were offered tenure-track positions.[14] The remaining 84 percent were hired into either part-time or full-time adjunct teaching jobs.

You might be thinking, "Being an adjunct isn't so bad." I won't weigh the relative advantages and disadvantages of being an adjunct here. My current concern is that adjuncts, who make up five-sixths of the new hires in this example, have fewer choices than their tenure-track peers when it comes to teaching. Adjuncts are often hired to teach at the common denominator of knowledge for the department. If, for example, a mathematics department needed to offer more sections of a pre-calculus course, they would probably recruit an adjunct to teach them. The adjunct might teach five sections of pre-calculus a year. It's irrelevant that his research interests are in the mathematical properties of tsunamis and hurricanes. Most departments wouldn't ask him to teach a course in that very cool area of applied math even though everyone in the department can teach pre-calculus and only this adjunct can teach the math of rogue waves.

From the point of view of the tenured faculty in the department, this approach to course assignment makes perfect sense. Perhaps some of those tenured math professors also teach pre-calculus from time to time, but most of them don't want to give up their favorite courses for every talented adjunct who comes along. Senior faculty cater more to the teaching interests of their new tenure-track faculty because they want them to stay. They probably want their adjuncts to stay, too, but they invest more time and money to fill a tenure line.[15] On many levels it's practical to reserve the prime teaching choices (and there probably aren't many in the first place) for tenure-track and tenured faculty.

A third frustrating component of the higher education system that leaves some faculty teaching what they don't know is the disorienting impact of graduate school.[16] New faculty fresh from graduate school are likely to believe that they are teaching what they don't know. On the one hand, this perception is grounded in reality; these instructors often need to learn new material when they teach broad survey courses like "World Religions" or "Introduction to Engineering." On the other hand, this perception is exaggerated by graduate school. If you have just left a role that was exclusively focused on your own sliver of research, you probably have a heightened sense that you are teaching beyond your knowledge base. After all, you just left a research experience where the standard for "knowing something" was extremely high and your tenacity for minutiae was eventually rewarded. Even though graduate students moan and groan about these impossible standards, they nonetheless internalize them.

When new Ph.D.s show up for the first day of class in their new jobs, these inflated expectations can cause real problems. New faculty can quickly become overwhelmed as they try to muster "expertise" on a new topic each week. They over-answer students' questions. They feel uncomfortable and underprepared, even though they have collected more examples than they will ever have time to use in class. Think of a small, pink-nosed mole that has just poked its head above ground after digging a great underground network of tunnels. Months (or years) of excavating every piece of knowledge on a topic can leave new faculty feeling a bit blinded by the sunlight. When asked to teach a course that covers a wide variety of topics, they go back to what they know best: digging deeply into each one.

Mounting Pressures

My last concern is the growing number of top-down initiatives that drive curricular decisions. Administrators carefully watch a variety of indicators to see how their institution compares with competing institutions, numbers such as their student enrollments, graduation rates, and national student surveys. Quite reasonably, colleges want to enroll the most desirable students, graduate more of them, and ensure that they are satisfied with their education. So these numbers are brought to the attention of the president, provost, and vice presidents as they do their strategic planning for the year. One result of this number-crunching is an increasing number of top-down initiatives to improve said numbers.[17] Some initiatives lead to adjustments in curricula and changes in the kinds of courses that faculty are required to teach, the way these classes are structured, and the types of learning activities that the instructors are expected to incorporate.

Although administrators have always watched these numbers, the pressure is growing because of an increased need for accountability. External groups—including parents, taxpayers, employers, and government agencies—are demanding reform in higher education. Parents want more for their tuition money. In 2005, the U.S. government issued a report calling for a higher percentage of students to graduate in five years and for those students to demonstrate greater proficiencies upon graduation.[18] Blame it on global competition from China or on rising college tuitions: whatever the cause, it's no longer sufficient that more students are simply going to college; they need to have more impressive skills when they leave.

Let's examine one national-level response to these pressures to get a better picture of the potential impact on university classrooms: the Voluntary System of Accountability (VSA). This may be the first you've heard of the VSA, but it's rapidly gaining a foothold in higher education.[19] To participate in the VSA, colleges and universities provide public information in a standardized way, on a standardized form, which means they can't hide embarrassing statistics or showcase only their best results. The central purpose of this system is to make it easier for parents and college-bound students to shop for the school that best fits their needs.

The VSA is an impressive collection of data about faculty, students, and learning outcomes, but it's not perfect. On the plus side, these reports should prompt many schools to create more stimulating environments for learning. If, for example, a participating institution finds that it repeatedly scores in the lowest quartile nationally when it comes to the number of students who worked with a faculty member on a research project, the administration might be motivated to allocate more funding and resources to faculty-student research partnerships. Priorities will shift and students (and, we would hope, faculty) will benefit from the added accountability.[20]

But there is a drawback to having administrators fill out these reports each year: their concern with the results is likely to fuel top-down pressures for faculty to teach a certain way. Administrators will probably target those areas where an institution is lagging behind its peers and place pressure on faculty to catch up with the now publicly visible norms. Courses are likely to become more uniform or formulaic to ensure that the school rates well. Mind you, there isn't a question on the VSA that asks, "How many of your faculty teach Plato?" Thankfully, it's not that prescriptive about course content. But institutions do have to report, for example, how much improvement students made on standardized tests of critical thinking between their freshman and senior year. We'd probably all agree that there are many ways to teach critical thinking skills. But you can bet we'll see more faculty committees on critical thinking because these test scores will become a quick gauge of an institution's success. As these committees identify "what works," they will focus more on the kinds of courses that should be offered and what faculty members should be teaching in them. The ideal would be for institutions to create flexible systems to encourage faculty to teach from their strengths, but with the trend to hire more temporary adjunct faculty, institutions may want to "help" new adjuncts come up to speed more quickly. And what better way to "help" someone quickly than to make it very explicit what she needs to be doing from Day 1.

Of course, this is a relatively new, voluntary system, and time will tell how it changes faculty autonomy at the classroom level. Several people have written about the very real concern that higher education is increasingly "managed" by administrators, given market forces and external accountability standards, rather than influenced by faculty.[21] My prediction is that teaching decisions will regrettably become less driven by a professor's area of expertise and more driven by these top-down initiatives.

We've taken a broad look at higher education and answered the two basic questions, "Who teaches outside of their expertise?" and "Why do they do it?" The answer to the first question is, it seems, "most of us," at least at some point in our careers. As for why, some instructors choose to challenge themselves and others are required to teach outside their specialty as part of their job. For many of us, it's a blend of the two.

But that brings us to a third question, "Why aren't we talking about it?" If it's so commonplace to teach what you don't know, and it's clearly hard to do, why don't academics discuss it? We could be trading best practices with one another, or complaining to whomever will listen. We might discover that some of us revel in this challenge because the pressure to learn something for the sake of teaching it rejuvenates us, pumps us full of risk-taking adrenaline every time we walk into the classroom. But we don't know whether this is true because most of us don't discuss this particular reality of the job. It seems to be taboo.

Some faculty, particularly junior faculty, would breathe a sigh of relief if the discussion got started. Early in my career, I was hoping that someone would broach the topic of teaching what you don't know and validate my experience, which seemed to involve teaching outside of my expertise on a weekly, if not daily, basis. In fact, when I first heard the phrase "just-in-time-teaching," I thought it meant "learning the material just in time to teach it." (I quickly found that it meant something else, so I kept my misunderstanding to myself.)

There are, of course, professionally acceptable ways to talk about teaching beyond one's expertise, and currently the code-word is "workload." Instructors are quick to agree that the work-load is much heavier than usual when you're preparing a new course. You can say, "I'm just a few days ahead of my students" the first time you teach a course, and everyone nods and sighs.

But these comments about workload are a little deceiving. They imply that faculty simply need a few more hours in the day to pour their well-formed knowledge into well-structured class notes. In some cases, this may be true. But in many cases, faculty haven't learned the information yet, or they learned it ten years ago. One of the real reasons it takes so long to teach a new course is that the instructor usually has so much to learn (or relearn). But this common and uncomfortable reality is hardly ever discussed. You rarely hear a professor say, "I spent most of the weekend making sure I could solve the problems on the exam," even though some of us do. Only in the most confidential conversations do instructors confess, "I don't know how I got through class today because this material makes no sense to me."

Although most instructors are reluctant to admit that they're teaching beyond their expertise, many will complain about teaching students they don't understand. Faculty members commonly joke, "My students are getting younger and younger every year." Or a professor might describe some egregious student behavior and protest, "I would never have done *that* as a student." But these comments are often expressed as criticisms of the students rather than as a reflection of the instructor's own ignorance, discomfort, or vulnerability. Although we can poke fun at the growing age gap between ourselves and our students, we are much less likely to say, "I don't want to get up there and make a fool of myself—I have no idea how to relate to them." And we'd be hard-pressed to find a faculty member who would candidly admit, "I'm not comfortable with the ethnic diversity in my class."

So why aren't we talking about this reality? We could externalize the issue. We could say that we don't discuss this aspect of higher education because it would frustrate parents and reduce our credibility with students. Both of these are legitimate concerns. Parents pay sizeable tuitions to put their children through school, and costs on average rise 6–9 percent per year, typically about twice the general inflation rate.[22] Given the sacrifices many families make to send their children to college, parents might well be outraged to learn that their investments are in the hands of faculty who are tempted to buy *Statistics for Dummies.*

Parents aren't the only ones who make a large financial investment, either. Students share that burden. On average, undergraduate students bear 19–27 percent of the costs of their four-year college education (depending on their family's income level), and many graduate students shoulder all of their educational expenses, which averaged $31,000 for the 2007–08 academic year.[23] In many cases, students are paying us to learn the material as well as teach it.

With our students, of course, it's more than just a financial concern. Students want to believe in their instructors, and we want them to respect our authority, knowledge, and experience. Students know that some instructors are better than others, but they want all their professors to inspire their trust and their confidence.[24] And we want students' respect in all the courses that we teach, not just in those select courses that fan our egos and tap our years of training. Many students might quickly lose confidence in a professor's ability to assign a grade to their essay if it were well known that the professor was still figuring out the material in the hours before class.

Tenure-track and adjunct faculty also have a very practical reason to be quiet about the fact that they're teaching what they don't know: job security. Tenure-track faculty are reluctant to admit anything that might be held against them in the review process. As Zach, the tenure-track chemistry professor, explains, "No one wants to do anything that puts them at risk. Why take that chance?" Adjunct faculty are in an even more tenuous position because their contracts come up for renewal on a yearly basis. Adjunct faculty often see themselves as replaceable commodities, and in many cases, they're right.

But in addition to all these very real and sometimes daunting external factors, if we can be honest with ourselves, another fundamental reason that we don't talk about teaching outside of our expertise is that it's one of the most revealing professional statements we can make. We may not be great teachers or we may not be great grant writers; we may not even write well, but gosh darn it, we know stuff. We should know things. That's the crux of what we, as academics, have been doing all these years—acquiring knowledge and creating new knowledge. To admit that we're teaching what we don't know would beg the question, "So what have you been doing?"

For some of us, pride is an issue as well. Our identity is often rooted in our small niche of professional expertise. We may not have highly lucrative jobs, but we have our expertise. And we want that knowledge to be valued. Pride in one's work is not just the vanity of junior faculty, either: it's an issue for professors at all stages of their careers. Senior faculty can be devastated when their nationally recognized work goes unacknowledged by colleagues in their department.[25] Professors can be a surprisingly insecure lot, and admitting that they teach beyond their expertise doesn't do anything to shore up their confidence.

My intention in this book is to end the silence on this issue and jumpstart the discussion. If teaching what you don't know is a reality of academia in the twenty-first century, then we need a language to discuss this predicament and permission to ask for support. If you're teaching outside your specialty, the faculty stories in the following chapters should reassure you that you're in good company.

To be clear, I've taught outside my expertise many, many times. It's much easier to admit now than it would have been five or ten years ago, when I was working very hard to make myself into the pedagogical equivalent of silly putty—I was always hoping that if I pressed myself into the right books and journal articles, I could peel away a smooth image of knowledge and authority.

One of the first courses that went far beyond my comfort zone was a class I taught at Carnegie Mellon University right after completing my postdoc and before landing a tenure-track position. The course was called "Research Methods in Child Development." Mind you, I had no children of my own. No one ever asked me to babysit, not even my own sister. (People often asked me to dog-sit, though. They would leave me detailed instructions about their dog and take their children with them.) To make matters worse, I had never done a research experiment with children. I had followed around a two-year-old once with a pen and paper, jotting down all the clever things he said for a linguistics class, but that was the extent of my practical research experience. It didn't matter. Much to my delight, the students in this Research Methods course never even asked if I had worked with children. I talked about my genuine areas of expertise and made them sound relevant, and no one questioned it. I got through the course unscathed, and my course evaluations were so strong that the other instructor who was teaching the class, a professor who had been doing ground-breaking research with children for more than a decade, wanted to see my syllabus.

To be honest, I didn't know any better. At that early point in my career, I didn't have much expertise in anything except a tiny wedge of cognitive neuroscience. Fortunately, I was bold enough to teach just about anything, so I quickly racked up a CV's worth of courses—as I said, the silly putty approach to pedagogy. But it was great fun, and as with any course that stretches you beyond your comfort zone, I learned a ton.

2 Why It's Better Than It Seems

Kevin Otos doesn't look like a stereotypical college professor; with his wavy red hair, playful smile, and tall frame, he looks more like an athlete. Kevin is an actor, and his specialty is physical, improvisational comedy. He is in the theater department at Elon University in North Carolina, where he teaches everything from advanced courses on classic Italian theater, "Commedia dell'Arte," to the classes most of us wish we'd made time for in college, like "Improvisational Comedy." But the year I met Kevin, he was teaching a freshman seminar called "The Global Experience." It's a general education course that most tenure-track faculty teach and that all students take, a rite of passage, so to speak. Fortunately, Kevin was able to wait until his second year to teach it. His office was finally unpacked, his kids were happy in their new school, and he was as ready as he would ever be to teach something he didn't know.

But he wasn't quite ready for what happened in week two. It seemed like a good day—the class had watched a video on global warming, had turned their desks into a circle, and were having a lively discussion, when Kevin made a general observation about why some people might not be changing their behavior despite reports of climate change. He explained, "There was a philosopher who once said that you can look at the history of human civilization and see people tolerating as much discomfort as possible. They tolerate that discomfort until they reach a threshold point where action must take place." "What's important," Kevin emphasized, "is that this action is not a gradual response to the problem. The problem has to reach a critical point, then action will proceed." Kevin paused to let the idea sink in, but the student on his left immediately replied, "I think that was Rousseau." This young woman, fresh from high school, recited the full quote from memory.

Kevin recalls the moment with horror. He didn't know what to do. He knew that Rousseau was a philosopher, and he knew that the Founding Fathers had been impressed by his works. But he'd never personally read Rousseau, and he certainly didn't know if the student was correct. In that moment, Kevin was sure that he could spell Rousseau's name, but that was about it.

When the student finished, he nodded appreciatively and took the discussion in another direction, keeping quiet on the topic of Rousseau. There wasn't much he could add. When we later talked about that moment in class, Kevin wondered if his own comment about "tolerating discomfort" might have been a tangent, that perhaps he had steered the discussion off-topic inadvertently. I could appreciate his concern—it's often hard to anticipate whether a comment will solidify an important point or ignite a heated digression.

But we can all relate to Kevin's story in one important respect: he wanted more than anything to steer the class back into familiar intellectual territory, back to the text or the video or something he knew with certainty. Let's be honest—it's hard to be shown up by a nineteen-year-old. It can feel as though everyone in the room realizes you know less than the student making the comment. As faculty, we all assume that we are reasonably well read and at least selectively well educated, but one or two "Rousseau-moments" can put those assumptions to the test. And the test seems so unfair when you never claimed to be an expert on the topic in the first place.

We all know the disadvantages of teaching outside your expertise, or at least we can imagine them: you could be outsmarted by your students, you could be asked a question you can't answer, you could spend hours preparing for every class, you could explain a difficult concept poorly (or worse yet, incorrectly), and you could have trouble sleeping at night because you're worried about any or all of the above. I've experienced all these problems at least once, several of them many times. As I interviewed faculty and read through the research literature, I learned some practical strategies for minimizing most of these difficulties. I'll share those strategies with you throughout this book.[1]

In this chapter, I focus on the aspects of this teaching experience that are easy to overlook: namely, the advantages to teaching outside your expertise. Teaching something you don't know very well can yield genuine rewards (and it's not just that you learn which sleeping medications work best). Both you and your students can benefit from the experience. You may not feel as though you're preparing enough when your students nimbly quote authors you've never read. But they bring strengths to the table and you bring strengths, and there are ways to build on both.

Before identifying the advantages to teaching unfamiliar material, we first need a way to distinguish faculty who are teaching comfortably within their expertise from faculty who, like Kevin in the Rousseau story, are teaching outside their expertise. Let's call the two kinds of faculty "content experts" and "content novices." "Content expert" is a phrase that's already widely used to refer to someone who has expertise in a specialized area. A "content novice" is someone who is either learning the content for the first time or relearning material he or she hasn't touched in quite a while. Most instructors are content experts in one field or another, but the question is whether they're teaching as content experts.[2] Let's consider a few examples. When Kevin teaches Shakespeare's *Twelfth Night,* a play he's both acted in and studied, he's teaching as a content expert. But when he teaches David Levitt's *Freakonomics,* he's teaching as a content novice. (*Freakonomics* may be a much more accessible read than *Twelfth Night,* but Kevin is still not an economist. It's one thing to read a bestseller like *Freakonomics* on a plane or in your living room and it's another thing entirely to teach it to eighteen freshmen.)

Within a single course, you might be a content expert one week and a content novice the next. Recall Dan Simons from the last chapter, the psychology professor teaching "Introduction to Experimental Psychology." He had plenty of knowledge about certain kinds of psychology, but with six major subdivisions in this far-reaching discipline, he was bound to be unfamiliar with some topics in the textbook. He still needed to teach everything from infant attachment to drug use, and during those weeks he probably taught as a content novice.

Like most dichotomies, this simple division into content experts and content novices is invariably too simple. Certainly some faculty members would fall somewhere between the two in their courses. For the purposes of this discussion, though, I stick to this simple dichotomy.[3] My focus here is on the opportunities available to the content novice and what these hardworking instructors bring to the classroom.

Why Would I Want to Teach Outside My Specialty?

As I interviewed faculty, I often asked them about the advantages of teaching outside their expertise. Most professors could list many. Some faculty, usually instructors who had just finished lecturing on unfamiliar material, could list only two or three. From these discussions I've identified four advantages that are worth noticing.

Advantage 1: Learn Something New and Interesting

The most compelling reason to teach on the edge of your expertise is that you get to learn something new and important. Academics, as a whole, typically love to learn new things. Maybe not every new thing—a college professor becomes just as grumpy as the next person when he has to learn a new voice-mail system—but most instructors love to dig into a new area of research. Intellectual curiosity is why some of us choose academia over careers in the "real world."

Some professors who teach outside of their expertise have the opportunity to delve into topics that they have been eyeing from a distance for years. Penelope, who teaches at William and Mary, said that her periphery course gave her "a productive outlet for all of the juicy interests" that kept pulling her away from the more boring, technical works she was supposed to be reading.[4]

Perhaps this goes without saying, but those of us who are content novices are often more effective learners because of the "fool factor." The fear of having nothing to say, or, perhaps worse yet, the fear of saying something that is contradicted in another part of the assigned reading, is highly motivating. It even helps some faculty overcome their mental roadblocks to a concept. Faculty who were once convinced that they couldn't make heads nor tails of Phylzpytt realize that they can glean something coherent from Phylzpytt after all when they have to get up and teach it in their 3:00 p.m. class.[5]

But the quality of your preparation for the class is just part of the story. You will probably gain a better understanding of material *as you teach it.* I've heard many people comment, "I didn't truly understand a topic until I taught it." Eric Mazur, a physicist at Harvard University who is known for his innovative strategies for engaging students in large lectures, noted, "I've always said that the person who learns the most in the classroom is the teacher." He believes that teaching a course is like writing a book. Both take a lot of time, of course, but in the process a thought transition occurs. The ideas become clearer to the teacher and to the writer, partly because they invest a good deal of time in the task, but also because they walk around the ideas as they try to make the language work for them rather than against them. It's one of the reasons Mazur has students teach each other in class (but we'll come back to that in Chapter 5).

Advantage 2: Connect with Faculty Outside Your Department

Teaching outside your comfort zone can lead to positive interactions with faculty in other departments. After all, the topic might be outside *your* area of expertise, but it could very well be the center of someone else's knowledge.

Interdepartmental connections aren't necessarily a built-in advantage to this kind of teaching—most faculty have to seek out these opportunities or foster the relationships themselves— but it is an important benefit that junior faculty might easily overlook. If you're relatively new to the institution, it's a good idea to make acquaintances outside of your department.[6] Befriending someone with knowledge that's relevant to your course can reduce the stress of undertaking a new topic. Better still, if this person is an experienced teacher, she can warn you about common misconceptions students have regarding the material they are about to learn.

Some of us find it embarrassing to approach an expert and admit our lack of knowledge. It's not a typical exchange between academics, after all: we tend to flash our plumage, not our soft underbellies. But most faculty members are thrilled to be recognized and called upon as the experts. Chances are their authority is challenged from time to time, just as ours is. All of us like to hear someone say, "I hear you know a lot about X." It's an easier conversation than you might think: "I'm teaching a class on X for the first time, and I know I'd do a better job if I could ask you a few questions. Can I take you out for coffee?" Make the conversation less about you and how little you know and more about the expert and his clever teaching strategies.

Some general education courses have "built-in" or structured opportunities to connect with others teaching the same course. For example, some schools have an orientation or monthly brown bag series specifically geared toward instructors teaching freshmen writing seminars. We're all busy and don't feel like we have time for another meeting, but attending one meeting and finding a mentor could save considerable preparation time.

Advantage 3: Broaden Your CV

Those of you who expect to be on the job market have a very real reason to teach outside your specialty: doing so allows you to add new courses to your CV. By teaching a course or two that differs considerably from the kinds of courses you normally teach, you expand your repertoire and make yourself stand out to potential search committees. You say to the world, "I am versatile." If you can learn to teach courses that are the cornerstones for your academic discipline, such as a 100-level introductory course or a 300-level methods course, then you can easily step into another school's curriculum. These courses almost always require you to learn something new because they sweep together the most compelling ideas and practices from every corner of the field. Of course, you want to be careful what you wish for. If you demonstrate prowess in teaching the methods or statistics courses in your field, courses that many instructors dread, then there is a very good chance you'll be asked to teach them at your next job, too.

Advantage 4: Develop a New Area of Research

You might not think of the classroom as the starting point for a new line of research, but if you're open to the possibility, it might just present itself. Some of the time you spend preparing for your class could also further your research agenda. Admittedly, this isn't going to be true for every course for which you need to learn new material. If you're teaching a large introductory course, chances are you'll be reading relatively watered-down accounts of classic theories and findings, not the cutting-edge research. And given the breadth of survey courses, you'll be teaching these ideas at a relatively superficial level, bouncing from topic to topic each week—not the best springboard for new scholarship.

But if you have the opportunity to teach a seminar to graduate students or to upper-level undergraduates that involves reading primary sources, evaluating their claims, and constructing new interpretations, then you've found a much springier springboard from which to launch new research. This could be a very intentional process—you could place sources on the syllabus that you've been wanting to read for a research project. I know several instructors who have taken this approach, so you'd be in good company.

A Club We'd All Like to Join: The Poised and Confident

Even though almost all faculty members seem daunted by the amount of time it takes to teach as a content novice, everyone has a different level of comfort with the experience. In my twenty-eight interviews, I found that most instructors fit into one of three categories. Some faculty belonged to what I'll call the "Poised and Confident" group. Instructors in this category weren't at all distressed when they didn't know the answer to students' questions. In fact, they were so comfortable teaching outside of their expertise that they intentionally sought out those kinds of courses. Other faculty fell into an "Undecided but Untroubled" group. They had mixed thoughts about this kind of teaching; they described being comfortable some of the time but not always. They might occasionally volunteer to teach a specific course outside their area of expertise, but they wouldn't do it too often. The final group of instructors were genuinely unhappy teaching as content novices; I'll call them the "Strained and Anxious" group. They said things such as, "I don't like it; I don't like it at all." Some sounded frustrated, some sounded anxious, but they all sounded tired and overstretched.

No one wants to be in the last group. But with some careful planning and strategic thinking, can you avoid it?

The short answer is yes, you probably can. Before I describe what can help, let's first rule out the factors that don't seem to matter. First, my interviews clearly revealed that a person's comfort level wasn't based on academic discipline, gender, the size of the department, or whether the general institution was focused on teaching or research.[7] My sense was that faculty could be confident (or miserable) teaching outside of their expertise just about anywhere.

Second, to my surprise, an instructor's level of prior teaching experience was not an accurate predictor of comfort level. Junior faculty who were feeling overwhelmed often envied their senior colleagues, whom they assumed had an easier time teaching unfamiliar material. But I also met senior, tenured faculty who felt extremely frustrated and overburdened teaching out-side of their expertise. Sadly, it doesn't necessarily become less stressful with practice. I also interviewed first-year faculty, fresh from graduate school, who loved the experience and were eager to do it again. If it doesn't matter how long you've been teaching or where you teach, what does matter? And can the rest of us learn to be more like the enviable Poised and Confident group? Or at least the Undecided but Untroubled group?

Perhaps you noticed that I said you can *probably* avoid being in the Strained and Anxious group, rather than you can defi-nitely and without question avoid that group. I hedged because one factor is most likely beyond your control. Two key factors, however, *are* within your control, and they can help you rise to the ranks of the Poised and Confident.[8]

Let's begin with the factor outside of your control.

In general, instructors were more anxious and overwhelmed teaching a course on the edge of their expertise when they *had* to teach it. These could be courses that the department chair assigned, that all faculty in the program had to teach, or that "should be taught in the department" but didn't really fit any-one's background. People in the last category seemed particu-larly frustrated with their situation, perhaps because they feared that their colleagues saw them as experts on these otherwise or-phaned course topics, which was usually far from the truth.

Sometimes you have to teach a course because you're the new person and they hired you to teach it. But in some cases, the rea-son is not so clear. These courses look voluntary from an admin-istrator's perspective, but if you asked the instructor, he'd tell you he really didn't have a choice. I'm thinking, in particular, of one person in the Strained and Anxious group. She was a tenure-track instructor when a senior colleague asked her to co-teach a course about which she actually knew very little. She could see that co-teaching would help her gain a friendly senior ally in her department and improve her chances at tenure. Some might say that this was her choice—she could have said no. But if you're on the tenure track and you're already scrambling to keep up with the conveyor belt of publications, you don't see much choice. You don't want to do anything to jeopardize your job; and on the flip-side, you want to do anything to secure it. The course was a stressful experience for this junior instructor, especially when the senior colleague was sitting at the front of the classroom. She was just relieved when it was over.

Faculty teaching outside of their expertise by choice had very different stories to tell. Yes, it was still a lot of work, but they were energized. In fact, in addition to developing new courses from the ground up, instructors in the Poised and Confident group found ways to be content novices in courses they knew well. Every year they would find new readings, change the theme of the course, or update their examples. Their perception was that teaching material that was new to them, even when it presented the opportunity to be confused, made them better teachers.

But simply because your department chair has assigned you to teach two highly unfamiliar courses doesn't automatically relegate you to the lifestyle of the Strained and Anxious. Most faculty have to teach outside of their expertise at some point, and I spoke with several faculty who were asked to do so regularly and still enjoyed it. What protected them? How did they approach their teaching differently? Two factors seemed to make the difference.

First, the Poised and Confident group tended to tackle directly what I call "the imposter issue."[9] Instructors who found a way to be honest with their students about their limited knowledge were much more comfortable teaching outside of their expertise. In contrast, content novices who pretended to be content experts were more likely to be Strained and Anxious. They felt it was important to appear more knowledgeable than they actually were, and this created tremendous pressure and more work, as you might imagine.

To some extent, many of us have felt like imposters in the classroom. As one professor explained, "Every faculty member, at some point or another, walks into the first day of class feeling like an imposter. But when you're teaching what you don't know, it's not just in your head. It's terrifyingly true." Although every content novice might grapple with the imposter issue, what distinguishes faculty is how they handle it. Instructors who were happy teaching on the edge of their expertise often diffused the imposter problem by saying to their students, "Here's what I know, and here's what I don't know," or "Some of this is new to me." They were frank about their limited expertise, and several were philosophical about whether they could actually be a true expert in anything meaningful. In Chapter 4, we'll look at the specific language these instructors used to reframe the issue.

Faculty who were Strained and Anxious were less likely to tell students about the limits of their knowledge. They talked to me instead about how much work they did to master the material, how they prepared pages and pages of lecture notes, and how they dreaded being asked a question that they might not be able to answer. They used phrases like "being exposed," "feeling vulnerable," and "feeling shallow." One woman said she envied her students because all they had to do was read the articles—they didn't have to do the readings *and* think about how to present the material in the most logical way. "They really have all the time in the world to just sit there in class and listen," she said.

(We'll come back to this comment and the assumption underlying it later.)

Some faculty feel like imposters with their peers as well as with their students. It's easy to assume that your senior colleagues have somehow always been content experts in their courses. This assumption leaves a new instructor thinking that she is somehow the first person in her department to machete her way through a new topic after being hired.

Is it possible to stop feeling like an imposter? I believe it is. I interviewed one instructor who was once quite miserable teaching as a content novice but isn't anymore, even though he still tackles new topics and courses. He eventually realized that "it's the pretending that gets you in trouble. You try really hard, but then there is a tension between you and your students. I think that tension begins before you even step into that classroom, because you're thinking that the students are out to get you, to expose you as the imposter." Today he tells students point-blank on the first day, "I don't know everything. I don't know anybody who knows the whole field. And you're not going to know the whole field when you're done with this class. We're here to see what the field *could* be about."

I've saved the second factor under your control for last because I think it's the most important, protective factor. Faculty who were comfortable teaching outside of their expertise and who truly enjoyed being content novices, the members of the Poised and Confident group, had developed teaching philosophies that did not require them to stick to their specialty to be effective teachers. These instructors explicitly said that they did not need to master the material. In contrast, people who were anxious and uncomfortable seemed to hold their expertise more dear. They focused on knowing as much as they could, and, un-

derstandably, that meant they were perpetually reading and preparing for class. They displayed what education author Maryellen Weimer referred to as "a strong allegiance to content."[10]

This group's anxiety isn't surprising. If instructors believe it is
essential to have mastered the content and have a wealth of examples, facts, and theories at their fingertips, then it would be
nerve-racking to teach with little more than freshly typed notes
in those fingertips. I spoke with one award-winning professor
who was anxious about knowing the details of each article, and
not simply the details in the body of each article, but the equations in the appendix as well. This is where the classroom discussions often landed—on these details and equations—and it
sounded like there was a competition among the graduate students to see who could recall the most minutiae. Another professor who seemed to have a love-hate relationship with teaching outside of his expertise talked about combing the text
multiple times, noting details so that he could turn to the exact
passage he wanted in class. Although he said he loved the challenge, he also described his "teaching anxiety" dreams. At the
time of our interview, he had recently had a dream in which he
was on the bus on his way to teach a class when he realized that
he hadn't read the book yet. He was scrambling to decide what
to teach instead—should he preview the midterm? Discuss the
candidates for president? This had never happened in real life
(he was always prepared), but that fear, he said, is with you always.

What about the Poised and Confident faculty, the instructors
who were relaxed about teaching as content novices? It didn't
bother them to be content novices because they didn't prize the
content in the same way. They still talked about how much work
it was to learn the material—it's work for all of us—but being a

dispenser of knowledge wasn't their chief priority walking into class.

A Different Model of Teaching and Learning

This points to a serious problem in higher education: many of us do, in fact, view ourselves as knowledge dispensers. The epitome of a "good" teacher is one who "dominates the classroom and its elements. She . . . disseminates information clearly and effectively so that students may learn it quickly, remember it well, and reproduce it upon demand."[11] We might not like to think that teaching can be boiled down to these coarse elements, but for many professors, I've just described a good day in the classroom.

Although we don't admit it very often, the classic, default model of college teaching is "teaching as telling." My job as the teacher, ultimately, is to tell students what they need to know. That doesn't mean that all faculty stand up and simply lecture to their students for hours on end—many instructors include interesting activities or organize their classes around interactive discussions. But the underlying assumption for many of us is that good teaching involves finding an effective way to structure and communicate complex information. I may not choose to spend the entire class period explaining the material to you, but if I'm doing my job, I should be able to.

But this model breaks down for those of us teaching outside of our expertise. "Teaching as telling" is a disastrous model for content novices because they have little to tell. Unfortunately, this is the model that the Strained and Anxious faculty tended to adopt. Recall the instructor earlier in this chapter who envied her students because they just get to "sit there in class and listen." She and well-meaning teachers like her had a great deal riding on their ability to master the material before stepping into class, and even more riding on their ability to get everything right in the retelling. Perhaps therein lies the true imposter syndrome. It's not just that I'm pretending to be a medical anthropologist when I'm not, or that I'm feigning expertise as a nuclear engineer when I'm so clearly not. What's bothering me is that at some core level, I'm also an imposter as a teacher. If I believe that teaching is about telling, and I'm teaching material that I don't know very well, I can't tell you very much. I can tell you some things, but I can't tell you nearly as much as I think I should.

"Teaching as telling" is also a problematic model for students. We'll hear more about this in Chapters 4 and 5, but research tells us that students don't learn more when we do all the work of lecturing at them. In most situations, students learn more when they actively engage with the material, when they need to do something more with the information than simply listening to it and writing some of it down when it reaches their threshold of necessity. I should clarify: research shows that there is, at best, one learning objective where lecturing is as effective as other teaching methods. If your goal is simply to transmit knowledge, to tell students something so that they can regurgitate it back to you, then lecturing is as good as other methods—not necessarily better, but comparable. But if your goal is to engage students in critical thinking or to have them apply a concept to a new problem, then telling them is not going to achieve those goals.[12] You need to present interesting challenges to solve, rather than simply explaining how other smart people have already solved those challenges.[13]

Why do I believe that teaching as telling is the classic, default model with which most of us are burdened? It's true that many faculty are incorporating other teaching strategies into their repertoire, and some disciplines rely heavily on other instructional methods, such as discussion in the humanities or case studies in business. But research indicates that lecturing is still the most common instructional method in most disciplines.[14] People may be lecturing a lot less than they used to, but most of us are still lecturing a good part of the time. (We may call them "mini-lectures" because we take breaks for "mini-discussions," but we still lecture.) And content novices often resort to lecturing despite their best intentions not to. I interviewed some junior faculty who regularly use collaborative and active learning when it's a topic they know well, but when they're teaching something novel, they find themselves lecturing again.

Moreover, if you ask an instructor, "What's a consistent dilemma you face as a teacher?" you'll frequently hear, "There isn't enough time to cover everything." We're all preoccupied with the coverage problem.[15] Faculty blame it on textbooks (they keep getting longer), on the number of hours spent in class (there aren't enough), or on the academic discipline itself (you need to know so much more to be a competent chemist or musician today). And the most efficient way to "cover" the topic is to lecture.

Because "teaching as telling" doesn't work very well, we need a different model, one that's manageable for faculty who are teaching outside their area of expertise, one that's attuned to students' different learning styles, and one that flexes with the expansion of knowledge.

An increasingly compelling model of college instruction redefines teaching as "creating a learning environment." The Poised and Confident faculty I interviewed took this approach. In this model, faculty see the course as a space where students can make sense and meaning of the key concepts, a space that supports the way students learn best. Although there are many theories about what makes a good learning environment, two powerful and practical principles stand out. First, students learn the most when we draw on their pre-existing understanding. No one is a blank slate—we all build on what we already know—and a good learning environment brings out that knowledge, challenges what's incorrect, and builds on the rest.[16] Second, students learn more when instructors engage them on a few topics in depth and provide them with several examples as meaningful anchors, rather than covering a blizzard of topics in fleeting specks.[17] These, among other things, should be features of our learning environments: identifying what students already know, building from that knowledge, and examining topics with enough depth that they have meaning.[18]

This is good news for content novices. It means we don't have to ask ourselves, "How much do I need to cover today?" or "What do I need to know in case someone asks it?" Instead we can ask, "What do students already know about this topic? How can I connect this new material to their knowledge? Which examples will be meaningful to them, and how can I structure time in class so that they can get the most from those examples?" The research shows that such a general approach will be better for your students, but it will also be more manageable for you, the content novice, because you're not posing as the omniscient one. You can build on what you know—you know which examples are meaningful for beginners because you just recently discovered which examples made the most sense to you.

Admittedly, the idea of creating learning environments is not new. Robert Barr and John Tagg created a stir about learning environments in the 1990s, and many education specialists have written about designing optimal environments.[19] I clearly stand in the shadow of giants on this one. Whereas others have advocated this approach because it benefits students, however, I'm hoping to add another reason for adopting this model. By focusing on the learning environment, you'll not only help your students learn more, but you'll be a much happier, less harried teacher.

What The Content Novice Brings to the Classroom

You might like the idea of changing your teaching philosophy but still find yourself preoccupied with getting every fact and concept nailed down when you're teaching something new. I know how hard that is—I've taught those kinds of courses myself. The obvious assumption is that students learn less from faculty who know less about the subject matter and learn more from faculty who know more.

But that assumption isn't correct. Evidence from cognitive science, organizational behavior, and educational psychology suggests that experts are not always the best teachers. If you've ever had a brilliant professor drone on at the chalkboard about something no one understands, then perhaps you're not surprised. You'll be relieved to hear that when you teach as a content novice, you bring several strengths to the classroom.

Strength 1: Realistic Expectations Lead to More Motivated Students

The content novice has an advantage over the content expert in motivating students. Student motivation is a complex topic, one that deserves an entire book unto itself, and I won't do it justice here. Suffice it to say that some factors affecting student motivation are student-driven, such as whether the material overlaps with students' career interests and whether an individual student thinks he's capable of learning the material.[20] Other factors are instructor-driven, and chief among them are faculty expectations.

Faculty expectations are a key element in student success. When instructors have low expectations of students, then students typically have lower expectations of themselves and perform at lower levels. When instructors have high expectations— regardless of the students' abilities—students are more likely to excel and meet those expectations.[21] This teacher-driven, self-fulfilling prophecy is often referred to as the "Pygmalion Effect." When you think back to your days as a student, you can probably remember a professor who encouraged you to achieve more than you originally thought you could. But that motivating professor probably didn't expect you to find a cure for cancer. I'm pretty sure she didn't ask you to translate the Bible into hieroglyphics, either. High expectations are motivating when they are realistic about how much effort and time a task requires.[22] If you give exams that are too long or homework that is too difficult, students feel that even their best efforts are not enough. They may make faces, complain to the department chair, any number of things, but they usually won't work harder when the professor's demands are repeatedly unreasonable.

This is where the content novice has an advantage. Four empirical findings shed light on the issue:

1. Everyone, regardless of experience level, tends to be overly optimistic about a beginner's performance. Both novices and experts tend to predict that beginners will take less time to complete a task than they actually do, and both groups fail to anticipate all the problems that are likely to occur.[23] (This could be one reason we all tend to assign too much reading.)

2. People who have a little experience are better at estimating the amount of time a task will take than people who have no experience at all. I like to bake and everyone likes to eat, so I'll use a baking example to clarify. If you've tried to bake at least one apple pie, you have a much better sense of how much time

it takes than someone who has never peeled an apple or dusted a rolling pin. This makes sense. What's surprising is that people who have a lot of experience and are regarded as experts are much worse at estimating the amount of time a task will take for beginners than are the beginners themselves. In fact, the experts' predictions are worse than those of someone *who has never performed the task at all.*[24]

3. People with a little experience are also better than experts at predicting how many steps another person will need to complete a task on her first attempt. They can better envision the steps that a beginner will take, what kinds of mistakes she'll make, and which steps she might have to repeat.[25] In our baking example, someone who has just made a pie or two knows you need to sprinkle flour on the table before you roll out the crust, and a novice can probably tell you how long it takes to clean up the mess if you skip the flour. The novice baker will factor in extra time because each step and misstep is a recent memory. A pastry chef will of course remember to flour the table when he bakes a pie himself—that's second nature—but he forgets that it won't be second nature to someone else, and that the novice might need to repeat several steps. He forgets to account for the sticking points, so to speak.

4. Lastly, someone who has not fully solved a problem does a better job of judging whether other people will be able to solve the problem than does someone who has already solved it.[26] If you're in the middle of baking your first pie, you'll have a realistic sense of whether it will look as good as the impressive picture in the magazine. If you're remembering that pie you made last Thanksgiving, you're likely to remember it as being prettier and easier to pull together than it actually was.

Are these skills directly relevant to college and university teaching? Absolutely. Faculty regularly need to estimate time on task. These findings imply that beginning students are likely to be discouraged by the unrealistic expectations of a content expert. Undergraduates in an introductory course in criminal justice may initially be excited to have a class taught by a leading forensic scientist, but that excitement will wear off quickly if the instructor forgets they'll need to do a long tutorial before they can do the homework. The students will be furious if no one can finish the first exam. In contrast, college students taking the same introductory class with an instructor who just learned some of the material will probably enjoy a teacher with more realistic expectations. The content novice is likely to warn students about the lengthy tutorial, perhaps even making the tutorial a homework assignment all by itself. Exam questions will be more accessible. Students new to the field will probably stay more motivated and, if they haven't picked a major yet, will be more inclined to pick criminal justice.

Of course, content experts have other tools at their disposal for motivating beginners. A forensic specialist might have fantastic stories about a double-homicide that she helped solve in Washington, D.C.—or she might present new evidence on Jack the Ripper. Content experts have insiders' knowledge that can motivate students in ways that a sensible homework assignment cannot. But not every content expert is a good storyteller. Nor is every expert interested in making their beloved field accessible to beginners. Content novices have many obstacles to overcome, but when it comes to realistic expectations, they're ahead of the game.

Strength 2: Concrete Explanations Lead to More Efficient Problem-Solving

All of us teach problem-solving. Math, science, and engineering faculty assign actual problem sets, but the rest of us assign different kinds of problems. An art professor might ask students to make a collage on a 3 x 5" card using black and white images to convey rhythm. Freshmen in a writing class might be asked to write a three-page persuasive paper on the future of books, given trends in reading habits, attention spans, and technology. Students are often engaged in problem-solving, even if those exact words don't appear in the syllabus.

The fact that you probably engage students in problem-solving points to another strength of the content novice. If you're teaching students how to solve a problem that you recently learned to solve yourself, research shows that you will probably provide more basic and concrete explanations than would a content expert. As a result, your students will probably experience fewer frustrations and more successes when they sit down to work on that problem.

This might come as a surprise. (Not the part about students' having fewer frustrations, but the part about your teaching a clearer solution to the problem.) Two empirical findings are relevant here. The first finding is that students who are taught by a content novice complete a problem faster on their first attempt and make fewer mistakes than students who are taught by a content expert.[27] The expert's students make more mistakes, which is part of the reason they need more time.

The second important finding is that students ranked content novices as significantly better than content experts at teaching problem-solving. Students thought the content novices provided much clearer instructions, so not surprisingly, students had an easier time solving the problem. In what ways were their instructions clearer? A professional observer noted that content novices used basic statements in explaining how to solve a problem whereas content experts taught using more advanced and abstract statements.[28]

It makes perfect sense that content novices would use more basic, concrete statements since they, by definition, lack an advanced understanding of the problem. What is surprising, however, is that content experts *don't* offer these helpful concrete statements. In one study, 90 percent of the content novices included a detail needed to solve the problem in advance, whereas only 9 percent of the content experts included that detail in their initial explanation.[29]

Content novices weren't star performers on every task, however. Specifically, they were less effective than content experts when they had to teach students how to transfer their knowledge to new contexts. Students trained by content novices were better at solving the original problem, but those trained by content experts transferred their skills more easily to novel problems. Don't get me wrong. The students trained by content novices could still transfer their learning to new problems—they weren't completely at a loss—but they solved the new problems a little more slowly and made more mistakes than the students trained by experts.[30]

Why is transfer easier for those who were taught by content experts? The researchers pursuing these questions, Pamela Hinds and her colleagues, believe it is because teachers who know the concepts well use more abstract concepts when they teach, which makes it easier for students to generalize to new situations. Of course, the abundance of abstract concepts and lack of concrete details in the experts' instructions make it harder to solve the first problem, but it's the second and third and twentieth problems that matter most.

How does this help you as an instructor if you have to teach as a content novice? One lesson to take from this research is that you're probably going to give students plenty of concrete instructions and clues that will make the first problem easier to solve. Your students will love you for that. But you'll need to make an extra effort to provide some abstract statements as well. You'll probably find some of these general principles in the textbook. Be sure to include these in your notes and spend time in class relating these abstract principles to the concrete steps and details that you're more likely to focus on naturally.

If you're not comfortable lecturing on the connections between the abstract principles and the concrete steps, raise the topic as a question for students to evaluate: "We know that Principle A is important to solving this problem. Why is it important? What are some of the different ways this principle might be connected to the problem?" Although most students won't jump in with suggestions, a few of the brightest students may have been dying for this kind of higher-level analysis to occur. Plus you've got the best of both worlds: first, you've provided the concrete steps and details because that's within your comfort zone, and those details will help students solve the first problem. Second, you've made sure to include more general principles, which will help students transfer the knowledge to future problems.

A second lesson to take from this research is that as a content novice, you'll provide the most helpful instructions if you first try to solve the problem yourself. If you pull an assignment from an impressive syllabus you find online but don't attempt to solve the problem ahead of time, then your advice and instructions will, I suspect, be lacking the kind of clear insights I've just described. That doesn't mean you need to write a ten-page essay with five references because that's the assignment you're giving your students. But it does mean that you'd probably do well to outline a sample argument and use Google or your library's online journal system to track down a few relevant articles. You'll discover things along the way that will improve the instructions you give, and you'll be able to describe a sample approach to the problem. You'll also be able to identify where, if necessary, you need to scale back the assignment.

Strength 3: Foster Deep Learning Instead of Surface Learning

Without even knowing what these terms mean, most of us would agree that we'd rather promote "deep learning" than "surface learning." It's like summer camp versus federal prison camp. One phrase is immensely more appealing.

Higher education researchers in Sweden, Great Britain, and Australia have been interested in deep and surface approaches to learning for years, and these concepts have recently been gaining ground in the United States.[31] The original researchers, Ference Marton and Roger Säljö, gave students an academic text to read and told them that they would later be tested on the material.[32] Students approached the text in one of two ways. One group tried to remember the facts from the text and spent their time identifying what they might be asked to recall later. Their memorization approach to the material was called a surface or superficial approach to learning. (Chances are you've known students who take this approach.) The second group tried to understand the meaning of the text, making connections to concepts that weren't directly mentioned in the book. Their more sophisticated approach was labeled a deep approach to learning.

In the thirty years since the original findings were published, researchers have learned a great deal about deep and surface approaches to learning. Deep learning is driven by the learner's intention to understand the ideas for him- or herself, so deep learners tend to look for the big picture and patterns in the material; they examine the logic of a claim cautiously and carefully, and they often try to relate the concepts in class to their own knowledge and experience. Surface learning, in contrast, is driven by the learner's intention to cope with the course requirements, so surface learners tend to focus on the details rather than on the big picture. They focus heavily on memorizing and reproducing those details, and they tend to treat the course as unrelated bits of information.[33]

Although we often categorize students as "surface learners" or "deep learners," research shows that no one is locked into one particular approach to learning. A student can adopt a surface approach to the material for one course and a deep approach in another, depending on her attitude toward the subject matter and the kind of encouragement she receives from the instructor.[34]

This is good news, because it means that an instructor has the potential to promote deep learning and discourage surface learning within the context of the course. We're not destined to a group of surface learners simply because we're teaching "Biology 101." But why is this malleability an advantage for content novices? It would seem, at first glance, that content experts would be in a better position to foster deep learning. They know so much more about the field than the content novice; they have a sense of the big picture; and they've invested a lot of their own time finding meaning in the material—all traits of deep learners—so it would seem they must be ideally equipped to engage students in deep learning.

Not necessarily. Keep in mind that a deep approach to learning involves helping the student find meaning in the material from the student's vantage point. It's the student's discovery of meaning, not the teacher's, that makes or breaks the deep learner. So who is better equipped to create that kind of environment of discovery?

I believe content novices are in a better position than their expert colleagues to foster deep approaches to learning in students. Again, it's more difficult for content experts to judge how much material is appropriate for the beginner. The research on surface and deep learning shows that students are more likely to take a surface approach to learning when there is an excessive amount of material in the curriculum.[35] When there's too much work, students become anxious about meeting the course requirements and turn to superficial studying strategies. They also resort to surface learning strategies when they are anxious about how they are being assessed. Both content novices and experts can have less than ideal assessment strategies—anyone can create a bad exam—but a content expert is more likely to be out of touch with the problems that students encounter. Content novices offer more concrete strategies for dealing with entry-level problems, and those strategies should reduce performance anxiety and students' fear of failure.

A content novice is also more likely than a content expert to relate difficult concepts to everyday, common knowledge, to something the student already knows, simply because the instructor doesn't have a vault of specialized knowledge on the topic from which to draw. And that's a key to deep learning: by encouraging students to build on their existing knowledge, we help them understand the material on a meaningful level. Let's say that you're teaching a course on election campaigns as a content novice. As an outsider to the field, you'll probably focus on popular recent elections. You'll work from examples you know best, and since you're a commoner like the rest of us, the examples you know best probably overlap, to some degree, with the examples the students at least vaguely know. Not true if you're a content expert. The content expert is burdened by details and knowledge that she doesn't share with everyone in the room. She's much more likely to be enamored with the controversial presidential race between Samuel Tilden and Rutherford B. Hayes in 1876 (which, I hear, was very close). A content expert with strong pedagogical skills will bridge this new, unfamiliar territory to the things students know, of course, but a content novice is already standing on the students' side of the bridge.

That's not to say that content experts are doomed—of course they're not. Many experts are fabulous teachers. A content expert who is focused on creating a good learning environment will do all the things I've just described. She will make the workload more moderate, give concrete instructions about handling problems she knows students will encounter, and explain concepts in terms of familiar, everyday examples. But if you're a content novice, this will come more easily to you. The fact that you're not enamored of the material in a new course in the same way you're wedded to the material in your expertise can make you nervous as hell, but it can also create teaching advantages that most of us overlook. In the next few chapters, we'll look at practical strategies for building on those advantages.

3 Getting Ready

If you've just been assigned to teach a course that's outside your specialty and you're barely hanging on as it is (meaning that you rarely see your partner or get any exercise besides running to the photocopier), you might have skipped directly to this chapter and bypassed everything else. That's fine. Welcome aboard. You might enjoy reading the previous chapters when the course is over and you've gone for a long hike in the woods or sipped your share of Chardonnay.

For now, it's understandable if you just want some survival strategies. Most faculty who teach on the edge of their expertise are concerned about making the experience manageable, appearing credible and competent, and teaching the course well enough that students learn something of value. The rest of this book offers concrete advice from faculty who have taught on the edge and have lived to tell the tale. We'll also look at the research literature to see why certain strategies work and others typically don't.

As the title suggests, this chapter identifies steps you can take before the first day of class. It's focused on course design and is written for people who are still picking the readings, creating the syllabus, and envisioning the course. If your class starts tomorrow or if you're already teaching the course, I'd suggest that you skip ahead to the last section of this chapter, "Four Common Mistakes Instructors Make in the Planning Stages." (You may already have made some of these mistakes—most of us have—but the advice might save you from repeating them. It comes directly from professors who've been there themselves.)

Planning Backward

Let's focus on two priorities first: you want to teach well enough that students learn something valuable, and you want to manage your time well enough that you stay sane. Some instructors think these two priorities are mutually exclusive. The working assumption among them is that in order to teach a new course well, you have to be exhausted all the time. That's certainly true if you expect to be a walking encyclopedia on the topic. If this is the case, then you'll never know enough. Yes, it's always a lot of work to teach a new course, even if you know the topic well. But you can reduce the pressure if you remember a lesson from Chapter 2—your goal is to create an effective learning environment, not to tell students everything they need to know.

Fortunately, you can turn to the proven educational principle of backward design, also known as planning backward, to organize your class in a way that maximizes student learning and focuses your daily preparation.[1] It's called "backward" design because you begin with the end product first: what do you want students to be able to do as a result of learning in your course? Note that the emphasis is on what students can *do*, rather than what they will *know*. If the question is simply, "What will your students know?" you could generate a long list of theories, names, equations, competing hypotheses, whatever, and call it a day. (We'll get to the disadvantages of this approach in just a moment.) Planning backward involves asking a difficult question at the outset—you have to picture what your students will be able to do differently once they know all those theories, names, or equations—but it can make for a much better experience for everyone once the course is under way because your teaching efforts will be more focused, as will students' learning.

We'll begin with Step 1, stating concrete learning outcomes. What do you want students to be able to do? In an "Introduction to Anthropology" course, you might want students to be able to use evidence to argue why every educated citizen, not just select researchers, should know something about primates. Step 2 is to outline the kinds of evidence that will be acceptable. How will you know that students have reached competency on your learning outcomes? To demonstrate that beginning anthropology students can argue persuasively about the benefits of primate research, you might ask them to write a two-page letter to the local school board arguing why students should learn about primates in public schools. This anthropology assignment is effective because you've given students three things: (1) a task—they are trying to persuade someone; (2) an audience—the local school board; and (3) a format—a two-page letter.[2]

Step 3 is deciding what you need to do as the instructor and what students need to do as learners to produce that kind of evidence. What materials will students need to read or research to write that letter? What strategic advice or background information should you provide, and what kind of practice will they need? They will probably need to practice analyzing evidence and making persuasive arguments from that evidence.[3] It's important that students remember to think about their audience—and what twenty-one-year-old has ever sat on a school board? As an in-class activity, students could review two or three sample school-board letters (which can easily be found online) to identify the features of a persuasive, worthwhile letter. If you haven't encountered backward design before, you can see how this approach differs from the way most of us naturally design our courses. We usually begin with the calendar: we outline the readings first, figure out how many papers, homework assignments, or exams to give, and somewhere in there, typically toward the middle or end of the process, draft some language about what we want students to know, which inevitably leads to squeezing in some additional readings or assignments. I've done this many times myself, so you're in good company if I've just described how you designed your last course. One problem with this approach is that it lacks an academic purpose. Basically it's designed to fill the calendar. You'll certainly achieve that, but in doing so you'll commit yourself to covering all that content—some or all of which you don't know—without more meaningful learning goals in mind. Beginning with the calendar also encourages a "coverage" approach to teaching, and the consensus among educational researchers is that trying to cover as much as possible does not promote deep student learning. In fact, the "coverage" approach reinforces surface learning, which is short-lived and fragmented.[4]

In contrast, a backward design ensures that there is conceptual glue to hold the course together. (After all, you can't rely on your expertise to hold it together, as you normally would.) Backward planning increases the likelihood that the way you spend your time teaching will align with what students need to be doing. And research shows that teachers who use backward design more successfully connect the content in the course with other meaningful topics, a strategy that promotes deeper approaches to learning.[5]

I've just outlined the classic model of backward design, but given that you're teaching outside of your expertise, it might help to reframe Step 1. When you're not a content expert and you've never been to the end of the course before, you may not be able to state, with as much certainty and precision as you'd like, everything that your students should be able to do by the last day. In this case you can use a variation on Step 1: what are the big questions you want your students to answer by the end of the course? Your first step is to identify the important questions that students should be able to answer more intelligently and more critically in Week 10 or Week 15 than in Week 1. In our hypothetical anthropology class, the question might be, "Why do individuals and society benefit when we all know something about primates?" You can imagine other big questions in other courses. How can we explain the unethical practices of big and small companies? Why are self-help books so popular? What is a mathematical limit and why do we care?

As a content novice, you may not have definitive answers to these big questions before the course begins, and that's fine. (Actually, if you're teaching a calculus course and you can't answer the last question about limits, you may want to set this book aside for a moment and pull out a math text. If memory serves me correctly, you can't get very far in calculus without that concept.) For the most part, you can design a syllabus and a course without all the answers to the big questions filled in. After all, students learn on the basis of what *they* do in your course, not on the basis of what *you* know.

Backward design clearly has its merits, but why is this a good approach for content novices? In other words, why should you try this approach now? In part, you should use backward design to ensure that the course holds together conceptually, as we've already said, but there's a better reason. You should use this approach because you're uniquely positioned to teach more

effectively this way. Research tells us that people learn more
deeply when they are trying to answer questions that they themselves have deemed important or interesting.[6] One of the pitfalls
and ironies of undergraduate education is that the learner typically isn't in charge of asking the questions. This makes sense
because the average eighteen- to twenty-four-year-old doesn't
know enough to ask the best questions, at least not the best
questions about medieval literature, particle physics, or Asian
pottery.[7] Many instructors whose approach is learner-centered
try to begin with questions that will be compelling to students
and that will eventually lead to questions that are compelling to
the teachers as well. But being an expert can get in the way of
seeing the issues from a student's perspective. After all, when
you're the expert, you're fascinated by the inner latticework of
the issues and often can't formulate questions that beginners
will relate to. I like to think of this as the focused fervor of the
well-informed. That focused fervor is a lovely thing when it
comes to writing an article or a book, but it can lose students in
the classroom.

The beauty of being a content novice is that you have an outsider's level of excitement and curiosity. Think of it as the fervor
of the uninformed. You see what's interesting and what matters
to someone who is new to the topic because you're new to the
topic, too, and you see how the topic relates to other problems and questions in everyday life. The expert might balk at
the idea of asking questions about how her life's work applies
to mundane, everyday problems like talking with your parents
about politics or deciding how to price something on eBay. But
questions that might be demeaning to the experts are enticing to
content novices, just as they will be enticing to your students.
Your students will be more interested in learning because you've
asked the right questions from the start.

So we now know that backward planning helps students maximize learning, but can it help you better manage your time? Let's consider this important second point. If you've planned backward and set out the questions that students should be able to answer by the end of the course, your work is more focused and less scattered than if you were to take a calendar approach. It will help you determine what you need to be doing as the teacher and what they need to be doing as the students. Once you've identified the important end questions, you'll have a better sense of which concepts you'll need to research more intensively before class (instead of simply doing additional research on every detail in the reading that's new or hard to pronounce). You'll have a clearer picture of which course assignments are necessary (which might mean you'll assign a more reasonable amount of work for students to complete and for you to grade). I believe that one of the reasons we become so exhausted when we teach as content novices is that we don't know what's important to know. It's like a floodlight is illuminating the entire field of possibilities, so we scurry around, trying to learn about everything that anyone might possibly see. That means our efforts are diffuse and we work as hard as we humanly can; there's some sliver of consolation in that—we couldn't possibly have done more. But if you set your sights on focused and worthwhile questions at the beginning, you've created a spotlight instead of a floodlight. Sure, someone could ask about something that's outside of the spotlight, and we'll talk about answering those kinds of questions in Chapter 4. But the experience can be more manageable for you because you've set limits on what you should know. You've set the stage and focused everyone's attention, including your own, on what matters for this course.

This one principle alone can help you make decisions about where you should invest your time in the planning stages. If you're like me, though, you'd like some practical advice as well, not just a principle. The rest of this chapter offers some concrete advice for planning your course, much of which follows from the notion of planning backward.

How to Generate the Big Questions

The principle of backward design rests on asking good questions right from the start. After all, the big questions drive the rest of your choices. You can do two things to ensure that you pick good questions: (1) find someone to talk to about the questions; and (2) read the texts before the course begins.

Find an Ally or Supportive Colleague

Before you begin teaching outside your expertise, it's valuable to find some supportive colleagues to whom you can talk. There are two different kinds of allies, and they're useful for different reasons. The first is someone who is knowledgeable about the topic you'll be teaching. (We already discussed some of the benefits of connecting with a content expert in the last chapter.) If you're designing your course by asking, "What important questions do I want students to be able to answer?" an expert can help you decide what those important questions might be.

If you're a careful reader, you're probably thinking that I've just contradicted myself. As we saw in the last section, an expert can become lost in the minutiae of an academic field and fail to identify the best questions for beginners. I stand by that reasoning. But you, the well-educated content novice, have the chance to be a filter between the expert and your students. What big questions matter to the content expert when he or she teaches these topics? Do any of those questions remotely interest you? If you've already drafted some of the big questions that you're thinking of using for the course, consider bringing them to the content expert for feedback. (I'll admit, that takes some courage.) A friendly expert can offer guidance on how to frame those questions so they connect with big issues in the field, or she might suggest some authors or resources that will help you.

Everyone can benefit from the first kind of ally. The second is helpful to people who are feeling anxious. If you see yourself as among the Strained and Anxious content novices, as we discussed in Chapter 2, you'll also want to find someone you can talk to *about* the fact that you're teaching outside of your expertise, someone who will listen supportively to your concerns. If you're lucky, that person will also happen to be a content expert in the subject matter, but most of us need multiple mentors or allies.

Why is this helpful? At the most basic, pragmatic level, you're likely to get some constructive ideas. As I discovered in my interviews, most instructors have taught outside of their expertise at least once, and if the person to whom you turn is reflective and insightful about his teaching experience, he might offer some savvy advice. At a more psychological level, the junior faculty I interviewed, particularly junior faculty who were Strained and Anxious, felt relieved once they had a chance to talk about their teaching anxieties.[8] Instructors who started off a conversation by tensely listing complaints almost always ended the forty-five-minute interview laughing and saying that they felt much better, even though I offered very little advice—I basically just kept asking questions. Simply verbalizing their concerns helped anxious faculty feel less overwhelmed. They came to realize that learning the material while you teach it is a common, stressful, and survivable part of being a faculty member.

Whom should you approach for this kind of support? Look for someone who will strategize with you without judging you or using this information to question your credibility. If your campus offers a teaching center or professional development office, this can be an excellent place to start. These offices usually have confidentiality policies that allow you to describe your teaching concerns and discuss the support (or lack of support) that you're getting in your department. They may even be able to recommend a sympathetic content expert in your department or college who could help you deal with this increasingly common teaching concern.

You could also turn directly to another faculty member. In an ideal world, I'd like to say, "Talk to anyone on campus," because more faculty *should* be talking about how hard it is to teach these kinds of courses, but I realize that would be politically naïve of me. If you think some senior members of your department might frown on someone admitting a soft spot, ask a junior person instead. Some of the people I interviewed said that faculty in their cohort (that is, instructors who started at the same time they did) made great confidantes. If you're teaching a general education course, you may find that the director of the program is a supportive ally. As the director, she probably realizes that general education courses often require faculty to teach outside their comfort zone.

Read the Materials before the Course Begins

You may be thinking this is obvious—or this may be the piece of advice that you least want to hear. I'll write about it anyhow because it will improve your teaching and make your life more manageable once the course begins. However busy you are now, chances are you'll be much busier once you start teaching something you don't know well.

The advice is simple: read what you're planning to assign before the course begins. If you can't read everything, then skim as much of it as you can.

Why is this so important? First, reading the texts beforehand can help you generate the big questions that drive the course you want to teach. As you're reading, you'll be drawn to certain issues and bored with others. Maybe you've already got some big questions in mind before you read the texts, in which case, great, but you still want to read the texts to ensure that (a) they provide some answers to those questions; and (b) you can clearly see the link between the questions and the answers. A content expert might see the links, but you need to see them, too. Second, if the course is outside your expertise, then you're probably wrestling with the texts for the first time. You'll need time to educate yourself before you focus on educating others. Michael Bérubé, a professor of American studies and disability studies at Penn State, calls it the difference between a "personal read" and a "teaching read." He does the personal read a few months (or weeks) before the course begins and the teaching read much closer to the day they will be discussing that material.[9] The point of the personal read is to give you the lay of the land and to provoke big questions. It also gives you permission to read the texts without feeling like you have to have a pen in hand and a perfect plan in mind. The teaching read allows you to capture any information that will help you and your students answer those key questions.

That brings us to another important point: one of the challenges to teaching outside of your expertise is that you often can't see the big picture, how the different pieces fit together. Andrew Mills, an associate professor of philosophy at Otterbein College, had an appealing analogy. Andrew explained that when you're teaching *within* your expertise, it's like you're trying to give someone a tour of your hometown. You know all the main roads and where the side streets will take you. Because you know where the course is headed, you can respond to brilliant but premature student comments: "What you're saying, write that down because in three weeks I'm going to ask you to repeat that."

Teaching *outside* of your expertise, Mills explains, is like visiting a foreign city. When you're teaching as a content novice, all you have is a map, namely, your trusty syllabus, as to what comes next. "In that kind of course," he notes, "you just have to give yourself over to not knowing where you are. The next guy in the book is just the next guy in the book—[you] don't have a good sense of what it has to do with Rousseau or Freire. It just comes later." You have to pull your map out often and trust that eventually you'll get where you need to go.

By reading the texts before the course begins, you see more of the big picture and begin to create your own internal map. You're still a tourist, so to speak, but you have at least walked the route once. Of course, walking that route quickly by yourself is still vastly different from leading students on that journey, but at least you have some firsthand knowledge of where you're headed.

But what if the textbook is seven hundred pages?

The advice to "read everything beforehand" came predominantly from faculty in the humanities (for example, philosophy, English, and theology), where students usually read a stack of books or articles for class. This approach seems less manageable for faculty in the sciences, health professions, or business, who teach from dauntingly large textbooks. Naturally, most of us don't want to spend our summer break reading a seven-hundred-page physics or management text cover to cover.

But this advice can be adapted for these kinds of courses. If you'll be teaching from a sizeable textbook, I would suggest that you do two "teaching" reads and no "personal" read: a cursory teaching read before the course begins and another, more focused read as you prepare each class day. In the first, cursory read, allocate forty-five to sixty minutes to skim each chapter you're planning to assign. (So if you're planning to assign fourteen chapters, you'd allocate eleven to fourteen hours for the entire text. It's certainly a good chunk of time, but perhaps less than you expected.) This kind of skimming is hard for academics. Be diligent. Set a timer if you need to. Keep in mind that for some of your students, this cursory skim is the only kind of reading they will do. As you skim, take a few notes on your computer. The following questions will help you frame your notes in that initial, cursory read:

- Does the chapter raise any big questions for you?
- Which items in this chapter strike you as the most/least interesting?
- Which theories, findings, events, cases, or equations are most important to the field, to the best of your knowledge? If you can't answer that question because the topic is too far outside of your discipline, which concepts seem to get the most coverage in the chapter?
- Which concepts or examples are the hardest for you to understand? It's worth noting them now because one of the best ways you can use class time is to help students make sense of ideas that are unclear from the text alone.
- What background information will help students understand this chapter? This may be one area where you can draw on your existing expertise.
- Is there any advice you'd like to give students before they read this chapter? Or try completing this sentence for students: "Come to class ready to . . ."
- If you, the instructor, could pick only two or three things that you'd like to learn more about before you teach this chapter, what would they be?

If you don't skim the text systematically beforehand, you set yourself up for a pacing problem once the class begins. Without a clear grasp of your priorities and what lies ahead in the book, it's tempting to work through each chapter lockstep, starting at the beginning and covering as much as you can before class time is up. That means you're probably overwhelming students by the pace and volume of information, and you may miss ideas that are important or harder to understand later. If you have big questions that you've developed from your initial skim, you're more likely to cover what matters.

Organizing the Course to Boost Your Confidence

This probably seems like an odd title. I realize it's akin to something like, "Calling your mom to lose weight." Independently, calling your mom and losing weight might both be good ideas, but the two don't seem very connected. (And they probably aren't.) But there are some ways that you can organize your course to boost your confidence. Having big questions that guide how you spend time in class is one important step, and there are ways to organize the syllabus to increase your self-assurance once the course gets under way. It's obviously good for you if you're feeling confident, but it's also good for your students. You'll be more open to their questions, you'll provide clearer explanations because you won't be second-guessing yourself, and you'll be more comfortable saying, "I don't know," which is an essential phrase for the content novice. (We'll talk more about the many different ways to say "I don't know" in Chapter 4.)

Map Out Key Course Topics

The first strategy in boosting confidence is to take stock of your situation. By asking yourself some basic questions, you can clarify which topics in the course diverge from your expertise and therefore might be the most challenging to teach. Your answers will help you place certain topics (or due dates) strategically on the syllabus.

Take out a sheet of paper and divide it into three columns. In the first column, note the course topics and readings that fall within the core of your expertise. In the second column, place topics that are further toward the edge of your specialty. Finally, use the third column to list any topics that are clearly outside of your expertise.

Depending on the length of that third column, you may now be thinking, "It's not as bad as I thought," or, "I am in deep trouble." But once you have a better grasp of which parts of the course are in the core of your expertise and which parts are on the periphery, you can think more strategically about where to place material on the course calendar. For example, if only a few topics are outside of your expertise, plan for those to be lighter weeks. Don't schedule major exams or long papers those weeks, if you can avoid it. You don't want to find yourself with a stack of thirty research papers to grade the same week you're learning (and teaching) the hardest part of the course.

This list may also help you decide which topics to include and which topics to exclude as you design the course. If possible, limit the topics from the third column to areas you're genuinely excited to study. Let's face it—you're going to spend a lot of time learning those topics along with the students, so they might as well be compelling to you. If a topic in the third column happens to be one that you dread teaching or that you think will be boring, could you skip it altogether? Or could you address a related topic instead?[10]

Let's take an example from my own experience to illustrate how to make a periphery topic more appealing to you as the instructor. Ten years ago I first taught a course titled "Sensation and Perception." "Touch" is one of the five senses—every eight-year-old knows that—and it was one of the chapters in our textbook, but I knew nothing scientific about touch. And I didn't care to learn. But, and I hope this doesn't say something terrible about me, I was very interested in studying pain. Why does it hurt so much but so slowly when you stub your toe? How can some people skip Novocain when they go to the dentist's, whereas my jaw hurts if I even see the needle? When I designed the syllabus, I planned to spend 75–80 percent of the touch chapter focused on the special topic of pain. I loved that week of the course. I was more confident and less anxious because I was so fascinated by what I was learning. I would go into class saying, "Can you believe. . . ?" By pursuing a closely related topic that stoked my curiosity, I suspect I did a much better job teaching about touch.

Start the Course from the Core of Your Expertise

We've already talked about organizing your course around big questions, and it's important to introduce these big questions early in the course, both in the syllabus and on the first day of class so that students see your vision and what they should be able to do by the end of the course. It also helps to spend some time early in the course on a topic within your expertise. These two suggestions, different though they may be, aren't mutually exclusive. The big questions can help you identify something within your expertise that's relevant to the course.

Let's say that you're a chemistry professor teaching a freshman writing seminar titled the "Common Intellectual Experience." (This isn't a random example—it's a general education course taught at Ursinus College, and Codrina Popescu is a chemist who was once caught in this very predicament.) One of the big questions for the course is, "What does it mean to be human?" As a chemist, Popescu could invite students to answer this question from several perspectives. What does it mean to be human from a biochemical perspective? From a psychological perspective? Or a religious perspective? If she begins with the biochemical perspective, she could help students identify the different elements in the body (a rather cut-and-dry set of facts) and then move into some of the complex questions that biochemists are asking about humans, such as, if we're all made from the same basic elements, why do individuals age so differently, even at the cellular level? (a much more interesting question).[11]

By starting the course in familiar intellectual territory, you can reduce your anxiety levels. You also build credibility with the class if you start from a place of confidence, where you have facts, terms, and examples at your fingertips. If you discover in the first week that yes, the students do respect you as an instructor, you'll feel more confident and adventurous going into topics you know less well.

Penelope, an instructor from the College of William and Mary, took this idea one step further. She was able to organize her periphery course so that the entire first half of the semester was comfortably centered in her expertise. The second half of the course ventured into new applications of those concepts, but she had already established her credibility and a strong rapport with students, so she felt more confident saying, "Honestly, I don't know, but let's find out."

Build Flexibility into the Syllabus

A common source of anxiety a few weeks into a new course is the concern that you're falling behind or running ahead of schedule. A class might move more quickly or slowly than you anticipated. Maybe half the class failed an exam and you find yourself devoting extra time to explaining the grading, not to mention reviewing the concepts that no one understands. It's always difficult to anticipate the pace of a new course, and from what I've observed, faculty usually fall behind the first time they teach a new topic. In a course you know well, it's easier to figure out what you can consolidate or even cut later in the semester, but content novices often feel they need to cover everything. (Although it seems more common to fall behind, it can be particularly stressful to find yourself suddenly *ahead* of schedule, with ten minutes left in class and nothing to say. It's not the comfortable kind of silence you seek in life. In Chapters 4 and 7, we'll build an Emergency Assessment Kit that can help you use an unexpected ten to fifteen minutes of extra class time.)

My advice in the planning stages is to build some flexibility into the schedule so that if you fall behind, you can catch up. One way to create flexibility is to list the topics and readings on the calendar by week rather than by individual class sessions.[12] Another strategy that I use when I teach a course the first time is to include a class with a very short reading and an ambiguous topic about half-way or two-thirds of the way into the course, simply to build in a catch-up day if I need it. You can also indicate in the syllabus that a revised calendar will be issued midway through the course if needed.

While many syllabi include statements such as "The instructor reserves the right to change the syllabus at any time," I'd caution against it. Though it leaves some handy room for creativity, it can be confusing and off-putting to students, who may entertain the idea that you're unpredictable or, worse yet, vindictive. As an alternative, try: "Your learning is my principal concern, so I may modify the schedule if it will facilitate your learning," or, "We may discover that we want to spend more time on certain topics and less time on others. I'll consider changing the schedule if such a change would benefit most students' learning in this course."[13] This lets students know that you have everyone's best interests in mind.

Plan to Use at Least One Case Study

Whereas the last two suggestions—to include a familiar topic early in the course and to build flexibility into the syllabus—are both small scheduling adjustments, this last piece of advice has more significant implications for how you organize the course. The suggestion is to include at least one, perhaps more, case studies in your course. As we saw earlier, one way to build your confidence and keep the teaching experience manageable is to put reasonable limits around what you need to learn and know. Designing the course around big questions is one global way to achieve that kind of focus. Remember—you want a spotlight, not a flood light. A second, more localized way to focus your efforts as the instructor is to use a few case studies.

Why should you add cases to a course that's already a lot of work? If you use a well-placed case or two, you don't need to prepare as broadly. You can focus your background reading for a case because you're not doing a cafeteria-style coverage of all conceivable topics. When I was teaching about toddler development in a freshman seminar, I had the students research a case study of an adopted child with a hearing-impairment. Rather than memorizing all there was to know about physical, mental, and social development in the first three years of life, we looked at the nature/nurture issue through the lens of this boy's case.

The suggestion to incorporate case studies came from Barb Tewksbury, a professor of geoscience at Hamilton College. She often leads workshops sponsored by the National Science Foundation (NSF) to help junior faculty become better teachers. When we discussed strategies for managing the workload of a course outside of her expertise, she strongly recommended building the

entire course around case studies. (I'd make the milder suggestion of including a few case studies, but I think I'm just more
timid that she is.)

Cases stimulate deeper learning. Students are more intrinsically interested in the topic when they are trying to crack a case-
based problem, which means they are less driven by grades
and more driven by their curiosity.[14] For anyone who is trying to
discourage surface approaches to learning and encourage deep
thinking about evidence and conclusions, or cause and effect,
cases are an excellent way to go.

If you've never taught with cases, here's a quick primer on
how to do it. A good case study usually involves three elements:
(1) a real-world scenario (sometimes embellished or simplified
according to the audience); (2) data or evidence that students
can analyze; and (3) an open-ended question without an obvious
answer. The third element is the "assignment" that you'll probably be grading. It might require students to make a decision,
propose a solution, or debate an issue.[15] One reason that cases
work so well for teaching unfamiliar topics is that students share
the burden of being fact-finders. The students have their text as
one source of information, but they are actively working to understand how all the pieces of the case fit together, rather than
passively waiting for you to assemble the pieces in perfect working order.

But you still have plenty of work to do. As the instructor, you
need to structure the case activity, be sufficiently well-versed on
the details of the case to answer students' questions about the
basic facts, and lead a discussion of the case either during or after the assignment. If you're using cases for the first time, you
can refer to step-by-step online resources for using cases effectively. It's not a difficult pedagogical strategy, but you can benefit from the advice of experienced colleagues. (Appendix B lists

different resources for case-based teaching by academic discipline.) Case studies are most readily available in certain disciplines (the sciences, social sciences, business, public policy, law, and health professions), but case studies in the humanities are becoming more available on the web.

This suggestion to use cases won't work for all instructors. Your academic discipline may not use cases often, or timing may be a problem: if you need to purchase cases, you'll have to make that decision as you order textbooks. Despite these obstacles, using cases can help focus your efforts and maximize student learning when you're teaching outside of your comfort zone.

Four Common Mistakes Instructors Make in the Planning Stages

This last part of the chapter may be helpful to anyone, but I've written it with a particular group in mind: instructors who are teaching an entire course (or almost an entire course) that's outside of their expertise. It's hard to prepare an entire course on unfamiliar content—there's no getting around that—but if you can sidestep some common mistakes in the planning stages, you can make it a much better experience for you and your students. I offer this list of common mistakes with the hope that I might spare you several late nights and give you a few more Sunday afternoons to spend as you like. I know my husband wishes I'd had this advice sooner.

Mistake 1: Underestimating How Much Time It Will Take to Prepare

I'm listing this as the number one mistake because faculty, both young and old, repeatedly told me that they always underestimate how much time it will take them to teach something new. Even if you're excited about the course and volunteered to teach it, it will zap your time and energy. Lydia McAllister, an associate professor of nursing at Seattle University, summed it up as follows: "You should assume that, midway through the course, you are going to be more tired than usual—and by the end, you'll need a much better vacation."

Mistake 2: Assigning Too Much Work

Why would faculty assign too much work? Part of the problem is related to the first mistake—it's hard to gauge how much work and time the class is going to take. As we learned in the last chapter, we all tend to overestimate task difficulty to some degree. There are two additional reasons you're likely to assign too much. You may be modeling the course after someone who had more content expertise, particularly if you're working from someone else's syllabus. A content expert can assign more work because it probably didn't take him as long to prepare the classes, research the answers to students' questions, and grade the assignments as it will take you to do the same tasks. And let's be honest—chances are that a content expert also got more sleep than you will be getting.

Some instructors assign too much because they are tempted to try a variety of assignments. And some variety is good. Part of providing a positive learning environment is giving students different ways to demonstrate their mastery of the material. Some students will excel on exams and others will think more clearly on a research project. But too much variety leaves you scattered and overwhelmed. If you try too many novel assignments, you could find yourself slogging through mounds of unexpected work. Even a tried-and-true assignment or project may take more time than usual when it's wrapped around a new topic.

The simplest, most concrete step is to reduce the number

of graded assignments by one. This may seem like a very small step. But by removing just one paper or problem set, you've saved yourself a considerable amount of time: the time it takes to create the assignment; meet with anxious students before it's due; generate grading criteria; grade the assignments; offer feedback; and wrangle with students about the whole process afterward.

Let's consider the grading, because it's easy to overlook how much time this is going to take. (I know an ambitious management instructor who realized after the course was over that he had graded and offered feedback on more than 800 pages of students' work.) Let's assume that you're expecting 24 students in the course and that you're using a pretty standard (though not your most exciting) assessment plan: you're envisioning three exams of 4–5 pages each, plus you want students to do a 10-page research project. That might sound reasonable, but if you do the math, assuming that two exams will be 4 pages each and one will be 5 pages, you're looking to grade roughly 552 total pages.

If you were to drop just one exam, you'd knock almost 20 percent off your grading workload. One word of advice: though it may be tempting, don't simply eliminate the longest assignment because that assignment may be the backbone of your assessment plan, the culmination of students' work throughout the term.

If dropping one assignment isn't an option, consider cutting the longest paper in half. A shorter paper can be just as challenging as a longer one if it's designed well, and shorter papers often require students to practice higher-order thinking skills, such as synthesizing and prioritizing, because they have to cut all irrelevant details.[16] I once saw a clever anthropology assignment that required students to use a picture or drawing of an everyday household object from the nineteenth century, like a rocking chair, and create a 300-word museum description of that object. They had to explain the object's importance in American society in language that would make sense to the average museum patron. I imagine those 1-page papers were delightfully quick to grade but still met the learning outcomes—namely, they demonstrated how well students understood what they had learned.

Mistake 3: Failing to Manage Other People's Expectations

This mistake is particularly common for new tenure-track faculty. By managing expectations, I mean helping people in your department have realistic expectations about the quantity and quality of work that you'll be able to do, and letting key people know when you'll be less visibly productive. Some new instructors don't say anything because they haven't come to grips with their schedule, and they see everything as equally impossible, rather than impossible in varying degrees. Others fear they will hurt their tenure chances if they admit that they need to cut back at all, for any length of time.

But in my experience and in my conversations with department chairs, I've found that most people have greater respect for someone who is honest and sets realistic, moderate expectations than for someone who either sets unrealistic expectations or, more commonly, avoids direct conversations about expectations altogether and then disappoints people. It's particularly important to talk with departmental colleagues who have a commitment from you. You don't have to fully disclose that you're teaching something you don't know—simply tell them that you're doing some new prep and it's a lot of work. Most people will understand.

Linda Gabriel, who teaches occupational therapy at Creighton University and was herself the vice chair of her department for eight years, explains, "Sometimes people just forget. You would hope that the chair or vice chair would say, 'Let's not ask Linda because it's the first time she's teaching this class.' But people don't think of it in the moment. They just know that something needs to be done and needs to be done well, and 'Oh, Linda would be good.'" What's her advice? "Just speak up for yourself. It usually works to say, 'I'm teaching this class for the first time and I'm really trying to put a lot of my energy in this.'" If you're collaborating on a research project or co-authoring a paper, discuss what you can and cannot contribute while you're preparing and teaching the course. If you're on a committee, talk with the chair and agree to take on more tasks or responsibilities later in exchange for a work reduction now.

If you're still wavering on whether you need to say anything, keep this in mind: if you're a new hire in your department, your colleagues will be trying to gauge your potential for future productivity. You want them to see that when you set a goal, you achieve it. You don't want them to see that when you make a commitment, you renege later.

Mistake 4: Forgetting What They've Learned

If you have taught other courses, chances are you've identified some strategies for sequencing the different parts of a course so that it's a good experience for you and your students. You've learned when the best and worst times are to schedule certain activities. Maybe your mantra is, "Never give tests on a Friday" or "Build in time for student meetings at midterm." Whatever strategies you've learned about structuring the timing of different events, remember those strategies and apply them in your periphery course as well. It's surprisingly easy to forget those strategies when you're wrangling with unfamiliar topics.

I can give you an example from Kevin Otos, the drama professor at Elon University. About eight weeks into teaching a course outside of his expertise, Kevin realized he'd ignored a tried-and-true lesson that he'd learned from nine years of teaching. In his theater courses, he ordinarily places more work-intensive assignments early in the course—harder texts, projects that require a lot of out-of-class group work, and so on. He finds that he gets higher-quality work from students if he schedules demanding assignments early in the course, and then glides into easier readings and assignments toward the end of the term, when everyone is tired and struggling to meet all their deadlines. But he forgot to apply this principle in his general education course, in part because he designed this course from a typical starting point—he began with someone else's syllabus.

The point is not to frontload your course with harder assignments (though there are certainly merits to this strategy, so that's a bonus piece of advice). The important point is to pay attention to the lessons you've learned in designing other courses because your wisdom applies here, too. It's fine to begin with someone else's syllabus because that can save you time and anxiety, but before you are lulled into complacency by their course design, step back and take fifteen minutes to think about your other teaching experiences. Whatever golden truths you've learned, honor them here, too.

4   Teaching and Surviving

You've probably heard of the Running of the Bulls that takes place in northern Spain each summer. At 8:00 every morning for about a week, a pack of six bulls is released onto the streets of Pamplona. A gate blocks the massive, agitated bulls from a group of nervous runners, each brave athlete dressed in spotless white with a red handkerchief carefully tied at the neck. Then a rocket is launched, the gate is lifted, and the race begins. Participants run in a teeming, confused mass through the walled and curving streets. The runners do their best to stay at least a few paces ahead of these scary animals, some more successfully than others. I imagine that everyone, bulls included, looks considerably less pristine and well-composed by the end.

Teaching outside your expertise is a bit like this nerve-racking event. There's mounting anticipation, a fair share of running, and a general sense of chaos. Of course, few faculty are trampled by their students, and we're all thankful for that. But for many of us, it can feel like a frenetic race to stay a few chapters or even pages ahead of the class. And we may feel walled in because, in the rush of the moment, we don't have the time to do those clever and creative things we'd originally envisioned for the course.

The runners at Pamplona have at least one obvious advantage over you. The famous bull run lasts, on average, about three minutes. Compared with your sixty- or ninety-minute class, that might seem like an attractive trade.

In this chapter, we'll examine teaching strategies you can use once the course begins. My goal is to help you be a credible, effective, student-centered teacher, while keeping the entire experience as manageable as possible. In other words, I'd like to help you stay ahead of the bulls and arrive at the end of the course still standing—maybe even smiling, with a sense of a job well done.

Establishing Credibility

According to James Eison, founding director of the Center for Teaching Enhancement at the University of South Florida, Tampa, "One secret to good teaching, passed on through the ages, is 'to appear to have known all your life what you learned earlier in the day.'"[1] It's so true. We'd all like to step into class with confidence and credibility on any topic. But how can you walk into a classroom and be credible when you're just a chapter ahead of the students?

The good news is that students view credibility as much more than just expertise in the subject matter. Your knowledge of the field may be the primary way that you earn credibility from your colleagues, but you have a different relationship with students and you establish credibility, respect, and trust in different ways. Research shows that instructors tend to *lose* credibility with their students when they:

- show up late to class
- lack familiarity with the text
- cannot explain difficult concepts
- rarely ask if students understand their explanations
- do not make any attempt to answer students' questions
- provide unclear expectations and vague answers to students' questions about course policies, tests, quizzes, or other graded assignments
- fail to follow the course policies outlined in the syllabus (particularly when they change grading policies)
- fail to remind students of upcoming deadlines and due dates[2]

A few of these items relate to the instructor's knowledge of the subject matter, and we'll return to those in a moment. But most striking about this list is that it suggests that much of your credibility arises from creating a positive learning environment, a key principle in Chapter 2. Credibility in the classroom is largely gained or lost on the basis of whether you show respect for the students, an interest in their learning, and a commitment to following the policies you outlined in the syllabus. It's like something your grandmother would have told you: treat others the way you'd like to be treated.

Fortunately, you can treat students well even if you're new to the material. There are several things you can do to create the kind of credibility that matters to students and the kind of environment where they feel supported in their learning:

- Show up on time for class, preferably early, so you have a chance to connect with students and find out if they have any questions.

- Periodically ask students if they understand the material. Research indicates that students pay attention in chunks of roughly fifteen to twenty minutes at the start of a typical lecture class, and if students are struggling to understand you, you may not even hold their attention that long.[3] Try checking in with students at least three times an hour. You obviously don't want to stop mid-sentence every twenty minutes, but there are times when it makes sense to ask students how well they understand the material. Some of the best times to check in would be after explaining a concept that you found confusing when you were preparing for class; when you're transitioning from one big topic to another; or whenever there is a long period when you're the only one talking. If students normally participate in your class every few minutes and fifteen minutes go by with no comments (or heckling), then it's time to ask which concepts they would like you to review. A prolonged silence could mean that students are absorbed in thought, or it could mean they're so lost they aren't even sure what to ask.

- Before assignments are due, provide clear reminders of your expectations. Set aside time in class to answer students' questions about the guidelines for homework, projects, and writing assignments, and clarify which material will be covered on an upcoming exam. It's important to communicate your standards for excellence so that students can generate their best possible work. If you're concerned that this approach is akin to "teaching to the test," try to look at it another way: if you can't articulate what you expect, students have little chance of knowing what that might be. And we're usually in danger of having less-defined expectations when we're teaching outside of our expertise, so it's important to be explicit, both for ourselves and for our students. Just as you'd expect a funding agency to provide clear instructions on the types of proposals they will fund, students want you to provide clear instructions on the type of work that's going to earn an A.

- Review the grading policies and due dates provided in the syllabus on Day 1 and adhere to those policies and dates unless something needs to change. Once you're teaching the course, you may discover that something simply isn't going to work. That happens. If a policy or due date must be changed, make it a priority to talk with your students about the reasons necessitating the change and discuss the potential alternatives. If possible, give students an opportunity to discuss and vote on which alternative they prefer. Students, like the rest of us, are more receptive to change when they have some input in deciding what that change will be.

Let's return for a moment to the list of practices that undermine faculty credibility in students' eyes. Two items are directly related to your content knowledge: a familiarity with the text and an ability to explain difficult concepts. We'll consider these in turn.

Staying on top of the reading assignments is time-consuming, obviously, but it's nonetheless important. I discussed reading strategies in the last chapter, but I mention this topic again because you can bet there will be weeks when you'll think that you don't have time to read through the entire chapter. Take a piece of advice from Mike Flynn, the linguistics professor from Carleton College who has taught twenty courses outside of his expertise: "Roll up your sleeves and read; there's no getting around it."

Explaining difficult concepts in ways that are clear and easy to understand can be a challenge for content novices. Before you begin ironing out a clear explanation, you first need to recognize which concepts are difficult. Because you're new to the material, some of the challenging concepts will probably be confusing to you, too. In this one instance, your confusion is good news—you can more easily identify where students will probably need help. The bad news, of course, is that being able to point to the hardest part of the chapter, book, or case doesn't mean you can explain it any better than the author does. (Later in this chapter I offer concrete guidelines for making hard concepts easier to teach.)

Although some difficult concepts jump out at you, not all of them will. Some concepts will be easy for you but still difficult for your students. Years of practice, even in a slightly different field, result in blind spots to some basic concepts and skills that have become easy for you but are still developing for your students. Blind spots occur often in teaching, even if you're teaching outside of your field. An art professor who, by some role of the dice, is teaching a music appreciation course might play a recording of a Bach concerto and say, "Now listen for when the violins come in." Those violins might be obvious to her, so she completely overlooks the fact that many beginning students might not be able to distinguish the sound of a violin from that of other instruments. It's easy to become preoccupied with how you'll explain the concept that gives *you* trouble, and in the process, you assume that everyone shares some other piece of knowledge you've had for years. So be aware that you might have blind spots. Ask your colleagues about the skills and knowledge students might not possess (again, a good reason to have an ally who's a content expert) or conduct some web research to identify common proficiencies or knowledge gaps. Better yet, ask your students directly—Chapter 7 offers ways to make it safe for students to admit what they don't know.

Jan Meyer and Ray Land have compiled a book of the academic concepts that routinely perplex students. Each chapter of the book, titled *Overcoming Barriers to Student Understanding*, is dedicated to a different discipline and offers examples of "threshold concepts" that students find troublesome.[4] For example, in economics, "opportunity cost" is considered a threshold concept. Undergraduate students in economics can often provide a textbook definition of opportunity cost, like the simple one I'm about to give you. Whenever you make a decision to do something, the opportunity cost is the value of the next most attractive alternative that you didn't choose. If you are choosing between going to a movie and taking your dog for a hike and you decide to go with the movie, you pay an opportunity cost to see the movie. That cost is the price of your movie ticket (obviously) plus whatever pleasure, companionship, and health benefits you would have enjoyed from the time with your dog in the sunshine (less obviously).[5] This kind of example is helpful because it makes the concept of opportunity cost accessible—we can all relate to making decisions about how to spend a Saturday afternoon—but it also tends to trivialize what is actually a more complicated concept. If students don't move past this kind of simplified thinking, they can't harness some of the power behind this idea. They are limited to the kinds of economic analyses they can already perform.

Threshold concepts like this one are troublesome and often counterintuitive in that they are specific to an academic discipline and typically require students to reorganize their existing knowledge. Because they are challenging, students often need to see them more than once. But the repetition is worth it. Once threshold concepts are understood, they "irreversibly transform the students' view" and open new ways of thinking.[6] In sociology, once you've begun to see the world through the lens of white privilege, it can be difficult to return to your previous way of thinking. In physics, once you've begun to see the physical world in terms of heat transfer, you don't see a cold metal doorknob the same way again.

It's worth doing a little research to find out if there are any threshold concepts in the new course that you're teaching. Threshold concepts are fundamental and central ideas in a field; these are core concepts you've probably studied, unlike the jargon that specialists use to discuss a nuance of the field. So if the periphery course you're teaching is in your department (even if it's a distant cousin to the courses you normally teach), chances are that you *do* know one or two of the threshold concepts that are troublesome for students. A good way to boost your credibility with students would be to spend class time helping them wrestle with those concepts.

Confirmation Bias

Ron Krabill, an assistant professor at the University of Washington-Bothell, shared an interesting observation about credibility: his students assume that he's teaching what he knows best, even when he's not. Ron's Ph.D. focused on the history and sociology of South Africa, but he now teaches in an interdisciplinary arts and sciences program. It is a generalist's dream and a specialist's nightmare. He's almost always teaching outside his expertise: "One thing that always strikes me in my teaching evaluations is how high students rate their confidence in 'the instructor's knowledge of the subject area.' My numbers for that question are always very high. And that's striking to me because I don't position myself as an expert." If anything, he explicitly tells students that he's not an expert on the material—but they still see him that way. I heard similar stories from several instructors who weren't scholars in the subject matter and didn't pretend to be. It's certainly reassuring to hear that students give some of us the benefit of the doubt, but why does this happen? And can we make it happen more often?

Some faculty might say that this is another indication that course evaluations are ineffective, but I'd like to propose an alternative explanation. Faculty teaching outside of their expertise may be seen as more knowledgeable than they actually are because students have a confirmation bias. A confirmation bias is a tendency to notice instances that are consistent with your expectations and ignore, downplay, or forget everything else. In other words, we tend to "see what we want to see."[7] If you believe that there is always a long line at the post office, you'll vividly remember every time you shuffle along in line, loathing the person at the counter with the unlabeled boxes. If you're like me, you'll probably forget those days when you walk right up to the counter. That's a confirmation bias. Or if you're a juror in a trial, you might form an initial impression of the accused. When evidence is presented that is consistent with your view, you'll accept it at face value and probably find it highly persuasive, but when evidence is presented that challenges your view, you'll either downplay it or submit it to intense scrutiny.[8] (You might also notice a confirmation bias when you talk politics with your in-laws.)

Students have confirmation biases about their professors, and these biases can work in your favor when you're teaching outside of your expertise. Just as you expect to see a line at the post office or expect the "real" evidence to align with your point of view, students expect you to know what you're talking about because you're the professor.

But first impressions are important. The research on confirmation bias in other situations predicts that if students believe that you're credible in Week 1, this belief will persist despite missteps later in the course. Cognitive psychologists call the impact of first impressions the "primacy effect." Researchers have shown that when people need to draw conclusions on the basis of evidence they gather over a period of time, the information that they gather early has a greater influence on their conclusions than the information they gather later. If you go to a new post office and there are no lines on your first two visits, you'll quickly come to cherish that post office. The research also tells us that once a person has developed a belief, that belief is very resistant to change, even in the face of contradicting evidence. This "belief persistence" shapes the way you take in new information. When new information is ambiguous (which is most of the time), people are more likely to interpret the ambiguity in favor of their beliefs. If you learn that the mail at that fantastic post office is often picked up a few hours late, you'll interpret this to mean you've got some extra time to drop off your mail, not that they have unreliable service. Your belief of the best post office is preserved. Belief persistence also means that when new information challenges existing beliefs, people are more likely to ignore it, forget it, or come up with a reason to explain it away as inconsequential.[9] What happens if there's a line on your fourth visit to the world's best post office? I'll bet you blame it on the time of day (or Congress, depending on your politics).

So how does this apply to your credibility in the classroom? If your students already respect you, they will rationalize away your less-than-brilliant moments. Erin Buzuvis, the law professor from Chapter 1, could see this happening with her students:

"When students are studying for the bar, if they find some detail on the books that contradicts something I said in class, they would probably think, 'Buzuvis must have been thinking about Massachusetts law and I'm taking the bar in Connecticut.' It wouldn't be a big deal. And that's if they even remember the details of what I said."

This news may not be earth-shattering, but the point is that a confirmation bias can help you. If students' initial impression is that you know what you're doing, they'll keep seeing you as competent, despite moments later in the term when you get confused in the middle of a story, write an equation incorrectly on the board, or give a wrong answer to a question. Students who believe in you will forget these missteps or explain them away. Of course, the confirmation bias can also work against you—if students' initial impression is that you're *not* someone they can respect and trust, then you might find it very hard to gain that credibility later. (Unfortunately, I've seen this happen for faculty who lose their temper the first or second week of class. They find it very hard if not impossible to regain the trust of the group.)

What are the practical implications for your teaching? First of all, try not to lose your temper the first week of class. More generally, start the course from a place of strength. When you were designing your syllabus, I hope you took the advice in Chapter 3 and placed some topics you know well early in the course. Teaching in familiar territory will boost your confidence and help establish your credibility.[10] Second, invest some time those first two weeks in introducing students to *your* way of thinking. I mean that not in a narcissistic sense but in a disciplinary sense. If you're a mathematician, why are mathematicians concerned with those big questions you described on Day 1? As an art historian, how would you approach the problem raised in the first chapter of the book?

These strategies from the research literature will go a long way toward establishing your credibility in the classroom, but some common-sense approaches can work as well. The way you introduce yourself on the first day of class helps frame your authority. You can introduce yourself as Professor Smith rather than just as Antoinette Smith. You can dress more formally for the first few classes, avoiding the tee shirts and jeans that put you on a par with your students.[11] (What you wear sounds trivial, but it can be especially important if you're female, young, or a person of color, because some students may question your authority.) You can mention your degree, your professional background, other schools where you've taught, places where you've traveled (if that's relevant), or cases you've worked on. Ideally, choose something that students will respect and value. I once worked with a voice professor at a drama conservatory who found that her students showed more respect when she began dropping the names of actors and actresses she knew. She preferred just to give her title and the years she'd worked on Broadway—saying anything more felt like bragging. But it was clear that name-dropping was the norm in her department and that students respected the famous names more than her years in New York. It took time, but she found ways to use this tactic that fit her personality. Admittedly, you may not have worked with Anthony Hopkins or Liza Minnelli, but chances are you have a few interesting experiences that will bolster your credibility.

Credibility Issues among Faculty of Color

Earlier I noted that confirmation bias helps *most* faculty gain quick credibility with their students. I said "most" faculty because, unfortunately, faculty of color often report that students directly question their credibility and authority, even when they are teaching within their expertise.[12] Any instructor, of course, might come up against this problem, but the empirical research indicates that it's more likely to happen to faculty of color. For example, faculty of color are more likely than their white counterparts to report that students interrupt class to state the exception to any generalization that the instructor makes. They also find that students are more likely to correct small mistakes that an African-American or Latino professor makes.[13] Many female faculty of color report finding it demeaning and frustrating to be asked, time and again, "Where did you earn your degree?" A female African-American economics instructor described having a line of twenty students waiting to argue their exam grades even though her white colleagues, who teach the same courses and use the same syllabi and exam questions, had no lines of contentious students.[14]

One of my friends is an African-American associate professor in her thirties. She notes that young female faculty of color often find themselves in a triple bind: they try to parcel out which aspect of their identity is causing people to see them as less credible than their peers. Or is it the combination of age, sex, and ethnicity? Trying to figure this out compounds the stress of being challenged at every turn. "I wear glasses instead of contacts just to look older," she says with a smile.

Although this is largely a problem with white students, it is by no means confined to them. Surprisingly, students of color often show the same lack of trust and respect as their white peers, hinting that the credibility problem is more insidious than just white students' assuming an unfounded superiority. At schools where both students and faculty are predominantly white, even students of color admit that they are more likely to question the authority and credibility of their African-American faculty.[15]

Fortunately, this is not the story for all faculty of color. I have read and heard the stories of many minority instructors who have not encountered challenges to their credibility and authority. But this phenomenon is common enough that it needs to be addressed.

So what can faculty of color do to establish and maintain credibility when they feel challenged by their students? It's still crucial to follow the advice we've discussed so far—stay on top of the readings, strive for clear explanations of difficult concepts, and show an interest in students' learning. Many faculty of color also insist on being addressed by their formal titles as a way to communicate their authority.[16] Some noted the importance of being well organized in class from Day 1, with handouts, Power-Point slides, or whatever materials seem appropriate to the learning experience. Although such evident care would raise perceptions of credibility for instructors of any race or ethnicity, faculty of color report that these visible demonstrations of professionalism help quell the challenges to their authority.[17]

Finding a mentor appears to be especially valuable for faculty of color, many of whom told me they sought out a mentor outside of their departments, someone who knew the culture and politics of the institution. Some faculty prefer colleagues of color as mentors, but others point out that white colleagues can be just as valuable and potentially more readily available if you're on a campus where there are only a few senior faculty of color who are already spread thin in their roles. The important thing is to find someone who is knowledgeable about diversity issues and in whom you can confide honestly about challenges to your credibility, particularly when you're teaching outside of your expertise.[18]

I had the opportunity to speak with Beverly Daniel Tatum, an African-American professor of clinical psychology and the president of Spelman College. One of her specialties is the role of race in the classroom, so I was hoping she might have some advice for faculty of color who are concerned about credibility issues. She recalled her own experience as a new tenure-track faculty member early in her career. She began teaching a course called "Psychology of Racism" at Westfield State College in western Massachusetts in 1983. "There were credibility issues for me," she explained. "First, I was a young instructor, having just finished my Ph.D. three years earlier. Second, the general student attitude was, 'You're not objective. You can't be objective as a black woman teaching in a mostly white environment.'" Even if she gave them an article to read that provided data about racist behaviors, students could shrug those findings away, rationalizing that she wasn't giving equal time to the articles they imagined must be out there debunking this view.

Beverly quickly discovered that students were less likely to question her credibility when she created situations in which they discovered and learned things themselves. She would send students on field assignments to collect data in different environments, at grocery stores or in libraries, so that they could rely on their own experience for authority. When they came back to class perplexed or outraged by some racist behavior they had observed, she could put her expertise to work to help them understand the theories underpinning those behaviors. This strategy not only increased her credibility but also made her a more effective teacher. I describe her story and this teaching strategy in more detail in Chapter 6.

Deciding What To Tell Your Students

Professors often wonder if it's wise to tell students when they're teaching outside their expertise. In my observation, instructors fall into three categories when it comes to talking with students about their expertise in a course. Some instructors are direct and honest with their students when a topic isn't their specialty. Most faculty I interviewed fell into this first group. Instructors in the second group are selectively less direct—they tell students in some courses but not others. The third group consists of instructors who simply have not broached the topic at all. Some instructors have intentionally avoided the issue for their own compelling reasons. For others, it wasn't a conscious decision—they just never thought to mention it.

I'd like to help you make a conscious decision. Why should you tell students that you're teaching on the edge of your expertise? Why not?

Reasons You Should Tell Them

The main reason to tell students that you're teaching on the edge of your expertise is to reduce the stress and pressure you experience. After all, it's a tremendous burden to be thought of as the all-knowing authority in a room when you're actually not. Among those I interviewed, faculty who were happy teaching outside of their comfort zone—the Poised and Confident group from Chapter 2—were typically direct with their students about their strengths and limitations with the course material. Many of them told their students when a topic or even most of the course was outside of their expertise.

By contrast, the faculty members who were the most unhappy about teaching as content novices were also anxious that students would discover that they were imposters. They did not tell their students they were teaching something new; in fact, they often felt pressure to maintain an illusion of expertise. The anxiety of being found out and the amount of work it took to recreate the illusion each day was incredibly stressful for these instructors.

By telling students when you're teaching outside of your comfort zone, you can also improve your rapport with them and build trust in the classroom. Lydia McAllister, an associate professor of nursing at Seattle University, said that one of her primary reasons for telling students is that she wants to set a standard for honesty: "If you want your students to be open and honest with you, then you have to be open and honest with them."

Another way to think of this is that if you take risks, your students will be more willing to take risks. In his book *What the Best College Teachers Do*, Ken Bain observed this pattern in the classrooms of outstanding teachers—when faculty were open with their students about their own struggles with the material, students reported feeling more comfortable with their own confusion.[19] Students felt that it was more acceptable to be ignorant in class when they knew that the material hadn't come automatically or easily for their instructor. They were more willing to make mistakes, think out loud, and ask more genuine questions.

Several people alluded to this risk-taking in my interviews. Recall the story of Codrina Popescu, the chemistry professor introduced in Chapter 1 who found herself teaching about the Declaration of Independence and slave narratives in a freshman seminar. These are not topics she knew well. Naturally, they weren't part of her chemistry training, and, having been raised in Romania, she didn't watch videos about the Underground Railroad in elementary school. One important lesson she learned from that course was that professors try too hard to be perfect. She certainly did. "But students don't learn more when you're perfect," she found. "They learn more when you make it an environment where it's safe to be confused and ask questions." When she admitted that she was learning much of the material herself and that she was personally shocked by these narratives, students began making more earnest comments. They asked about dignity and cruelty, about what people were thinking and what humanity was capable of doing. It was as though there was less pressure to be people with answers and more room to be learners with questions. Her risk-taking paid off.

If you're teaching only a few topics that are new to you, you might find it surprisingly energizing and liberating to walk into class and admit your utter confusion. David Green, an adjunct instructor in international studies, told me about a time when he basically announced, "I've tried to make sense of this. I know it's a classic text and that's why I've included it on the syllabus. I understand parts of it, but I find other parts really confusing. So I'll tell you what I think, but I'm very interested in hearing how you read this." He said his admission generated one of the best discussions the class had all term. Even chronically quiet students spoke up that day, trying to squeeze meaning from awkward passages of text. Obviously, you couldn't take this approach every class day for ten to fifteen weeks, but used selectively, this kind of candid conversation can be a powerful way to spark discussion.

Reasons You Shouldn't Tell Them

For most instructors, openness will reduce stress and foster better student inquiry. But it may not be the right choice for everyone.

If you can't admit your lack of expertise in a positive way, don't do it at all. If you know that you'll make it sound like a complaint, please stay silent on the issue. I spoke with an assistant dean of a business school who had received student complaints about an accounting instructor who made the following announcement in class: "I was a philosophy major. I don't know much about accounting, but I didn't have much choice in the matter, so I'll do what I can. You're on your own with the text-book, and don't expect me to be able to answer all of your questions." Of course, this was a student's memory of what was said, but the clear message was that "learning this material is your problem, not mine." If you fear sounding resentful because the course was thrown at you at the last minute or you simply don't want to be there, then don't tell students that you're teaching outside your training. You'll most likely make your life more difficult, not less, by doing so.

If you believe your authority and credibility are likely to be challenged in most courses that you teach, you may want to think twice about telling students you're teaching on the edge of your expertise. As we saw earlier, faculty of color often receive more direct and indirect challenges to their authority, even when they are experts on the topic. A female instructor in a field that's traditionally dominated by men (such as law, medicine, engineering, or computer science) may also think twice before standing up in front of a class and saying, "I don't know as much as some other professors do."

But some faculty of color pointed out that it's all in how you say it. Beverly Daniel Tatum could appreciate that if instructors weren't receiving the respect they deserved from students, those instructors would be highly reluctant to reveal when they were still learning the material. But, she said, "For me, it's valuable to be authentic. When I was teaching a new course at UC Santa Barbara or Westfield State College, I would be honest with my students and say, 'This is new for me as well.'" And then she laughed. "But I wouldn't say, 'I just read the book.'" She found ways to be honest with students but she used "discretion in disclosing the details," to borrow a phrase from the literature on time management.[20] If it wasn't her expertise, she played up her other strengths. When she was teaching "Qualitative Research

Methods" for the first time, she admits that she didn't feel completely on top of the subject matter. "But I didn't go into class and say, 'I'm not completely on top of it.' Instead, I talked about what I did know."

Frame the Experience Positively

Let's assume that you've decided to tell students that you're teaching some material that's new to you, but you're wondering what to say. You don't want to admit, "I have no idea what I'm doing," or "I'm sorry you're stuck with me." The most important thing you can do is to frame the experience positively. This was a clear pattern in my interviews. Faculty who were excited about teaching outside their comfort zone (the Poised and Confident group) had ways of presenting the situation that were affirming and realistic rather than frustrated and grim. The literature also suggests that if you can frame a situation positively, students will be more receptive to the material. When you frame a set of circumstances so that people see the situation as a personal gain rather than as a personal loss, they will be more accepting of those circumstances.[21]

Survey Courses

If you're teaching a broad survey course that encompasses topics you know well in addition to topics you're still learning or relearning, begin by framing students' expectations. Imagine that you're a history professor teaching the all-encompassing "Western Civilization" course: "This is a survey course, which means we'll learn interesting things about key world events and we'll identify the political, social, and economic forces that have contributed to Western culture. I'm an expert in some of these topics but I'm certainly not an expert in all of them. We'll be surveying 2,000 years of history—I couldn't possibly be. But I can help you make sense of the most important issues and help you see why each topic is important to understanding Western culture and society." As the course progresses, you can draw attention to topics that fit your expertise by providing some context: "My Ph.D. is in the early history of Christianity, so I've really been looking forward to this part." When students like a professor, they like to hear about his research. For a topic on which you're particularly rusty, you might say, "It's important that we learn about imperialism. We want to see how Europe came to dominate Asia and Africa because we can trace a good number of today's problems in those countries to that empire. But I want to admit upfront that it's not my area of expertise." By framing it this way, you've reduced the pressure on yourself to be the knower of all things.

Courses in Cutting-Edge Disciplines

If you're teaching a course in a rapidly changing discipline, such as genetics, climate change, or popular culture, let students know that it's essential to be focused on the topical issues: "For this course to be meaningful to you, we need to cover the most recent developments, things that change literally on a yearly if not a monthly basis. I'll be learning along with you as we examine some of the big issues that have just emerged and the little issues that are important but not well known." You're presenting yourself as an astute guide who can help them judge what is and isn't important, even if you're just learning the facts yourself.

Lab, Studio, Methods, and Statistics Courses

You may be teaching students how to do something, such as how to make a lithographic print in an art class or how to use a mass spectrometer in a physics course.[22] Compared with teaching facts, teaching procedures and methods that you don't know well can be daunting. You need to remember not just *how* to do each step but *when* to perform it. (If the steps are out of order, the procedure probably won't work; worse yet, it could be dangerous.) It's hard to anticipate mistakes students will make, and the workload is high because you typically need to structure new activities for each week in the lab or studio. Some weeks you may be setting up equipment you haven't touched since you were in college—or that didn't exist back then. The list goes on.

You can ease a fraction of that stress by letting students know that the nature of being a researcher or an artist is to be a specialist in solving certain kinds of problems, so you use certain methods more frequently than others. Explain that it's important that they learn a variety of methods so they can choose the test or technique that's most appropriate for the problem they're trying to solve. On those lucky weeks when you're teaching a method you know well, show them why that method fits the types of problems you like to solve. This will offer a glimpse into your expertise and help them see that ideally, the problem drives the choice of methods, not the other way around.

General Philosophies for Framing the Experience

In addition to these strategies for specific types of courses, there are general ways to frame the experience positively and realistically for yourself and for your students. Here's a sampling of clever ideas generously offered by the people I interviewed as I wrote this book. Perhaps one of their strategies will work for you; if not, I hope their solutions will give you the confidence to formulate your own positive framework.

"Let's conquer this together."

I hate to use a military metaphor, but here it is. One strategy is to treat the material as a common enemy. I can say to students, "I'm with you. This guy is hard. What can we do?" Now

I'm free from having to be the expert; at least I don't have to be the expert on this text I don't understand yet. I can align myself with something I'm more comfortable with—the methods and how to tackle difficult texts, battles the students might lose without my help. I shift the conception of my expertise, so it's still worth their tuition money. This works best for really hard material, like Hegel, but if you're teaching outside of your expertise, it can all look like hard material.—Andrew Mills, Philosophy, Otterbein College

"You're the first pancake."
The first pancake is never perfect. It's true—it's never perfect. And the second pancake isn't quite right, either; something is always a little off. But by the third time, ah, then you've adjusted everything and you've got it just right. And I tell my students, "You're the first pancake."—Michael Bérubé, American Studies and Disability Studies, Penn State University, author of *What's Liberal about the Liberal Arts?*

"What's impossible isn't worth doing."
My belief, as a teacher, whether I'm teaching little kids or Ph.D. students, is that it's impossible to know all the content in your field. Ever. Ever. You could sit in your office and do nothing but read one article after another and you still couldn't keep up with it. So I always have this pragmatic philosophy that what's impossible isn't worth doing. And what's impossible for me to do is not worth imposing upon my students. There are certain things that students need to learn, such as how to ask a meaningful question. That's really important! You can't survive if you don't learn that. But I'm not going to make you remember, "Here are five studies and here are all the different conditions in those studies, and here are all the effects from each of the conditions."

I'm just not going to make you remember all that, because I don't. I kind of use myself as a meter, and I say, "I'm not going to make you do the kinds of things that I haven't been able to do."—Junlei Li, Developmental Psychology, Director of Applied Research and Evaluation, University of Pittsburgh

"What are people thinking right now?"

In the sciences, virtually nothing that I teach now in any of my courses bears any resemblance to anything I learned in graduate school or undergraduate school. The science changes so fast. Let me give you an example. I'm teaching planetary geology this semester. I only teach it every other year. The last time I taught it the big news was what the Rovers were discovering on Mars, and now, two years later, the big news is all of the stuff coming back from Mars—all the orbital spectrometry data. It's a very different course this time because we know different kinds of things, things that were uncertain in 2005 we're certain of now. And now we know that some of what we thought was true in 2005 was wrong. They were hypotheses, and we now have the data. It's a lot of fun because students know I'm learning along with them, and we'll say, "What have we learned? What are people thinking about right now? What are the big questions that are left?"—Barb Tewksbury, Geosciences, Hamilton College

"Uncertainty drives excellence."

When I'm teaching in a field that doesn't come naturally, the thing that's richest for me is the uncertainty. I am not comfortable being certain. It isn't what learning is. It isn't what music is—you can practice, practice, practice for a performance and still be out of tune or play a wrong note. And it isn't what the law is—you can study, study, study and do the best you can, but when you have that oral argument or file that brief, something might have evolved that you couldn't anticipate. The uncertainty of teaching in a field that is ever-changing is what makes me get better and better.—Jill Ramsfield, former music instructor; Professor of Law, University of Hawai'i

"Expertise isn't what you think."

I think you just have to be honest with the students about where you are. I try to explain that the reason I'm not an expert in this topic is that this is how a scholar's life works. The life of a scholar is to always be learning. We don't have time to be experts in everything, so we experience the same thing you do as students. Each time you take a new course you start over again as a novice in that discipline, and it takes years and years to become an expert. And there's no way that anybody over a lifetime can be an expert in more than one narrow field. So I joke with students. I say, "At one time I considered myself one of the two or three experts in the world on the last three stanzas of Canto 12 of Book III of *The Faerie Queene*." It's true! Who else would want to be an expert in something so tiny, especially when it's not like it's a real important field? And if you had to be a true expert, those three stanzas might be the only thing I could ever teach. But the point is that you can't truly be an expert in anything. As a critical thinker, you learn how to navigate through an idea even when you're not an expert.—John Bean, English, Seattle University

"We all have something to learn."

When I'm teaching any course, whether it's a topic I know well or a new course, I set up ground rules and we discuss the assumptions that I bring to class. One of my assumptions is, "We all have something to learn." And that includes me as the professor. Another assumption is that we all have to listen and learn from one another. Students may hear something that differs from their experience. And I may hear or read something that differs from my experience and my training. By discussing those assumptions in the first week of class, I have more room to admit when I learn something new.—Beverly Daniel Tatum, Clinical Psychology; President of Spelman College

Drawing on Your Strengths and Interests

When you're teaching something new and unfamiliar, what's immediately striking is how different the texts are from what you're used to reading. The terms are different, the authors and arguments are new, and in some cases, what constitutes evidence may be very different from what you consider scholarly. Despite those differences (frustrating though they may be), take a step back and think about how your expertise might apply to this new topic. If you can draw on the best skills or material you've already developed, you can make the experience more manageable for yourself and more interesting for students.

Reuse Material

Although it may sound crass and too simplistic, let's face it, it's strategic to reuse good material from courses you know well. You don't need to reinvent the wheel every moment in class. You'll probably need to make some changes so that material from another class applies to the new topic, but if you choose well and make explicit connections between your reused material and the big questions, you can save time and create an effective learning environment.

We've already described one way to reuse material—by reinforcing threshold concepts, the ideas that are fundamental to a discipline but hard to understand. Another approach is to focus on your favorite classes, on the days when you went home and told your partner how well your class went. If you're in biology, perhaps you taught a class on the "physiology of being frazzled." If you're in philosophy, how about the lesson you developed on free will using *The Matrix?* Where do your past memories of teaching passion connect with the course you're teaching now?

Although it's gratifying to think of your finer moments, you're also trying to identify classes when students were truly wrestling with hard ideas and weren't letting go. Have you had a class day when most students wanted to keep talking after class was supposed to be over? I'm picturing a day when students said, "Wow. I've never seen it that way before." Thinking about those classes can help you identify material that's worth using again. It can also put you in a mindset of teaching at your best, of creating an environment in which students are truly changing the way they think about the world.

Find an Entry Point that Interests You

Boredom, specifically *your* boredom, can be a real obstacle in these periphery courses. If you're teaching as a content novice because you're eager to learn about the content, that's one thing, but some faculty have to teach outside of their expertise to fill a hole in the curriculum. Parker Palmer, the author of *The Courage to Teach,* told me that when departments are tediously marching along to meet the needs of the curriculum, it doesn't take long before they stomp out the topics that are most alive for the professors. "I would say to people who are caught in that kind of lockstep curriculum, once you've listed what you must teach, how do you preserve the pieces of the field that are most alive for you? I think that's kind of Pedagogy 101," he explained. "If it's not alive for you, it's going to be dead on arrival for the students."

If you have to teach a topic that doesn't interest you, find an entry point that does. You're looking for some way to frame the topic so that it's more compelling for you and your students. My favorite strategy is to use Google to search for the dreaded topic plus some topic that is personally motivating. Trust me, the personally motivating topic can be completely unrelated. In fact, if it's unrelated, the surprise factor can work in your favor to grab students' attention.

Take personality and ice cream. Personality is my dreaded topic. In Parker Palmer's words, it just wasn't alive for me. I've never taken a course in personality theory and have never wanted to, much to the surprise of people who expect that of all hard-working psychologists. Of course, personality theory is important to the field of psychology (not to mention my colleagues in the department). So when I was teaching the "Introduction to Psychology" course, I knew I couldn't skip the personality chapter. The first time I taught the intro course, the week on personality was not a proud moment in my teaching career: I gave a litany of definitions, theories, and researchers—boring and forgettable lists.

But I did redeem myself a year later. The second time I taught "Introduction to Psychology," I began the week on personality very differently. If we had to learn this topic, we could at least frame it with something I find interesting—ice cream. I started the class with a personality test, a "flavorology study" commissioned by Edy's Grand Ice Cream, which supposedly told you something about your true nature based on your favorite flavor. If your freezer is stocked with strawberry, then the analysis predicts that you're shy and detail-oriented; if you crave a pint of chocolate, then you also crave being the center of attention.[23] I put up a slide describing these personality profiles and we had a good laugh. I then asked the class to compare the ice cream profiles to traditional personality theories. Which features make a valid test or theory of personality? Why might people have such strong reactions to personality tests—why are some people excited to take them while others are highly skeptical? By starting with something we could make fun of, we could acknowledge that this cute ice cream test was the kind of transparent, multiple-choice survey that the average person thinks of when she hears the phrase "personality test." From there, we could build an understanding of legitimate theories of personality, define how psychologists use the word "validity," and discuss a variety of other abstract topics that could now be grounded in something concrete. Although I still didn't find the legitimate personality theories exciting, we could at least all agree that the real theories were more reliable and predictive than the ice cream test.

So you teach physics? You might be surprised what a little internet research can produce. When I conducted a search for "physics" and "ice cream," I learned that several physics laboratories are researching ice cream. They study the freezing process of ice cream; the physical properties of this delicious substance that is not quite a solid and not quite a liquid; ways to avoid heat shock; and so on—all legitimate areas of physics research. From a teaching perspective, ice cream can also be used to illustrate basic principles such as Newton's law of cooling or Boyle's law and the relationship between microscopic and macroscopic properties. Whatever your dreaded topic might be, I challenge you to try my Google approach to teaching it.

You probably won't design an entire course this way, but this kind of fun approach will give you an entry point for the rest of the material. And if it's more fun for you, students will remember it. My colleague who taught the course in personality once asked me, "So what is this ice cream test I keep hearing about?"

Explaining Difficult Concepts Clearly

How do you give a clear, accessible, and compelling explanation of a complex idea? Unfortunately, clear explanations can't be prescribed in a simple, three-step formula. And what constitutes a good explanation of a concept can differ considerably from one academic discipline to another. An English professor, for example, would explain a "fatal flaw" very differently from an engineering professor. The appropriateness of your explanation will also vary from student to student. One student may find that your baseball analogy makes everything clear, while another student is simply more confused by it.

Nonetheless, an essential element of good teaching is the ability to explain a concept clearly. This is a problem when you're teaching as a content novice. It can be hard enough to offer clear explanations for material that you know well, but when you're just piecing the ideas together yourself, you might find yourself fumbling more than usual or giving examples that seemed insightful at first but that actually complicate the issue. You might know when you've just given a bad explanation, but simply seeing that everyone is lost doesn't help you formulate a better one.

Below I list a few general principles to giving a good explanation. These aren't strict rules. If you have a lot of time, you can probably find some strategies specific to your discipline, but I'm pretty sure you're short on time. These basic principles will help you make a hard concept easier to understand.

Start with Common Knowledge

The key to a good explanation is to begin with something that's familiar to your students and easy to grasp. If you're trying to explain a very difficult and abstract concept, then it's especially important to begin with something that's common knowledge. By "common knowledge" I mean something that students knew long before they walked into your course, something that's rich with experience and easy for them to discuss. It isn't something that was covered in a course last semester, and it certainly isn't something you just taught last week.

That last statement may seem obvious, but it's an easy mistake to make. We all suffer from the illusion that because we taught it, everyone understood it. More times than I'd like to admit, I've thought to myself, "Well, we learned about X in class on Monday, so that's something everyone knows." And from that unchecked assumption, I launch into a plan for class that's efficient and convenient for me but rocky for everyone else: "I'll do a quick review of X (reviews are good, right?) and then make the connection to the really hard concept Y." Fingers crossed.

It *is* important to make explicit connections between different concepts in a course, so connecting the dots between X and Y is good teaching (or at least basic teaching). But X is not your best starting point if you think students will struggle with Y, and you'll run into trouble if it's your only starting point. Some people may not have understood X in the first place. Other students probably have only a partial or fragile idea of X if you just covered it in class. There's another risk to this approach: some students will be more confused about X by the time you're done with Y. If you try to build a much more complicated idea on top of a newly learned, freshly formed, tentative base without any other supports, it's like trying to build a house on freshly poured concrete. If you've just poured that concrete, you need to let it dry, or everything will be lopsided.[24] Build on something that's already solid and well understood. Make complex ideas as accessible as possible by starting with an idea you're sure the students understand.

It's also important to use common language at first so that the concepts are more intuitive. You can introduce the jargon a little later into the explanation; if you begin with jargon, you give unmotivated students a ready excuse to tune out. If you can use some vivid imagery as you introduce a complex concept, students will have an easier time both visualizing and remembering that concept. "Let's picture four short bald men and one tall red-haired man standing on a dock" is a better opening than "How do we explain variance?" Concrete starting points are better than abstract ones.

You might be thinking that these techniques underestimate students' abilities and don't belong in a college classroom. I can appreciate your reservations, and I would have agreed with you a few years ago. But I became convinced of this approach by watching outstanding teachers use it to make opaque and complex ideas as clear as glass. Let's consider an example.

It's 1:50 on a Friday afternoon and an electrical engineering professor begins to set up his materials for his 2:00 class. More than one hundred students shuffle into their seats, many looking tired from a long morning of recitations and a week of labs. The instructor starts the class by asking everyone to take a blank sheet of paper from their notebooks: "Today we're going to learn about microwave frequencies. And the best way to understand microwave frequencies is to begin with an example. So take your sheet of paper and draw a line down the middle of the page. Write Baked Potato on the left side and Microwaved Potato on the right." There's a lot of movement and sarcastic commentary as students tear sheets from their notebooks, and most of them are either smiling or looking skeptical. The instructor gets their attention again: "Now, take a minute to list all of the ways that a baked potato differs from a microwaved potato." Again, a little chatter, and then one student raises his hand and asks, "What if you've never had a microwaved potato?" Students around him laugh. The instructor replies, "Have you ever been to Wendy's? No? Just take your best guess." The lecture hall settles down quickly enough and people begin writing.

While the students are generating their lists, the instructor writes "Baked Potato" and "Microwaved Potato" on the board. After a few minutes, he asks students to call out some of their answers while he records their ideas for everyone to see. When he's satisfied with the list, and once most students are just offering variations of the same ideas, he sets down the chalk and turns to the class: "So you've read the book for today and you know we're going to be spending the next few weeks on microwave frequencies. This will make more sense if we begin with something concrete. I'm going to explain to you how a traditional oven and a microwave oven heat food differently. When we're done, we'll come back to this list and see if the science can account for all of the differences that you've identified." He slides the board with the potato properties up toward the ceiling, revealing the blank board behind it: "And once we've applied all the science we know, if there are any differences left over, we may just have to blame a less-than-perfect potato on human error." He smiles broadly and looks at the student who asked a question earlier: "I mean, honestly, it's a big mistake to go to Wendy's for their 'baked' potatoes." He gets a laugh and turns back to the board to draw a rectangle with a sine wave through it. Students fold back their notebooks and begin to write.

This example captures many of the elements we've described for introducing a complex concept. The electrical engineering professor eases into the topic by beginning with something familiar, potatoes. It's true that not every college student can relate to the difference between baked and microwaved potatoes, but many can. The professor also uses common language, at least so far, and ideas that are easy to visualize. Cleverly, he calls on other senses, such as taste and touch, to create some highly vivid images that students can build on as they learn about the more abstract properties of microwave frequencies.

It's also worth noting that he began his explanation by polling his students. One way to ensure that you're connecting with students' existing knowledge is to ask them what they know. By asking students to list the differences between the two types of potatoes, the professor can be sure that his explanations of microwaves are connected to students' existing knowledge.

I heard about this potato activity from a colleague who used it in class. The colleague was not an electrical engineer but a specialist in German and Indian literature. It's a long, long story why this humanities professor had to give a lesson in microwave frequencies, but he did, and this potato example allowed him to do so quite effectively and with more confidence than he would have had otherwise. It's a fantastic example of someone teaching a difficult concept clearly outside of his expertise.[25]

If you're a physicist or an electrical engineer, you may be thinking, "But comparing a microwave oven to a conventional oven isn't the best way to describe microwaves. Microwaves are used in many technologies—in sensors, semiconductors, even in your BlueTooth headset—so a microwave oven is a highly limited application." That's true. It may also be true that kitchen appliances have little to do with how most scientists and engineers use microwaves in their research. These are excellent observations to make later in the course, but not yet. When you're introducing a complex concept, you're not looking for the most technically precise definition. Nor are you looking to explain sophisticated applications that will be relevant three years from now. You're looking for something that's relevant to your students today, when they're trying to hold onto this shaky new concept and they want to know where to put it. Once they understand some basics about microwaves, you can introduce them to more complex scientific applications. As Ken Bain notes, "Good explanations start with ways to help the learner begin to construct a good understanding; they are not necessarily the most accurate and detailed way of putting something."[26]

Weave in Technical Terms and Theories

What do you say after you've finished your baked potato list? In other words, how do you introduce the more difficult, technical language or abstract theories? One effective strategy is to begin with a simple summary statement that connects with students' existing knowledge and opens the door for you to teach more specific details. For a physics or engineering class, where students have probably learned about electromagnetic waves in their other classes, you might begin, "A microwave is an electromagnetic wave that has a lower frequency than light but a higher frequency than FM radio waves." For a nonscientific audience, you might begin with a summary statement that uses more common language and touches on more common concepts: "A microwave is a type of wave, like a light wave or a radio wave. Scientists define different types of waves by their frequency. What do I mean by frequency? If you've ever stood by the ocean and watched the waves, you know that sometimes they are frequent with very little time between each wave, and sometimes they are slower, with more time between waves."

After you've connected with their knowledge, students are more prepared to hear technical language and abstract theory. But most students won't learn much if they're just doused with a fire hose of theory. For the theory to make the most sense, you'll need to include concrete examples in your explanation. I raise this point because some instructors claim that students need several days' or even weeks' worth of theory before they can appreciate a concrete example. (It's true. I won't name any names or disciplines, but I've seen several professors organize their syllabus this way. Weeks 1–5 are theory, and the examples begin almost begrudgingly in Week 6. They contend, "But they really can't appreciate any examples until they've heard the history of the theory and they've seen me derive it.")

I can appreciate why instructors decide to teach theories before examples—it's a deductive approach to a problem, and it seems to be the natural way of teaching for many of us. The instructor begins with a broad theory, generates some hypotheses from that theory, and then looks for evidence to support those hypotheses. Textbooks are often organized this way, reinforcing this approach among instructors. Plus, many of us love the power of our favorite theories, and it seems like a convincing place to begin an explanation. Unfortunately, this doesn't work for most students, who seem to learn best inductively.[27] As we'll see in Chapter 6, most students want to begin with something concrete, something tangible and observable. If they prefer to begin with examples, not theories, they will probably also prefer to take an inductive approach to the problem—they first want to look for intriguing patterns in those examples, then generate some potential hypotheses. Finally, having laid the right groundwork, they can appreciate the full-blown theory. As a result, most students in classes that spend a full class or a full week on theory without any examples probably understand little of the theory. Cognitive research on how we learn abstract concepts shows that most people benefit from frequent, explicit connections between abstract theory and concrete examples.[28]

Give Them a Picture

If your examples are familiar to students, you're likely to see the greatest gains in their reasoning skills. If you can't make the examples familiar, do your best to make them easy to visualize. (Concrete and vivid is always better than abstract and amorphous. "Ben & Jerry's" or "a tennis racket factory" is better than "Company A," just as "elephant" or a "small, gray mouse" is better than simply "animal.") Include some pictures in your Power-Point slides, or pass around an object if you have an interesting model or artifact. Maybe you're discussing economic policies in China—even passing around some Chinese currency, the yuan (if you have some), would make it more real for some students.

Research shows that when students learn something from a visual image, they represent the information twice, once verbally and once as a visual image. By comparison, when they learn something from a verbal description, they typically represent the information only once, verbally.[29] So if I ask you to picture a potato, your mind represents a potato two ways: as a picture and as a word. If I say the word "potato" in a sentence, you're likely to simply represent it as a word. This isn't just an issue for visual learners, either. It's true that some students prefer to learn through visual images, but all students benefit when they have multiple ways to represent a hard idea.

Building on this imagery idea, when you're explaining a difficult concept, try to offer multiple ways to represent the same ideas. If you can describe a concept in words and draw a diagram on the board or show a picture of an everyday example, then students have multiple ways to represent the same idea. If you're explaining wave frequencies, you can describe them verbally, draw two different sine waves on the board, and describe how a piece of paper flaps in front of a fan at different rates, depending on the speed of the fan.

Summarize What You've Said throughout Class

To reinforce a difficult concept, it's important to give intermittent summaries, not just at the end, but throughout the explanation. "So far, we've been talking about . . . and we've learned that. . . ." or "The next step is to ask ourselves an important question. How does this lead to. . . ?" These summaries help you transition into the next concept, and they clarify the most important points, or "take-away" lessons. Periodic summaries also prompt students to ask questions if something you've said does not make sense. Some educators refer to these intermittent summaries as "signposts." Frequent signposts help students follow the path of your thinking as you wind through complex concepts where students otherwise might get lost.

Additional Strategies

A demonstration is another effective starting point for a difficult concept. Demonstrations are used frequently in art, science, engineering, and technology courses, but with some creativity, they can work equally well in the humanities and social sciences. In a management class, instead of listing why companies comply or fail to comply with environmental regulations, try a role-playing game in which students represent different companies that need to make strategic choices about compliance. In a history class, instead of describing the elements of a historical argument, start the class by making a historical argument or watching one on DVD. Then step back and analyze it with your students.

Other basic strategies can help you explain a difficult concept. Try pausing from time to time to give students a chance to ask questions or catch up with their note taking. When you're teaching something complex that you don't know very well, you may feel an urge to get through it all quickly. That's perfectly natural—none of us wants to linger on something confusing. Instead, picture yourself as a storyteller. You pause naturally when you're telling a good story or a favorite joke. The topic you're teaching may pale in comparison to a good story, but the basic idea can help you pace yourself. Keep in mind that the students are more confused than you are.

If you started class with an example or activity that provided an overly simplistic notion of a concept, return to this starting point later and question it. The electrical engineering professor might want to go back and critique the baked potato activity. Just because students can successfully evaluate the strengths and limitations of an example later doesn't mean you chose a poor starting point. Rather, it demonstrates that students understand the concept well enough to critique their earlier understanding. Think of a child learning to ride a bicycle. After relying on his training wheels, he's terrified to see them removed; but as soon as he can ride without them, he'll take a great deal of pleasure in scoffing at them.

It also helps to step back from a difficult concept and analyze it with the students to identify the parts that are clear and the parts that need more explanation. You can literally step back from the board or the PowerPoint slides and say, "This is a tricky concept. I'm guessing that some of it is beginning to make sense and other parts are just as confusing as when we started, maybe more so. So, first tell me, which parts make sense?" Another approach would be to ask, "What do you think might be unclear to you later when you review your notes?" This approach cleverly suggests that though students might understand everything now, concepts aren't always as clear once they leave the magic space of the classroom. The idea is to take the students' perspective, to show them that you're on their side in trying to make sense of this difficult issue. As you'll recall from the section on credibility, students feel much better if they know the two of you are trying to tackle the hard concepts together.

Handling Students' Questions When You Don't Know the Answers

Even when you're teaching a course on a topic you know well, there are bound to be days when someone asks a question that you can't answer. When you're teaching *outside* of your expertise, there are bound to be more of those days, when the student in the front row wants to know the birthplace of Karl Marx or the average lifespan of a chicken.

On the face of it, it seems as though you should just be able to respond the same way you'd respond to any question you don't know. But "not knowing" often feels more revealing in a course outside of your expertise, and many instructors hesitate to answer honestly when the moment arises. Perhaps it's the fear of being exposed as an imposter. Or maybe you're certain that the (astonishingly basic) answer will appear in the next chapter, which you haven't read yet. (Personally, I hesitate to answer truthfully in those moments because if I worked hard all weekend to prepare for class, it feels cosmically unfair that I might be stumped by a question about a chicken.)

It helps to walk into class realizing that it's not the end of the world if you don't know every answer. It's not a sign of weakness. Students know that you're human; if not, it's fair to remind them. Most students don't complain because an instructor couldn't answer a question in class. (But most will complain if they're treated rudely for asking hard questions.)

If you're the first instructor students have met who is open about what you do and don't know, they may respect you even more for your candor. Let's return to Barb Tewksbury at Hamilton College. As we learned earlier, Barb teaches only one course in her expertise each year. (Her situation is repeated at small colleges across the country. She's one of only five full-time faculty members in her department, so everyone has to teach outside of their research area on a semi-regular basis.) She is often faced with questions she cannot answer, and she's quick to admit when she doesn't know. And she hears about it on her final course evaluations in glowing terms: "One of the things I really like about her class is when she doesn't know, she says she doesn't know. She goes and finds out, then we come back and have a good conversation about it." She's earned respect, not by hiding her ignorance, but by being genuine about it and by demonstrating that students' questions are insightful enough to drive her learning as well as theirs.

Clarify the Question

Be sure you understand the question. It's easy to misunderstand a question when you don't know the topic well, and students often ask ambiguous questions. In your area of expertise, you probably find it easy to spot an ill-formed or vague question and turn it into something meaningful. As Mike Flynn the linguistics professor explains, "When someone asks a question in class that I just luckily happen to know something about, I'm very grateful. I can massage the question into one that's more interesting or more important. I know where it's going, what they are really thinking about, and students appreciate that." When you're teaching outside your expertise, it's hard to know when a question is vague and even harder to make it more interesting or relevant.

The first step is to gain a better understanding of the question. Rephrase the question back to the student and verify that you've got it right, or ask the student to repeat or rephrase it. It could be that the student is asking a question you *can* answer, but because it's framed poorly or because your confidence or energy level is low, you might hastily jump to the conclusion that you can't answer it.

Acknowledge the Student or the Question

Let's assume you're asked a clear question. A good approach to answering any question, whether you know the answer or not, is to provide a two-part response: (1) acknowledge the student or the question, then (2) answer the question.[30] I've noticed that when instructors don't know the answer to a question, they sometimes quickly become preoccupied fashioning a witty or salvageable answer and forget about the person asking it. When you recognize the person or the question, you set a tone of respect. You don't have to say much; simply saying, "That's a good question, David," or "I'm so glad you asked that" is plenty. (Or, if your students appreciate your sense of humor, "I was afraid someone might ask that.") If a student asks a question at a bad time, set it aside for later, but give a quick acknowledgment: "That's an interesting question, Emily, but it takes us a bit off topic," or "I can see why you'd ask that, but I'd like to hold off on that for now." These little phrases may seem overly formal or unnecessary, but researchers find that students are more likely to show up for class on time, listen quietly without disrupting class, and generally behave themselves when their instructors treat them with respect and recognize them as individuals.[31]

Ask the Class What the Answer Is

Some faculty find it very effective to turn the question back to the class. You probably don't want to do this for every question, but this strategy is particularly helpful if you think you might know the answer and just need a minute to think about it.

This approach is also effective if you think someone in the room has specialized knowledge and is likely to know the answer. Dan Simons, the cognitive psychologist, recalls one class in which a student had done considerable independent research on animal cognition, an area that Dan hadn't personally studied. When a question would come up about canine pack behavior or bee memory that Dan couldn't answer, he could always say, "Joshua, you're our expert on animal cognition. Know the answer to that one?" It reduced the pressure on Dan, and the student appeared to love the attention. Not every student wants to be in the spotlight, of course, but many seem to appreciate being recognized for their specialized knowledge.

Some books on teaching recommend that you ask students to research the answer. This approach shares responsibility with students and helps them learn through the research process, but it has clear disadvantages. Some instructors said it was akin to punishing students for asking creative questions, which might deter them from asking further questions. Another professor said she wasn't sure that students would always return with a correct answer. She's got a good point—you would probably recognize a truly bad answer in your area of expertise, but it's much easier to be led astray in a topic you don't know well.

One last piece of advice on asking the class for the answer to another student's question: use this strategy occasionally even when you do know the answer. It's an effective way to get students to interact with one another. You'll also have more credibility if you use this technique on occasions when you can provide the answer as well as at times when you cannot.

Admit You Don't Know

If the question is clear and you still don't know, and no one else knows the answer (or if you've decided not to ask the class), admit that you don't know. Or admit that you're not sure. This was the one unanimous piece of advice that I received from every instructor I asked: *you need to admit that you don't know.*

Since you'll probably need to say "I don't know" several times over the course of the term, you'd do well to have a variety of phrases to draw on. Here are a few of my favorites:

- "What a good question. I wish I had a good answer."
- "I haven't read that literature."
- "That's a very reasonable question, but to be honest, I haven't the faintest idea."
- "I'm not sure of the answer, and I don't want to lead you astray. Let me think about it."
- "That's a very precise question, and it deserves a precise answer. Let me get back to you on that."

Offer an Educated Guess

After you've admitted that you don't know for sure, you can offer an educated guess. You might say, "I'm not entirely sure what the answer is, but if I had to make an educated guess, I would say . . ." or, in the words of Michael Bérubé from Penn State, "Here's a tentative answer. It's only tentative. It's something I'll have to look more into and then I'll get back to you on it." Some instructors offer a glimpse into their thinking process by saying, "I'm not sure that I know the answer, but we can use what we *do* know to come up with an educated guess." This is valuable because it demonstrates how you think through a problem, something students might not see every day. Students who like and respect you as a teacher will pay attention to how you think about complex problems. Later, when they encounter a new problem or question that they can't answer (and keep in mind that they encounter these questions even more often than you do), they can try to retrace the steps you took.

Offer to Find an Answer

Most instructors I interviewed said that they offer to find an answer to questions they can't answer. They jot down enough information to remember the question (either during class or right after class—you know your own memory best), and they come back with an answer the next class or the next week. Researching the answer is a good strategy because it shows that you respect your students and take their questions seriously. If you tell them which sources you used, you inadvertently teach them where to look for good answers.

Students can be highly impressed by faculty who go in search of answers. Michael Bérubé, author of *What's Liberal about the Liberal Arts?*, distinctly remembers when he was a graduate student almost twenty years ago and asked the famous philosopher Richard Rorty a question about Heidegger that Rorty couldn't answer. The professor looked at him directly and said, "I really have no idea." But Rorty came back with an answer about a week later. "I was so impressed," Michael recalls. "At first, I thought he was just blowing me off. I mean, here he is this completely august, leading philosopher in the country, and I go and ask him a stupid question. And then he came back to me a week later saying, 'I thought more about that question. I'm sorry I didn't have a better answer for you.'" Michael wasn't expecting an answer or an apology, and he was struck by the entire exchange.

If you don't have an answer within a week or so, at least give the class a quick follow-up on your research: "I didn't get a very clear answer when I did a search on Google, so I sent an email to Professor Biggs, who teaches in the design department. I'll let you know when I have a good answer." Of course, only promise to find an answer if you will genuinely follow through. Students remember when you make promises you don't keep.

Warning: Never Fake It

It's always a mistake to pretend that you know the answer if you don't, or to present a potentially incorrect answer as though it's correct. First, students could prove you wrong. A student with a laptop can quickly Google the answer in class. Even if no one catches you in the moment, someone might find the correct answer after class, either online or, more embarrassing, in the textbook. Second, if you always act as though you know and you don't successfully distinguish the times when you *do* know from the times you don't, the act of pretending will undermine your credibility and students' confidence in you. Some students need only a little nudge to lose respect for an authority figure. As one instructor said, "They smell weakness like sharks smell blood."

It's a mistake I made the first time I taught a particular course about eight years ago. It was early in the course, perhaps the third or fourth week, and I guessed at an answer to a question without explaining that it was a guess. No one said anything that day or the next, and I would have forgotten about it entirely, except that at the end of the semester it came back to haunt me in my student evaluations. Four students all made the same basic comment: "She gave a wrong answer to a question, and the answer was right there in the book . . . I can't believe she didn't know what she was talking about." Their language was so similar that the four of them must have talked about it. It was a painful lesson for me. It was a tiny moment in class, but it was clear that it had made an impression on them.

Note to Tenure-Track and Adjunct Faculty

You might be thinking to yourself, "All the quotes in this section have been from tenured faculty. It's easy to say 'I don't know' when you have nothing to lose." I'm highlighting their stories because these seasoned faculty have been saying "I don't know" successfully for years, so the take-home message should be that instructors can adopt this approach and still receive tenure. Faculty at all stages and career tracks find that they gain more than they lose when they are honest with their students.

Common Mistakes Instructors Make Teaching outside Their Expertise

Faking expertise when you're asked a question is certainly a mistake you don't want to make. In this last part of the chapter, I review three other common mistakes that faculty make in their periphery courses.

Mistake 1: Over-Preparing for Each Day in Class

It's easy to over-prepare every week for a course that's outside of your comfort zone. It seems tantalizingly possible that you could, with enough effort and caffeine, bring a course into your comfort zone. This is a catch-22 of teaching what you don't know. You can be lured into thinking that if you prepare as much as you possibly can every week of the course, then you'll have more expertise going into each class. You'll have more examples, details, theories, or whatever else in your holster, and you'll feel like a more capable teacher.

Preparing *before* the course begins is an excellent investment of your time. The problem is routinely over-preparing week after week once the course begins. If you prepare too much for each class, you can become exhausted and resent the students.

You might feel frantic about squeezing in everything that you just worked so hard to learn. And if you're cramming the night before to research just a few more sources, you won't have time to organize it all. You can see how over-preparing during the course is tempting but stressful and counterproductive.

So how can you avoid over-preparing for any given day? Let's walk through how the problem might arise. You begin with an ambitious notion that you need to cover four key concepts (A, B, C, and D) for tomorrow's class. Five would be ideal, but four is manageable. Plus, with four you'd be caught up with the syllabus. You take copious notes on Concept A, leafing through other books for clever examples—after all, you want to know more than just that one example from the course textbook. You do the same thing for Concept B, jotting down what you learn as you learn it, but you're trying to filter a little bit more now because it's getting later in the afternoon, and your partner just called with a reminder that you have dinner plans that night. By the time you get to Concept C, you've already prepared enough lecture notes to fill the class period. You begin Concept C in less detail, but you actually *like* this concept and remember a great story you heard in graduate school. You go back through your notes to mark some places on Concepts A and B where you might be able to skip some things, but you're reluctant to cut anything because you just spent the last few hours learning it all. A quick glance at the clock reveals that you need to leave for dinner before you even start Concept D, which means you have a late night or early morning ahead of you. Or you could accept that you're going to get behind by half a class (which is feeling increasingly inevitable).

How do you avoid falling into this time trap? Robert Boice suggests preparing for class in short, regular intervals, adding ideas that you'd like to address in class as they come to you, rather than committing a long period of preparation time that is likely to have diminishing returns after an hour or two.[32] For example, when you arrive at the office in the morning, spend fifteen minutes reviewing the first half of the chapter, putting notes in the margins of key concepts. In the thirty minutes before lunch, open your file for the class and jot down a few notes based on what you read that morning and a new idea that's come to you. In the twenty-five-minute window you usually have after class but before you go home, do some internet research and add these ideas to your notes. I like this strategy because it means that you keep approaching the material when you're relatively fresh.

My concern is that Boice's approach probably works best when you already know the topic well, but that it would be harder to generate teaching ideas in short periods when you're still building your own understanding of the concepts. An alternative strategy is to begin by identifying your three to four learning objectives for the day and outlining the class according to these learning objectives. We discussed backward design for the entire course—this is basically backward design for each individual class day. Create an annotated outline of your class before you fill in the details. What do you want students to be able to do when you've finished addressing Concept A? It can be hard to answer this question when you're still learning the material yourself, but on the basis of what you've read about Concept A, what would you reasonably expect students to be able to do? (Or, what are you now able to do with Concept A, since you just learned it?) Perhaps you want them to be able to give examples for a concept, perhaps you want them to explain the author's choice of language, or perhaps you want them to apply a rule or equation to a new problem. The trick is to keep moving through your learning objectives before you fill out the detailed class notes for Concept A. What should students be able to do when you've finished addressing Concept B? Concept C? The key differences between this process and Boice's are that (a) you're focusing on what you want students to be able to *do* with each concept, and (b) you've written down what's most important about Concept D before you begin fleshing out Concept A in belts-and-suspenders detail. Although it takes a little time to generate this outline, you'll be more efficient and strategic in deciding what you do and don't need to prepare for class when you fill in the details.[33]

You may, of course, over-prepare for a very different reason: perhaps you want to be sure that you have enough material to fill an entire class. Some instructors dread the awkward day when they won't have prepared enough lecture notes or discussion questions and find themselves nearing the end of their prepared material ten minutes too early. Those ten minutes are easy to fill if the class is in your expertise, but it's much harder to improvise if you're literally only a chapter ahead of the students.

If you're concerned that a class might end early and you'll be staring out at a sea of expectant faces with nothing brilliant to say, I suggest that you put together an "Emergency Assessment Kit." No, this isn't a bar of expensive chocolate for you and an educational video for the students. The Emergency Assessment Kit is a folder containing an assessment activity that you could use at any point in the course. (You can label the folder something less revealing, such as "In-class Assessment Activity," if you find the word "Emergency" too strong.) In Chapter 7, I'll describe several classroom assessment activities that take about five to seven minutes to complete from start to finish, activities such as a "Clarity Grid" and "Survey Says." Before the course begins, look through these activities and find one that you like.[34]

Once you've selected an activity, prepare a handout (without a date so that you can use it at any time) and make enough copies so that you'll have one for each student. If you're teaching a large class, you can have one copy for each group of two to three students. There's one last important step: write a brief introduction so you won't need to think of one in the moment. Find a large sticky note or simply tape a sheet of paper on the inside cover of the folder that reads, "I was hoping we'd have time for this today, and it looks like we do." Put the introduction at the front of the folder so it's easy to find. Perhaps you're talented enough to improvise an effective introduction, but it's better not to leave it to chance. I've seen professors improvise activities and frame them very negatively, as in, "Well, I guess we don't have anything else to do, and someone told me I should try this." No one feels invested with that kind of introduction.

Chances are you won't finish the same class early twice, but it can happen, especially if you're teaching that course for the first time. Once you've used the activity, you can find another in Chapter 7 that suits you and restock your emergency kit.

Mistake 2: Lecturing too Much

Another common mistake that faculty raised in my interviews was the tendency to lecture too much. This was particularly common for junior faculty who were teaching outside of their expertise for the first or second time. They said that though they normally incorporate active learning, discussion, or even performance elements into their traditional courses, when they taught as content novices they found themselves reverting to lectures. Despite their best intentions, they found it hard not to lecture. I feel for these instructors because I've been there myself, and I've done it enough times to see the sad irony in this fall-back strategy. If you're still making sense of the material the night before you teach it, it seems as though you *wouldn't* want to be the fount of knowledge at the front of the room.

Why is it a mistake to rely so heavily on lectures? First, lecturing takes a lot of time to prepare, so it compounds the first mistake of over-preparing for class. Lecture prep is particularly time-intensive if you typically use PowerPoint slides for every class and concept. Second, despite all your efforts, your students may not learn as much when you lecture at them. There's no getting around it—research has shown that students learn more deeply and demonstrate better recall and reasoning when they engage with course material in some active way.[35]

Why do we resort so readily to lectures when we teach content that's outside our comfort zone? For one thing, discussions and active learning are much less predictable than lectures, and the instructor has less control. When you're in lecture mode, students are less likely to ask questions that you can't answer. Moreover, new faculty tend to think that lecturing will save them preparation time. You're taking notes as you read and learn the material, so the easiest thing to do is to use these newly constructed notes as your lecture notes. You don't have to step back from the material and analyze it for the most thought-provoking discussion questions or reorganize your notes into a well-structured activity. You can just staple your notes and go.

Some instructors would argue that even if they had the time, it's difficult to analyze the material because they are still integrating that knowledge into their own understanding. Maria Ferreyra, an assistant professor of economics at Carnegie Mellon, notes that this is a big difference between courses she knows well and courses she's still learning: "When I know what I'm teaching, that material is fully incorporated into my cognitive structure—it belongs somewhere; it's related to other knowledge; it has a 'home.' The main drawback to teaching something

I just finished learning is that I haven't found a 'home' for the material yet."

I appreciate all these reasons. Instead of trying to get rid of lectures altogether, try incremental steps to reduce the time spent in lecture. Consider using one of the ten active learning activities in Chapter 5; some take as little as two minutes of class time, so you can get back to the comfort of lectures quickly if you like. You can also try inserting mini-discussions into your lecture, as we saw with the microwaved-potato example. That instructor was leading into a lecture on the properties of microwaves, but he began with a brief discussion to stimulate interest in the topic and promote critical thinking before diving into the lecture.

Mistake 3: Focusing on Lists

Lists are a specific kind of lecturing problem. When instructors teach outside of their expertise, their lectures tend to be heavily peppered with lists, such as the "eight most powerful political parties in India," or the "twelve steps to designing an effective web page." (I did the same thing when I first taught personality theory. The "big five" personality traits come to mind.) Eugene Fram, professor of marketing at Rochester Institute of Technology, brought this common problem to my attention. In his fifty-one years of teaching, he's been tempted to rely on lists when he takes on a new topic, and he's seen his junior colleagues make this same mistake. In part, faculty who are new to the material may rely on lists because they provide pre-packaged, well-organized information. After all, you can simply spend time in class reviewing and explaining a particular list, which takes virtually no time to prepare.

So what's the harm in using lists? Indeed, these facts or steps may be important conceptual building blocks, but students can often get this information directly from their textbooks or, perhaps even more quickly, from the internet. And as Fram observed, you probably don't add much to students' understanding by reciting these lists in class, except to communicate that yes, everyone needs to know this list. Furthermore, you might be sending the message that you value rote memorization. If that's one of your primary learning goals, then reviewing a list is a fine approach. But chances are you want students to understand these concepts, not just list and recite them.

Your goal should be to engage students in examining the relationship among the items on the list. Why are some items on the list and not others? Why is the list organized this way? One general strategy is to construct the list using students' input. Write the title and first item from the list on the board, then invite students to generate the rest. If the list is already in their textbook, direct their attention to two or three items and help them explore the relationship between those items. If you're teaching about political parties in India, you might pick two parties and discuss the issues that are most important to each, the ways the parties differ geographically in their membership, and how one of the parties came to be more powerful than the other. Although you're only focusing on two of the many parties, you're helping students build a more meaningful representation of key concepts.

By narrowing the focus, you also help students bring their existing knowledge to bear on the new information. In this example, students are able to map what they know about geographical differences between Republicans and Democrats onto these new, unfamiliar parties. Students are less likely to make those connections if they are trying to memorize a list of eight new parties and their current leaders. It's still reasonable to expect students to memorize these facts, but they can do so outside of class. Use the time in class to construct the meaning behind the list.

If you're teaching a procedure or a sequence of steps, such as the "twelve steps in web design," try the active learning strategy titled "Sequence Reconstruction" in Chapter 5. In this activity, you list the steps in random order, and students place them in their proper sequence. Because students are constructing the sequence, they are engaged with the material, and there is reduced pressure on you to perform. This activity takes a little time to prepare, but not as much as a lecture on the same material.

Another advantage to constructing the sequence with your students is that you give the highly experienced students in the class the opportunity to challenge the sequence that's proposed. Some students have had jobs or internships that give them specialized knowledge, and they may know how to optimize the process, or they may have discovered that in most cases, a step has to be skipped because it's impractical or the resources aren't available. I've called this an advantage because when students raise these kinds of practical concerns, as long as they do so politely, you've engaged more people in the room. You may feel threatened by students who disagree with you or with the text, but if they are saying something meaningful about the content, they can make the class a more rewarding experience for you and the other students. Students who know more, or who think they know more, often sit at the edge of a topic, arms crossed, and egos sorely under-acknowledged. If you can pull them into the conversation, even if it's through their skepticism, you've done your job well.

When you feel challenged, an easy and honest response is, "I haven't run into that problem before." It's also reasonable to trust that the information you have is accurate. So treat this student's experience as an exception to the rule: "Interesting. It's really helpful to learn from exceptions. Why do you think you ran into that problem?" Or you could engage the entire class in analyzing the problem: "Why do you think the authors included step 5 if it's difficult to implement?"

I'm not saying that it's always easy when students challenge what's being taught. It can be intimidating, particularly when you're not an expert on the material. Teaching outside of your expertise is risky business, but you don't need to know everything to create an environment in which students are learning new things. Remember Codrina the Chemist's advice: "Students don't learn more when you're perfect." They learn more when you're human and you make the classroom a place where it's safe to ask questions.

5 Thinking in Class

My mom's side of the family is Slovenian. Sadly, I don't know what Slovenians do for fun back in the old country, but I know that when they came to America, they picked up bowling. My family loves to bowl. Indoor bowling, outdoor bowling, you name it. When my mom was a little kid, the Slovene Center (where the neighborhood used to go when there wasn't a party on someone's porch) wasn't a bingo hall or a place where people sat around playing checkers—it was a bowling alley. I can recall two pictures of my grandmother as a young woman—in one picture, she's wearing her wedding gown and in the other picture she's wearing a bowling jersey. I've managed to carry on at least part of the family tradition. Few people know this, but I had my bridal shower at a bowling alley. (Not at the Slovene Center, though. We went to a bowling alley that played something a little catchier than polka music.)

Lest you think I'm actually good at bowling, I should mention that my all-time high score is about 120. I'm usually excited if I break 100. If you've ever gone bowling, you know that the highest possible score is 300, so a 120-point game is not impressive, especially for someone who's been bowling since she was three.

For me, and I think for most people, the trickiest part about bowling (once you figure out the shoes) is a split. In a split, there are only two pins left, one standing defiantly on the far left and the other on the far right. When I'm faced with a split, I try to send the ball straight down the left or the right side of the lane, but at best I hit only one pin that way. (Actually, the ball usually veers into the gutter long before it gets there.) The strategy is ineffective no matter how you look at it, and it limits me from getting much better at bowling.

According to Mark Cracolice, chair of the chemistry department at the University of Montana, the limitation I've just described is exactly like the limitation to be found in the standard lecture classroom. Just as I send the ball hopefully down one side of the lane, most faculty lecture at their students, hoping that's enough. Given the spread of abilities in the classroom, instructors know they will miss roughly half the students because they aim too high or too low. But instructors don't feel they have many options, especially when they're relatively new to the material themselves. As for the students, how do they perform in lecture classes? In some cases, students perform well enough that the instructor has no compelling reason to change, but in other cases, an unacceptable number of students don't understand the material as well as the instructor would like. Even in those lecture classes where students do perform well, most don't dazzle the instructor (or themselves, for that matter) with their insights. For both the professor and the student, there's the small victory of hitting one of the pins but not the excitement of hitting them all.

You probably know what's missing from my bowling game. I need to learn to put a hook on the ball when I'm faced with a split. If I could hook the ball properly, I could learn to hit both pins in the same shot, and suddenly I'd be playing a whole new game. With enough practice, a 200-point or even a 300-point game would become possible. (Well, maybe not for me, but certainly for my cousins and probably for you.)

According to Mark Cracolice, adding active learning to your classes is like adding that much-needed hook. You reach more of the students. More students pass, and students who would have passed anyway produce higher-quality work. There's a transition period—if your students are used to a passive lecture classroom, they might find it awkward at first to turn around and talk with their neighbors, just as I'm sure I will fumble around the first time I try to hook a bowling ball. But research has shown that after some regular practice, students soon perform at a much higher level than when the instructor simply lectured.[1]

This isn't just a convenient bowling analogy—study after study demonstrates that students learn more when instructors give them opportunities to think about the material in class.[2] Students leave class with fewer misconceptions, show stronger mastery of abstract concepts, and have better attitudes toward the course when interactive activities are introduced.[3] And you don't even have to restructure your entire class. In one study, researchers compared two sections of the same course—students in one class listened to a typical forty-five-minute lecture each day, and those in the other class listened to a slightly truncated lecture on the same content for thirty-nine minutes, but they took three two-minute breaks throughout the class to compare their notes with their neighbors. The question is, who learned more? Is the outcome obvious? Even though they had less lecture and content from the instructor, the students who had the brief opportunity to think about their notes in class showed significantly better recall and comprehension on the final exam than students who just took notes.[4] As faculty, we often feel conflicted about the coverage issue, but here's one of many cases where instructors who covered less material found that their students learned more.

Overcoming the Obstacles

As you might have noticed, this chapter is titled "Thinking in Class." I already know that *you're* thinking in class—probably harder than you'd like to. But for most of us, it's less clear whether our students are thinking in class or what they're thinking about. I hope you'll agree that if students in your periphery courses thought just as actively and just as hard as you do every day, they would come away knowing volumes. As Ron Krabill succinctly put it, "If they connect the dots on their own, they'll remember it. If I do it, they won't." In this chapter we'll look at active learning techniques that prompt students to think harder in class. Although there are many definitions of active learning, I like the simple one used by Michael Prince, a chemical engineer at Bucknell, who refers to active learning as "any instructional method that engages students in the learning process."[5]

I won't review the exhaustive literature on why active learning is much better than lecturing alone. In the last chapter, I described some of the limitations of lectures, and I've just given you a quick taste of the research that compares student learning in the two kinds of classes. I also realize that if you're dead-set against trying active learning, a dozen research findings probably won't convince you.

This chapter is primarily for faculty who already know about the benefits of active learning but aren't sure how to make it work when they teach on the edge of their expertise. This is a common frustration. It's partly a time problem—you probably don't have the time or the energy to prepare tailored, thought-provoking activities for your periphery courses. The class already consumes too much time. It's also an idea problem. Instructors say that they can identify or create a good activity for a topic they know well, but those activities aren't self-evident when they're so close to learning the material themselves. And for most us, lecturing is the safe default when we're teaching outside our comfort zones.

I asked Eric Mazur about the difficulty of promoting active learning in a periphery course. As we learned earlier, Mazur is a Harvard physicist and science education researcher known for his work on active learning in physics classrooms. He developed the peer-instruction technique that we'll discuss later in this chapter. Mazur understands why we would fall back on lectures when we're teaching something we just learned, "but," he notes, "you're not doing your students a service." He points out that "nothing clarifies things better than putting it in your own words. And I think by standing in front of a class and thinking out loud, in a sense you're reinforcing your own knowledge. But that doesn't justify the lecture approach. That should never, ever justify lecture. Because we're not teaching to teach ourselves. We're teaching to teach others." You may feel good about lecturing on a new topic because that time in class helps you clarify your thinking, but students don't necessarily share that experience just by listening to you. If talking about a subject helped you, it's a safe bet that it would help students, too.

This chapter is also for instructors who've thought about trying active learning but aren't quite convinced that it's worth the effort. If you're in this camp and have a lecture style that works, you may be wondering, "Why introduce a new challenge in a course that's already difficult to teach?" If comfort is your goal, this is probably not the best time to experiment with active learning techniques. But if a rich and rewarding student learning experience is your goal, you may want to give active learning a try.

Lastly, I'd like to appeal to the adventurous, "what the heck" aspect of your personality. When you teach outside of your expertise, you're doing something different. You're reading new books, preparing new materials, taking new risks. Why not try a new activity? If it doesn't work, then at least you've tried. It's not as though you're teaching in your specialty and students would be missing out on a brilliant lecture you've perfected over the years. If the active learning exercise *does* work, and it probably will, then you can enjoy students' gratitude at the break from lecture. (I don't expect to convince every hardened skeptic with that reasoning, but I'll settle for softening a few.)

Selecting an Activity That Works for You

Since you're probably pressed for time, you don't need a list of forty or fifty activities to wade through. With that in mind, I've chosen ten of my favorites.[6] In some ways, these activities are like bubble wrap—they can be wrapped around most any topic, and you don't have to be an expert in handling the topic to use them. Some activities fit certain disciplines better than others, but I've tried to pick activities that can be adapted for most disciplines. I've seen these activities used in engineering lecture halls as well as in art studios, in everything from teaching finance to teaching fiction.[7]

Realistically, three factors will affect your selection of an activity: (1) the amount of time it takes to conduct the activity in class, (2) the amount of preparation time you'll need to invest, and (3) whether the activity uses individual, pairs, or groups. Since these factors are easy to identify, I've provided information on each for the ten activities below. Ideally, you should also select an activity on the basis of your big questions and educational objectives, but another chapter would be required to outline all those possibilities. Generally speaking, longer activities engage more higher-order thinking skills (such as creativity and hypothesis-testing) than do the shorter activities.

The activities I've featured are ordered roughly from those that take the least amount of time in class to those that take the most. The shortest can take as little as two minutes and the longest can take as much as sixty minutes. You might be wondering why you'd want a longer activity, but trust me, there will come a time. On those nights when the rest of your household has gone to bed and you're still preparing for tomorrow's ninety-minute class, an activity that occupies a full thirty minutes of class time will seem like a blessing.[8] For each activity I've noted roughly how much time you'll need to prepare (none, minimal, some, or a great deal), with extra suggestions for activities that take more preparation.

Activities of Two to Five Minutes

COMPARATIVE NOTE-TAKING

Preparation: None

Structure: Pairs

Activity: This activity is described at the beginning of the chapter, and it's almost too simple for instructions. Just take one to two minutes to have students compare their notes with a neighbor. Research suggests that attention spans lapse in a standard lecture every fifteen to twenty minutes, so plan to schedule this activity every twenty minutes to recapture students' attention.[9] Or use this activity after covering a particularly difficult concept. It will give students an opportunity to rework notes that aren't clear while the ideas are still fresh in their minds and while you're poised to answer questions. Christopher Lucas and John Murray go one step further and recommend asking students to exchange notebooks with a neighbor for a quick review and different perspective.[10] Whichever approach you take, when the time is up, expect students to have some questions. They will often realize that their understanding was unclear, incomplete, or contradictory when they go back and review their notes with a partner.

PARTICIPATION PREP

Preparation: Minimal

Structure: Individual

Activity: As suggested by the title, this activity helps students prepare for class discussion. Tell students that you plan to ask them a question in a moment, and everyone is to write down an answer. They can write the answer in their notes—you're not going to require them to hand in anything—but afterward you will call on a few people to share their answers. Pick a question that requires some thoughtful analysis, not just a slingshot answer from memory. If you were using this activity in a religion class, for example, the question, "Which deities are in the Hindu and Buddhist creation stories?" wouldn't stir as much analysis as the question, "Would you expect Buddhism and Hinduism to have similar creation stories? Why or why not?" If you give the class a chance to write before the discussion begins, some students who normally just listen will be more likely to participate. Giving students time to structure, evaluate, and even rehearse their answers can boost their confidence and create space for new voices.

INTENTIONAL MISTAKES

Preparation: Some (see Suggestions at the end)

Structure: Individual or in pairs

Activity: Present students with an inaccurate statement, incorrect proof, weak argument, or illogical conclusion; their task is to find and correct the error(s). Provide the problematic item on a transparency or on a PowerPoint slide and ask students to jot down a corrected version and the reason that the original is incorrect. You're trying to draw attention to a common mistake that students are likely to make or an item that's confusing. If you find yourself getting confused about a topic, this activity might be a good way to understand it better. Once students have taken a few notes, ask to hear some suggested corrections and reasons the original is wrong.

A word of caution: You could also write the problematic sentence or passage on the board, but this takes more time in class, and most students are trained to believe that anything on the board is correct. If a student arrives late or leaves early and sees the incorrect statement but doesn't hear the explanation, she may write it down in her notes verbatim.

Suggestions on preparation: You'll need to create an erroneous statement for this activity, which can take a little time. If you've taught the topic before, then you might know some common mistakes from previous exams, but if the subject is outside of your expertise, you'll need to start from scratch. Try searching the internet for "common misconceptions" and your topic area. Other people have probably posted plenty.

Activities of Seven to Fifteen Minutes
THINK-PAIR-SHARE
Preparation: Minimal
Structure: Pairs
Activity: If you've ever been to an education conference, you've probably participated in this activity. As James Lang observes in his book *On Course,* if you can get past the *Sesame Street*–sounding name, this can be a very effective technique for getting students to generate and compare ideas.[11] The activity is

simple and involves three steps: first, ask a question and give students a minute or two to think about it and perhaps jot down a few notes (that is, *Think*). Second, ask students to pair with someone next to them to compare their answers to the question (that is, *Pair*). Third, after a few minutes of focused conversation fills the room, bring the class back to order and ask a few students to share what they've learned (that is, *Share*). As with the Participation Prep activity, Think-Pair-Share is most effective when the question is open-ended and encourages analysis, interpretation, or calculation, rather than just a simple memorized answer. Of course, you can take memorized terms and ask the class to apply them. In an accounting class, you might ask, "When should a company use a backflush costing system instead of a job-order costing system?" Asking about the conditions surrounding a new concept prompts students to utilize higher-order thinking skills. Good starters for those questions include, "When would . . ." or "Under what circumstances would . . ." For example, "When is a critic deconstructing the text and when is she just plain-old analyzing it?"

When students compare answers, they validate or challenge their reasoning. "I thought backflush costing only made sense for small businesses" might be one possible misunderstanding. ("I thought 'backflush' somehow referred to sewage treatment" might be another.) Because these assumptions are challenged in the pairing stage, students often have new questions during the sharing stage.

A Think-Pair-Share activity is invaluable for classes outside of your expertise because it's often difficult for a content novice to tell which concepts are clear to students and which ones are confusing. It's also hard to predict when you've said something that is ripe for misinterpretation—it's often the first time you've said it. (I always find it a bit ironic that instructors, myself included, often put a tremendous amount of energy into saying something that's clear and organized but rarely turn to the students and ask if they've been successful.)

SEQUENCE RECONSTRUCTION
Preparation: Some (see Suggestions at the end)
Structure: Individual or pairs
Activity: The idea is simple. Begin with a sequenced list of items and jumble the items in the list. The students' task is to reorganize the list. The list could be a sequence of steps in a procedure, a list of ranked priorities, a series of decisions in a flow chart, or a set of historical events. Maybe it's the flow diagram for the fermentation process in a biology class. Or it might be the priorities when a new client walks into a manager's office. In a sociology course, perhaps the "sequence" is actually the different parts of an APA-style citation.

Where do you find the sequence or list? I often develop lists from figures or tables in a textbook because the information is already sequenced for you. (It's so easy it feels as though you're not really working. Trust me—good teaching isn't always hard work.) Use a list, diagram, or timeline from a textbook that isn't part of their homework but that still relates to what they've been learning in class. You probably have a stack of books by your desk or some bookmarked web pages to use as source material.

The simplest approach to running the activity in class is to provide a list on a PowerPoint slide or on the board and ask students to resequence the items as they copy the list in their notes. You can also distribute a handout with the jumbled items at the top. You can have students work alone or with a partner (if they compare and revise their lists with a peer, they once again benefit from explaining their rationale). Just be sure to review the correct answers as an entire class. Ask students what they put as the first step, second step, and so on. You'll often find that some steps come easily whereas other steps are harder to sequence, which reveals common misunderstandings you can address.

Suggestions on preparation: After finding the list, alphabetize the items to make jumbling it quick and simple. A little more preparation is needed if you put the list on a handout, but doing so will save class time because students won't need to copy the list by hand.

PEER INSTRUCTION OR CONCEPTESTS

Preparation: A good deal (see Suggestions at the end)

Structure: Pairs or small groups

Activity: I've worked with faculty in many disciplines who use this technique, and it seems to be a student favorite, particularly with undergraduates. Developed by Eric Mazur, the activity is similar to Think-Pair-Share, but with several notable differences.[12] As with Think-Pair-Share, students are given a conceptual question on a PowerPoint slide or overhead transparency and a few minutes to generate an answer. They then compare their answer with that of their neighbor, working together to figure out a correct answer.

An important difference, however, is that when you give students the question in a ConcepTest as opposed to a Think-Pair-Share activity, you also give them four or five multiple-choice answers. Keep in mind, you've asked a conceptual question, so the answer should require some thinking and should not be immediately obvious. The question should require students to apply a concept they've learned to a new problem (hence the name "ConcepTest"). If you're teaching a course in nursing and you've been learning about diabetes, you might ask, "A forty-year-old male who has been taking insulin for his diabetes for five years has been admitted to the ER for taking an overdose of aspirin. What should you closely monitor in this patient? A. Hypoglycemia, B. Excessive insulin secretion," and so on. This question requires students to think about the type of diabetes this patient probably has as well as the potential interaction of aspirin and insulin. Students make their own individual guess first and then you ask them to talk with their neighbor about why they chose one answer over another. Students who really understand the topic get a chance to practice explaining it to someone else, and students who are less certain discover the weak parts of their reasoning. In essence, you're giving students the opportunity to teach one another, hence the name "Peer Instruction."

Why is the peer instruction part of this activity so important? Students solidify their learning by telling someone else. You know this firsthand as someone teaching outside of your expertise. When do you have the clearest understanding of the material you just learned? Is it while you're still reading the text? At the start of class, notes in hand? Or would it be at the end of class, when you've just finished teaching about it? My guess is that most people, if they are honest with themselves, will pick the last option. (Maybe you said, "when I practice explaining it to my partner the night before class," but that's underlining the same basic point.)

The peer instruction step is helpful to the students; what comes next is helpful to you. Bring the class back together to discuss the correct answer. Before you reveal that answer, ask students to vote on their best guess. You could simply read down the list of possible answers and ask students to raise their hands when you come to their best guess, but this is problematic because students are swayed by the group consensus. It's hard for two or three students to be the only ones raising their hands for a particular answer, which means you could be misled into thinking that more students understand than is actually the case.

To get around the problem of peer pressure, have everyone vote simultaneously. Mazur and many other faculty use Classroom Response Systems (or "clickers"), which are basically handheld electronic devices about the size of a small stack of credit cards that allow students to select an answer by pushing a key.[13] This is a fantastic technical solution that quickly generates statistics and bar charts of the students' answers, allowing you to see how many students were drawn in by a plausible but incorrect answer. Students can also vote anonymously, which creates a safe environment for taking their best guess.

There are different variations on this activity. Some instructors have students vote, discuss their answer with a neighbor, and then vote again, all before the instructor gives any new information. This vote-discuss-vote approach lets you see how much the vote changes after students have had a chance to think through their answer with a peer. (And the votes often change.) Or students can simply discuss their answers with a peer and vote once.

Whereas some people are drawn to peer instruction because of the technology component, others are turned off by it. The drawback to using the clickers is that you need to be using PowerPoint in a wired classroom, and you may have reasons for not using PowerPoint. If you'd prefer a simultaneous voting strategy that's less technically intensive, you have several alternatives. One low-tech strategy that I've used is to pass out colored sticky notes. The first time I do this activity in class, each student receives four colored sticky notes—one each of yellow, blue, green, and pink (or whatever the bookstore has in stock)—and I ask them to keep the notes stuck to the inside cover of their notebook. When I prepare my multiple-choice answers, I color-code them by adding a little colored square next to each answer. Answer A is yellow, B is blue, and so on. When it's time to do the voting, students select the colored sticky associated with their best guess, and then vote on the count of three. Each student raises his or her sticky note, and I get a very quick sense, as do they, of everyone's answers. Like Mazur, I then ask students to give the reasons for their answers: "Can I hear from someone who voted for yellow and why?" The colored sticky notes are easy to see even in a large lecture hall, and I've seen this work in business and engineering classes of fifty students or more.

As I learned from my colleague Jeffrey Anderson, an even simpler method than the sticky note approach is to have students raise the fingers on one hand. They raise an index finger if they think the answer is no. 1, two fingers (index and middle finger) if they think the answer is no. 2, and so on (you'll want to give a little instruction so that students aren't rude in their finger choices). This only works well in a relatively small room where you can easily see everyone. But this approach minimizes preparation and fosters spontaneous questions on your part.

Whichever polling strategy you use, this is a proven way to learn where students have clarity and where there is confusion, and it's a great way to raise the energy in the classroom if it's beginning to droop. I've seen this activity used effectively in statistics, economics, anthropology, nursing, chemistry, and mechanical engineering, to name just a few. Entire books have been written on peer instruction, and you can turn to these for additional advice and examples.[14]

Suggestions on preparation: This activity involves some preparation because you need to generate a question, an answer, and a few plausible but incorrect alternatives. Depending on the voting system you use, this activity can require quite a bit of advance work the first time you use it, but it will take less preparation the second or third time because you'll have a voting system in place. If you've never used clickers before, factor in some extra time to adjust to the technology; you may even decide that it's too stressful to try clickers in a course where you already have your share of stresses. Then again, you may be more open to experimentation and playing with novel approaches in this periphery course, so you be the judge.

THREE-WAY INTERVIEW

Preparation: Minimal

Structure: Small groups of three

Activity: This activity helps students feel more personally connected to a topic that's otherwise distant and intellectual. The basic concept is that students will take turns interviewing one another on a topic related to the class. Divide students into groups of three. You want three students in each group so that one person can record the answers, freeing up the other two people to have a good conversation. (If the number of students in your class isn't divisible by three, have two groups of two students each, rather than one group of four. A larger group will be at a disadvantage with the time limits.)

At the start of the activity, distribute one sheet of blank paper per group. Instruct students that there are three roles in each group: an interviewer, an interviewee, and a recorder (or scribe).[15] Write these three roles on the board to help students remember. The interviewer asks the interviewee the question, the interviewee answers, and the recorder takes notes on the sheet of paper. The interviewer should begin by asking the prepared starter question that you've provided, but after asking that starter question, the interviewer can ask creative follow-up questions to gather more information about the other person's story. After two to three minutes, announce that it's time for everyone to take a new role within their group. The recorder passes the answer sheet to someone else in the group; a new person becomes the interviewer, and so on. After two to three minutes, the roles rotate a final time, allowing all three members of the group to play each of the roles.

What kind of question should you ask? Because it's an interview, pose a question about students' personal experience so that you can connect the day's topic to something personally meaningful for them. As you may recall from Chapter 2, students are more likely to take a deep approach to learning when they find something meaningful and interesting in the material. For example, you might be planning to discuss the worldwide boycotts of the 2008 Olympic torch in an international studies class. You could lead into the topic by doing a three-way interview on the question, "When have you encountered a boycott or protest? What influenced your decision to participate or not participate?" Give students an easy way to refer back to the question: write it on the board, present it on a PowerPoint slide, or circulate it on a handout.

When the final interview is complete, ask the recorder to draw a line across the page below the last interview. The final task for each group is to look for themes or common elements across the answers offered by all three members of their group. Give students one to three minutes to look for themes, depending on the complexity of the issue. Afterward, ask a few groups to report on their common themes or any surprises from the interviews.

Activities of Fifteen to Thirty Minutes

CATEGORY BUILDING

Preparation: Some to a great deal (see Suggestions at the end)

Structure: Individual or small groups

Activity: This is one of my favorite small-group activities; I learn so much about students' understanding as I watch them perform the task. The basic idea is to give students two or three concepts and a long list of features. They then sort the features around the correct concepts.

For example, in an art history course, you might have two concepts, the Art of the Ancient Near East (say, Mesopotamia and Iran) and the Art of Ancient Egypt, and a long list of features. Students work in pairs or small teams to sort the features into three categories: Ancient Near East, Ancient Egypt, or Both. You could stick to two categories, but I like to include a column for "Both" because it challenges students to think of higher-order properties that both art forms share. You could even add a fourth category, "Neither," if you want to take the time to generate unusual features that do not apply to either category, but it can be hard to think of plausible, fictional properties if you're not an expert in the field.

How do you generate the list of features? Tables and figures are my favorite sources. It's hard to go more than a chapter or two in most traditional textbooks without a figure that consists of two column headings and a list of distinguishing properties— the differences between macroeconomics and microeconomics, federal law and state law, or bases and acids. Use a table or figure from a textbook or article that you haven't assigned for class, so students are working with some familiar concepts and some novel ones.

There are different ways to conduct this activity in class. The quickest is simply to distribute a handout with the categories and the list of properties. Students work individually or in small groups to categorize each property. Since I use outside sources to generate the properties, I let students use their textbooks. (Perhaps it's just me, but I find it exciting to see them apply the text to solve a problem.) When they finish, review the groupings together to discover which items caused confusion.

If you're willing to put in a little more preparation time, a superior way to do this activity is to make it more like a game: break students up into teams and give each team slips of paper with the different properties.

Before class: Type up the category names and the properties in a large font (20–28 point) so that it will be easy for you to see students' progress as they work together on the task. Cut the items apart so that you have one property per slip of paper (a paper-cutter makes this a quick task). Clip the slips together or put them in envelopes so that you can distribute one packet per team.

In class: Break students up into two-to-three-person teams and give each team a packet of materials. Instruct the students to sort the items into groups. The beauty of using little slips of paper is that you can walk around the room and see students' understanding of the concepts emerging on the basis of their groupings. Properties that students sort quickly are usually well understood, but in some cases, their initial groupings reveal a knee-jerk misunderstanding. You can also see which properties are giving students trouble or causing debate because those properties are usually set aside while they work on easier concepts. I've even used this activity with international students who would talk in their native language in their small groups, but because the slips of paper were in English, I could readily see what they were discussing (at least, what I hope they were discussing).

When I use the "slips of paper" approach, I often tell students that each group is allowed one hint as I walk around the room. Sometimes the hints are very vague, such as, "You've got two items sorted incorrectly." This usually leads to frustration followed by a rallying cry as they refocus their efforts. Sometimes I invite each group to direct their hint: "Decide where you most want feedback." Groups get very strategic about this. Some will ask, "How many items should be under 'Ancient Egyptian Art'?" whereas others will zone in on specific items, "We can't decide where to put these last two items—any hints?"

However you decide to structure the activity, it's important that everyone comes back together to review the correct answers and discuss the items that were hardest to categorize. Be sure that students have some record of the answers to take home and review. The first time I tried this activity with small groups, students were so focused on seeing how well their team scored that many of them forgot to write down the correct answers.

Suggestions for preparation: It takes some time to find the list, jumble the items, and add a few items to the "Both" category. It requires more preparation to do this activity with movable slips of paper than with a simple one-page handout. But the gains are great because you'll learn more about students' knowledge: as you watch them slide slips of paper around their desks, you quickly learn what students know well, what they know tentatively, and what they don't know at all.

VIDEO PREDICTIONS
Preparation: A great deal (see Suggestions at the end)
Structure: Small groups

Since this activity takes more preparation time than most of the other active learning exercises, I'll explain why it's so effective before I explain how to do it. You deserve to be convinced if you're going to try this one.

If you like to use videos in class, this learning activity is probably for you. It makes videos more educational and helps students pay more attention to the parts of the video that are most important to you. Now you might be thinking, "As soon as I turn on a video, students are already paying more attention." I'm sure this is true.

But what students learn and recall from a video may be very different from what you hoped they would learn and recall. Shannon Harp and Amy Maslich have conducted research on the power of what they call "seductive details" to distract students from the harder conceptual aspects of a lecture.[16] A seductive detail is information that is tangentially related to the main concept and that stirs interest in the topic, but that doesn't contribute to students' understanding of the main concept. For example, in a physics class on the way lightning is formed, a seductive detail would be the number of golfers who die each year in the United States from a lightning strike. It's an interesting statistic and you're likely to remember it (as will your students), but research shows that when these kinds of distracting details are presented in class, students pay more attention to these irrelevant details than to the key concepts, such as how an electrical charge builds in a cloud.[17] Seductive details make a topic more interesting, but they interfere with a student's success in learning the main concepts.

Seductive details abound in videos. Producers add them to keep the viewer interested and to provide a sense of place and context. I often use videos in my neuropsychology courses to help students understand rare or misunderstood cognitive disorders. But if I just put in the video and press play, students will remember charming but irrelevant details. When we watch a video of a split-brain patient, almost everyone will remember that the patient with severe epilepsy works in an egg-packing factory (which I agree is surprising) but completely forget the point of the two research studies he performed in the lab. To make the important concepts just as memorable as the seductive details, I developed this "Video Predictions" activity.

Activity: In this activity, you'll ask students to predict part of the video. You ask them to predict something very specific and particular, which helps focus their attention, after which they watch the video to see if they predicted correctly. When students are asked to describe the details of what they expect to see on the basis of what they've read or heard in class, they are often surprised to discover that the vague image they had in mind differs so sharply from what they see on video. The conscious disconnect between what they expect to see and what they actually see creates, I suspect, a deeper approach to learning.

Students could work by themselves, but it's more educational and energizing to have small teams of three to four students generate predictions together. Students have a chance to think through their predictions with their classmates, and when one of their team members makes a spot-on prediction, the whole team celebrates.

Obviously, the surprise factor is greatest when students have not seen the video. Good candidates include PBS specials, documentaries, recordings of research experiments or people with unusual behaviors, historical reenactments, interviews, news programs, foreign films, and so on. If you wish to show a video that you suspect at least some students have seen, then ask them to predict something unusual that they probably haven't noticed. If you wanted to use the movie *The Matrix* in a religion class, for example, you might ask students about all the references to Christianity in the first fifteen minutes of the film.

Your instructions for the activity will vary depending on your class and the type of video that you're watching, but I'll offer a few general suggestions. Begin by having students watch part of the video. They will be resistant to making predictions or describing their expectations with no context, so have them watch a few minutes to gain a sense of the setting, people, story, testing apparatus (in science and medicine), and so on. Then stop the video and give a general overview of what's going to happen next without providing any specific details. For example, if you're watching a documentary about labor practices at Wal-Mart, you can let students know that they are about to watch a manager interviewing a job applicant for an entry-level management position, and this person has made it through the initial paper screening. Ask students to work in small groups to generate written predictions about what they expect to see. One person in each group has a sheet for recording the groups' predictions. (By limiting the materials to one sheet for the entire group, students are forced to work together.) Ask for specific details, preferably concrete measurable details. What gender, race, and age do they expect the manager to be? How about the applicant? How long do they expect the interview to last? Do they expect it to be public or private? What four questions do they expect will be asked? By focusing students' attention on specific issues, you've created a context for them to discuss their assumptions and state their existing knowledge.

Before you start the video, be sure that each group has divided up the responsibilities for testing their predictions. Several of their predicted events could occur in rapid sequence, and if everyone is looking for the entire list, one or two events can easily be overlooked. In our example, one person could time the interview and two others could take notes on the four interview questions, just in case the questions are asked and answered quickly. When you stop the video, be sure to allow time for discussion. Most students will be eager to justify why something did not play out the way they expected. They might have questions about whether the depiction in the video was typical. You've created a very teachable moment.

Suggestions for preparation: This activity requires a good deal of preparation because you have to track down a video, preview it, select the part that fits your learning objectives for the class, and generate questions that will focus students' predictions. But I think you'll be well rewarded for your efforts. When students have to predict what they will see, you push them to describe the images they have in mind. Chances are they aren't even aware that they had any expectations going into the video. You learn about their misconceptions and naïve theories, and you often gain a concrete picture of how they interpreted (or misinterpreted) important concepts from the reading. You're also ensuring that they pay attention to and recall much more than those seductive details.

Activity of Thirty to Sixty Minutes
FISHBOWL (OR CONCENTRIC CIRCLE DISCUSSION)
Preparation: Minimal
Structure: One medium group and one large group
Activity: This activity is popular among education faculty and works well for discussion classes. In many traditional discussion classes, a few students dominate while the rest of the class remains silent. A fishbowl provides a way to engage a greater number of students in the conversation. A fishbowl consists of two concentric circles of students: an inner circle of six to ten students having a discussion around a table, surrounded by a larger group of students who listen to the smaller group's discussion.

To set up the activity, ask for volunteers for the inner circle. The talkative students who normally dominate will be the first to volunteer. That's fine. They have a chance to participate in a more fast-paced and animated discussion than they would in a normal class, and the silent students on the periphery get to observe a livelier version of the discussion. Provide the inner circle with discussion questions and a time limit. Give the outer ring different roles. At the very least, their job is to observe and document the discussion dynamics. Which topics are discussed most? Which arguments or pieces of evidence are raised and discussed, and which ones are raised but relatively ignored by the rest of the group? When do emotions appear to be running high? It's also a good idea to ask someone in the outer group to be a timekeeper and let the inner group know when they have just a few minutes remaining. When it's time to end the discussion, you might give the outer group the opportunity to de-brief the discussion they just witnessed. In this way, there is first a discussion by the inner circle and then a discussion by the outer circle.

A more dynamic variation on this activity is to give students in the outer circle a way to join the discussion by simply "tapping in." Any person from the outer circle is allowed to tap the shoulder of someone in the discussion and swap seats. This not only gives outer-circle students an opportunity to add something important to the conversation but also creates a way to censor a dominating student. If you're going to allow students to "tap in," you might want to add some rules. For example, someone who has been "tapped out" needs to wait until three other people have tapped in before they can tap in again.

This activity is a stress reliever if you're teaching on the edge of your expertise because it requires you to generate only the initial question to launch the discussion, rather than a full twenty to forty minutes' worth of discussion questions. Some faculty who are still learning the material are reluctant to lead discussions because it's challenging to generate a series of effective questions. In a fishbowl, you ask the initial question and then step back and let students do the rest. Of course, the initial question needs to be open-ended and interesting enough that students can discuss it for twenty to forty minutes. For example, in a modern American history class, you might ask, "Some people have argued that the Cuban Missile Crisis was the most dangerous event that's happened in the United States in the past fifty years. First, why would someone claim that, and second, to what extent do you agree or disagree?" This open-ended and controversial question will generate a more effective discussion than the relatively closed question, "Who was crucial in making the key decisions in the Cuban Missile Crisis?" Along the same lines, you want to avoid asking questions that simply require students to respond with a straightforward list. Lists are problematic because they often rely on rote recall and fail to prompt interesting discussion. "What events led up to the Cuban Missile Crisis?" is a relatively boring question that would lead to a relatively boring fishbowl in most classes. Even personal lists are relatively boring, such as, "What are two things you always try to do on the first day of class?" because they don't require members of the inner circle to listen to one another. As a general rule, it's best to begin these activities asking "how" or "why" rather than "what."

I'll admit that a fishbowl sounded strange until I tried it; it was one of those things I would read about, then nod my head and move on. Now that I've been a student in one, I know how effective they can be. Most of the success of the activity rests on the quality of the question you give the group, but once again, the good news is that you only need one or two good questions. I particularly like the "tapping in" variation because it pressures the inner group to have a high-quality discussion, and it motivates the outer circle to pay more attention.

A Final Word about Motivation

Now that you've read about some of these activities, you may be thinking that active learning is best for classes in which students are highly motivated. After all, if you're going to ask ev-

eryone to rearrange their chairs into two circles or predict what
will happen in a video, you might think that students need to be
falling out of their seats with excitement for these to work. On
the contrary, these active learning techniques usually work even
when students aren't excited about the topic. One of the reasons
they're so successful is that they often stimulate interest in a
topic that isn't generating much on its own.[18]

In fact, these active learning techniques are probably even
more necessary and more valuable in a course in which students *aren't* intrinsically motivated. When students are motivated, they will engage in active learning on their own time.
They will put the lecture notes in their own words, find a study
partner to help them plod through the densest parts of the text,
or predict the results of an experiment. It's when they're *not*
motivated that you need to create the structure and incentives to
engage them with the material in class because you can't rely on
them to do it on their own.[19]

Eric Mazur shared a story from his own days as a student
to illustrate the interplay between motivation and active learning. It's a surprising story from someone who's internationally
known for his dynamic physics classroom:

> The class I learned the most in was taught in the Netherlands by
> the most abysmal professor that I've met in my life. It was a quan-
> tum mechanics course I took as a physics undergraduate. The only
> place where you could hear what he was saying was in the front
> row. He would come in, shaking nervously, and he would start
> with his back toward the class, and start writing on the blackboard
> in beautiful handwriting, at the top left corner, and he would
> mumble and write and mumble and write. I would sit in the front
> row, sliding my table and chair as far forward as I could, furiously
> writing down everything I could. After an hour he would get to
> the bottom right corner of the board and then ask methodically,

"Does anyone have any questions?" but nobody understood enough to even ask a question. Then he would walk out, smoke a cigarette outside for ten minutes, come back, erase the board, and start the second hour, writing once again from the top left to the bottom right. I would go home and spend hours trying to decipher what I'd scribbled in my lecture notes (which I've kept to this day as a relic of the past). And by forcing myself to rewrite those lecture notes, I learned a lot. Even though it was an abysmal performance, I learned a tremendous amount.

"What that means," Mazur continued, "is that if you have students who want to learn, you can do whatever you want; it doesn't matter as long as you give them a source of knowledge." But if your students aren't passionate about learning in your class, then you need to give them more than just the knowledge. You can't just scribble and mumble (which is how I'm sure I sound to my students from time to time, especially when I'm not very confident about what I'm saying). You need to give them the chance to practice working with the knowledge in class, while the ideas are still fresh and before they're distracted by something else. We may all wish to have a room full of students like Eric Mazur, edging their desks forward to catch every last word, but most of us don't. Even he, a professor at Harvard, doesn't have those kinds of students as often as he'd like, which is potentially why he began looking for better ways to engage students in the first place.

6 Teaching Students You Don't Understand

The final exam was halfway over, and I knew I had an unpleasant phone call to make. Matt hadn't shown up. I kept hoping that he'd shuffle in late, drop his backpack on the table with an apologetic nod of his head, maybe even ask to borrow a pencil. But he never even stepped into the room.

It was the first class I had ever taught on my own and I had named it "Attention and Awareness." I was teaching at Carnegie Mellon University, an elite high-tech school, so these fourteen students were paying top dollar for my first teaching adventure. I poured my heart into that course, and to this day, I remember most of the names and faces from that room. Matt had a crew cut and wide, husky shoulders, and when he came to class, which wasn't often, he sat on my right, toward the front.

I'd like to think that I did all I could for Matt. The first few weeks when he would miss a class, I would send an email and he would apologize. He didn't whine or make excuses, which surprised me; his sense of being responsible for his irresponsible behavior made the experience almost pleasant. I sent him a concerned note when he missed a writing assignment and reminded him about the final. But at some point, I have to admit, he stopped showing up altogether and I stopped asking.

All in all, I shouldn't have been surprised when he missed the final exam, but in my mind, it was one thing to miss a string of classes and small assignments but another thing to miss the final. When I got back to my office with everyone's bluebooks, there was a message from Matt on my voicemail. Oddly, he gave no explanation except that he had overslept. When I called him back, he apologized rather formally and unhurriedly, asked to make up the final, and explained that he needed to pass this last psychology course to graduate. Two competing voices emerged in my head: "Of course you can make up the final because I would never stand in the way of your graduation"; and "Did you consider setting a second alarm?" The first voice won out, as we knew it would, and Matt and I agreed that he could take the exam in my office the next morning.

Can you see where this is headed?

He didn't show up. I waited by the door to our office suite, looking up and down the hall, thinking perhaps he had gotten lost, but there was no sign of him.

I didn't know what to do. I had made every accommodation I could in good conscience, but no matter how generously I did the math, Matt wasn't earning a passing grade. To add to the pressure I was feeling, he wasn't going to graduate. My first foray into teaching as a twenty-five-year-old grad student and someone wasn't going to get his degree from college because of me. The guilt was tremendous. After waiting almost thirty minutes for him to show up, I went to my teaching mentor, a brilliant and funny professor by the name of Ken Kotovsky. Thankfully, Ken was in his office.

Ken reviewed the entire story with me and then said with a

shrug, "So he fails. You did everything you could. Welcome to the club, kid." I had already tried reassuring myself that it wasn't my fault, but I didn't want anyone to fail. Should I have sent him an extra email a few days before the final? Was one out of every fourteen students destined to fail my classes? (Remember, this was my first real teaching experience, so I over-analyzed a lot.) Ken studied me for a moment, leaning heavily into his armrest: "Maybe this student wanted to fail. Some students choose to fail, you know; they probably don't consciously choose it, but at some level they do. Maybe Matt never wanted to be a psychology major." Then Ken snapped his fingers as though he'd just realized something. "Maybe his dad wants him to go into the military as soon as he graduates and by failing your class, he can avoid boot camp. Who knows?"

This was definitely beginning to help, but his most important piece of advice came next: "Look, kid, you might as well learn this now—not everyone is like you. You can't imagine failing because that would be the worst thing for you, the absolute worst thing, but for some people, it's not so bad. It may even be a good thing because it gives people an out. It's a tough lesson to learn, but you'll have a much easier time and you might even enjoy teaching if you realize that not every student is like you."

It's true. On the one hand, we know rationally that our students aren't just like us. They are unique individuals, and intellectually we appreciate that. But on the other hand, most of us are probably still taken aback by some of the differences, by some of the things that students say or do (or, in Matt's case, fail to do). If you're like most of us, you'll find yourself looking at your students from time to time, thinking, "Why did they do that? I would never have done that as a student."

Just less than a year after that "Attention and Awareness" course was over, I saw Matt in the hallway. His crew cut had grown out and he had lost some weight, so I didn't recognize him at first. But he stopped me and said hello, in the same formal way he had always addressed me. He explained that he'd changed majors to information science and that he was still going to graduate, just a year later. The most surprising moment of that quick conversation in the hallway came when he thanked me. He didn't explain, he just thanked me.

Ken was right. The sooner you realize that your students are different from you, the easier and perhaps happier your teaching life will be.

In this chapter, we'll examine the many ways your students simply aren't like you. And we'll explore some strategies for dealing with those unavoidable differences.

How They're Different

In some ways, you're different from your students because you chose the life of a scholar. As Myra Strober, an economics professor at Stanford, observed, "They're not like me. By and large, most of the students in my classes don't have the desire to go into the library and spend a couple of weeks there." Most students will endure the repetitive cycle of reading and writing for a few years in college (or, if they're in the sciences or the arts, the equally repetitive cycle of reading and problem-solving). But you, the college professor, chose to pursue that training regimen as a career. So let's be honest—you weren't actually like everyone else when you were a student. You probably spent long hours in the lab, at your keyboard, or on stage when other people were out on the quad.

These aren't just my musings about how well you did or didn't fit in at your alma mater (I'm sure you were very popular). Researchers have compared the learning styles of faculty and students and found, not surprisingly, that these two groups differ considerably in what and how they prefer to learn. In fifteen years of collecting data on college students, researchers such as Charles Schroeder have concluded that approximately half of the students in college can be categorized as "concrete active" learners, which means they learn best when they can see things directly and when the concrete applications of an idea are immediate and obvious. They want to stand in front of a museum case and see a real lung blackened with emphysema; they don't just want to hear about the probabilities of lung cancer in different populations. These highly pragmatic learners want to begin with an example and eventually move to the theory. They are more interested in hearing what happens when the CEO of a major corporation makes a bad ethical decision than in debating the abstract implications of cultural relativism.[1]

The problem is that most of their professors revel in phrases like "cultural relativism." Or they like to daydream about numbers. Sure, professors like to go to museums to see the exhibits, but as faculty, we can be lured into a fascinating problem simply because it's a complex, enticing problem. We don't necessarily need to see the crusty, blackened lung to be drawn in. And most professors don't prefer to approach things pragmatically. (You already know this, of course, if you've ever seen one of your colleagues try to figure out why a photocopier is jammed. We can have amazing persistence when it comes to arguing an idea, but we aren't always the sharpest tools in the shed when it comes to solving practical problems.) Whereas 50 percent of students are concrete active learners, Schroeder and others have found that less than 10 percent of faculty members are.[2] So in a department of ten faculty members, you might expect to have at most one instructor who prefers to approach problems and questions pragmatically, the way that most students typically do.[3]

What about the nine other members of the department? How do they prefer to learn? Most of them would probably be categorized as "abstract reflective" learners. These types of learners are interested in "an idea for the idea's sake" and prefer compelling theories to concrete applications. They prefer to move from theory to practice, not the other way around. And when abstract reflective individuals are learning something, they prefer to maintain a high degree of autonomy. They want to create their own structure; they don't want to be told what to do at every turn. Once again, we see the rift between learning styles. In the sample of 4,000 students described earlier, only about 10 percent preferred to learn in an abstract reflective way.[4]

So students and faculty generally prefer to receive information in different ways, which might explain some of the frustrations you're having with your students (and some of the frustrations they're having with you). If students keep asking you to jump to the problems in their homework, you may assume that they're just focused on getting good grades. Or if they complain that your "real world" example from 1998 isn't real or current enough, you may think that they are apathetic about important world events. It may help to realize that you probably prefer, and perhaps have always preferred, a different type of learning experience from that of your students. If your seniors ask for step-by-step instructions for their senior projects, it's not necessarily the case that they lack creativity (though they may); it could be that they are seeking a much more structured and linear learning experience than you probably sought when you were twenty-two years old. Even when you were a student, your fascination with open-ended problems was probably not shared by everyone in the room.

Another problem, of course, is the generation gap: students today *are* different from students ten or twenty years ago. Even if you had a grasp on your students a few years back, you might find yourself complaining that young people don't seem to be as engaged or as focused on their schoolwork as they once were. According to the research, you're correct: students today invest much less time on school-related activities than once was the case. Think for just a moment about how much time you spent reading for class, doing your homework, and working on papers or projects when you were in college. My guess is that you spent at least fifteen hours a week, maybe even twenty or thirty hours a week. In the 1980s, you would have been in the majority—73 percent of students reported that they spent more than fifteen hours a week preparing for their classes. By the 1990s, only 65 percent of students were spending more than fifteen hours a week studying. Although fewer college students were putting in the kinds of hours that you invested in your homework, it's nice to see that they still constituted more than half of the student body. By 2008, that number had dropped to roughly 35 percent of students. In fact, the average number of hours students spent preparing for class—and this is for all their classes combined—was only thirteen hours a week in 2007 and 2008.[5] This was about half as much time as faculty expected students to spend.[6] And no, students aren't working at lightning speed. When students invest that little time, they can't get all their work done: roughly one in five first-year students and seniors reported that they often go to class without finishing the readings or the assignments.[7]

One reason students are putting fewer hours into their classes is that they're spending more hours earning money. For decades, there has been a slow but steady rise in the number of students who hold down jobs while they take classes. And students are working longer hours at these jobs. In fall 2006, approximately 22 percent of all undergraduate students nationwide were working twenty to thirty-four hours a week. Another 10 percent of students were working thirty-five hours a week or more. Combined, that means that one in every three students in your class is working at least twenty hours a week at a job in addition to managing their coursework.[8] That's a considerable proportion of your students. You may not be impressed by these numbers if you worked two jobs to put yourself through school, but the demographics have shifted: the students who are working these kinds of hours aren't just the most highly motivated students. They aren't like you—they probably won't graduate magna cum laude or choose between great graduate programs. Spending long hours at an outside job is increasingly the norm for average and below-average students, those who truly need to be putting more time into their coursework but regrettably are not.

Students who are working full-time are categorized as "nontraditional students." "Nontraditional" is a catch-all term that ironically now describes more than half the students attending college. Nationwide, almost three out of every four students (73 percent) are classified as nontraditional, meaning that on top of doing their homework, they may be working full-time, caring for a child or an aging parent, still finishing a high school degree, or returning to school after several years in the workforce. While these numbers are higher at community colleges (89 percent), the percentages at four-year public and private institutions are higher than you might expect (58 percent and 50 percent of the student body, respectively).[9]

Students are also more notably pragmatic than their counterparts even a decade ago. They are increasingly interested in undergraduate degrees that look like job titles at Verizon or Sony. Students are choosing to major in business and communications like never before. In 2007, more than 327,000 students graduated with a bachelor's degree in business, compared with approximately 164,000 students in the social sciences and history, 55,000 in English, and 21,000 in the physical sciences.[10] This increase reflects a 45 percent growth in the number of business majors in ten years, compared with an average growth in the three other fields of only 18 percent.[11] Most departments are graduating more students simply because college enrollments have increased substantially, but students aren't spreading themselves equally across campus—they are choosing more applied fields.[12] Whereas English and literature grew a paltry 13 percent over a decade, communications and journalism saw a whopping 58 percent increase in majors. If you want to teach in a place where students take classes for the pure love of learning or for a well-rounded education, you're out of luck at most institutions.

Students are also more racially and ethnically diverse than ever before. The proportion of students of color doubled between 1976 and 2007, from 15 percent to 32 percent of the total undergraduate population. Which groups are increasingly represented on our campuses? Although some people primarily think of African-American students when they hear the phrase "students of color," most of the growth has been in the number of students from Asian, Latino, and Pacific Islander origins.[13] Students of color are also having more success in graduate school: between 1991 and 2006, students of color went from constituting 11 percent of students receiving master's degrees to 22 percent.[14] You may have also noticed that a higher percentage of your students are from eastern Asia, Europe, and the Middle East. Although international student enrollment declined for a few years following the terrorist attacks of 2001, the numbers began to climb again in 2006, with a 10 percent increase in the number of new students starting their first year of college in the United States.[15]

This may seem like an avalanche of numbers, but the point is that students have changed considerably in the past few years. Keep in mind that you're dealing with two issues simultaneously: you're teaching students who aren't like you, and you're teaching an increasingly diverse group, a group that's more diverse than when you were a student. That students are ever more different from one another—and from you—can make it very difficult to know the best way to teach them.

Of course, the national numbers can't predict the exact composition of students in your classes. If you're at a private institution, you probably have more students from higher-income families than if you teach at a public university. If you teach in California or Texas, you've probably been teaching ethnically and racially diverse groups of students for most of your career.[16]

But there is another, more subtle discrepancy that you may have encountered. As we've already seen, today more students are working full-time while they go to school, and more have heavy responsibilities at home. On the basis of these findings, you might expect to walk into class tomorrow and face students who are pedaling as fast as they can, students who have even more practical, real-world experience than some of their instructors. And yet when I ask faculty, "What kinds of things surprise you about students today?" they don't tell me about students who need to leave class early to pick up their toddlers from day care. Instead, they tell me about students who don't know how to use a dustpan and a broom. They are surprised and often frustrated by students who seem to be very sheltered and bring less practical experience to the classroom rather than more.

Consider Al Greer, a physics professor at Gonzaga University in Washington. Gonzaga is known in recent years for its men's basketball team, but as a medium-sized Jesuit school, it also has a tradition of providing students with an excellent undergraduate education. Al grew up in a blue-collar home, and when he first started teaching fourteen years ago, he had a fair number of students in his classes who were first-generation college students like himself, students who had worked at construction jobs or waited tables over the summer to help pay for college. In contrast, students in Al's classes today seem removed from what he considers to be everyday practicalities: "They can all use their iPods, they can all use their cell phones, they can all surf the web, but they don't have any hands-on experience in a working environment. A lot of them have no idea how to change the oil in their car. It's a sort of disconnect with the day-to-day reality that most folks have to deal with."

This limited experience changes the way Al teaches his physics classes. If he wants to use a car example to discuss friction or torque, he can't talk about the clutch on a manual car because fewer and fewer students have looked under the hoods of their cars (and they may not see a clutch if they did). He can't even describe torque in terms of the wrench you'd use to change a flat tire because most students haven't changed one. "I can talk about power antennae going up or about power locks," he explains, but what does that get you in a physics class? Part of the issue is that cars have become more automated and computerized, but he points to the broom and dustpan example or to the fact that most students haven't changed a flat tire as evidence that these students have diminished real-world, problem-solving experiences. It makes labs slower and harder to teach today—when a piece of lab equipment doesn't work perfectly the first time students try it, they don't fiddle with it or try to diagnose the problem. They simply sit back down on their lab stools and wait for Al to come fix it. He's learned to be patient with it, but his experience is that an increasing number of students have grown accustomed to pressing a button, paying a professional, or relying on their parents to accomplish tasks that were once considered basic skills.

How can we reconcile stories like these with the research literature that shows an increasing number of nontraditional students who have had to solve and juggle all kinds of real-world problems just to get into college? Sylvia Hurtado, professor and director of the Higher Education Research Institute at UCLA, explained to me that the research literature reports a second phenomenon: a generation of highly sheltered students. It's the problem of "helicopter parents," so named because many parents of the Baby Boomer generation hover over their children, ready to swoop down and take care of annoying, everyday tasks like changing a flat on the side of the road.[17] (These types of parents have also been dubbed "snowplow parents" because "they try to clear the way for their children.")[18] On Sylvia's own campus, just like on most campuses today, faculty, deans, and department chairs regularly receive meddlesome phone calls from these well-intentioned parents. Sylvia told the story of one department chair who received a call from a father complaining that the questions on his daughter's final exam were unreasonable. The department chair agreed to talk with the student and asked how to reach her; the father replied, "She's in the exam now."

So on the one hand, we have some highly dependent students on their cell phones to their parents during an exam, and on the other hand, we have other, highly independent students who are coming back to school part-time at age twenty-six, commuting an hour to their jobs each day, and putting themselves through school. What professors are seeing in their classes is an extreme dichotomy. As Sylvia Hurtado explains, "You have polar opposites in the classroom. You have very nontraditional students who have extreme responsibility with family and work, and then you have the other extreme of students who are forever in the nest. And by the way, those sheltered students? They are going to move back home when they graduate."

Thus far, most of the research findings and anecdotes about student differences have focused on undergraduates and part-time master's students. If you teach doctoral students, you might be wondering whether they've changed as well. The short answer: it depends. If you emulated your graduate advisors and wanted to follow in their footsteps when you grew up, then sadly, your graduate students are probably not like you. That's not to say that you're a poor role model. Research in the University of California system shows that today's graduate students lose the desire for the academic fast track.[19] After a few years in graduate school, neither men nor women see the tenure-track lifestyle at research institutions as being family-friendly, and they don't want the harried lives of their advisors. Myra Strober sees it in her students: "My doctoral students aren't as interested as I was in proving I could do this. They don't need to show the world they could have a job at the most prestigious school. And why aren't they trying to do that? They say, 'In all honesty, Dr. Strober, I don't want to work as hard as you do.'"

The Easy Part: Learning about Your Students

So when you walk into a new class, whom do you encounter? Are you about to teach a room of highly responsible but over-extended nontraditional students who themselves are a very diverse group? Or are you facing a cohort of protected students who are used to being coddled and receiving high praise promptly for their work? (That's another dimension of the sheltered "Generation Y" students. They are accustomed to receiving prompt and typically positive feedback on their work.[20] I'm guessing this isn't news to you.) You might be able to guess by students' ages as you glance around the room, but that's often hard to judge, and age isn't a perfect predictor. Likewise, if you teach at a private school where tuition is high, you probably have more sheltered students. But I've taught at private schools, and I've watched the number of full-time working students go up in my classes each year.

Given these extremes and given how hard it is to know whom you're teaching, you need some simple and quick strategies for learning about your students. If you take a few steps to learn more about them collectively, you can be a much more effective teacher. If you find out what they already know about the course you're about to teach or what they hope to get from the $150's worth of books they just bought, you can build from their knowledge, interests, and motivations.

On the first day of classes, I usually ask students to complete a background knowledge probe, sign up for a quick meeting with me, and work together on a syllabus activity. I'll describe these activities and several others I've discovered in the course of my interviews. Use what makes sense to you.

Background Knowledge Probe

Thomas Angelo and Patricia Cross call this activity a "background knowledge probe." It's a short, simple questionnaire that asks students about the knowledge they bring into class on Day 1. The simplest version would consist of a list of key terms or concepts related to the course. A more complex version would include short problems to consider. So far, this sounds like a traditional quiz, right? What distinguishes a background knowledge probe from a quiz is that students tell you how much they know or don't know, rather than actually defining the concept or solving the problem.

The best way to understand this is by example. Let's say that you're teaching a course on the civil rights movement and one of the important concepts is separatism. On the background knowledge questionnaire, students would see the word "separatism" and five possible ways to rank this concept:

1. Have never heard of this
2. Have heard of it but never really knew what it meant
3. Have heard of it and could have explained it once, but cannot recall now
4. Can recall what it means and can explain it in general terms, but cannot explain how it applies to the civil rights movement in the United States
5. Can recall what it means and can explain how it applies to the civil rights movement in the United States

Before I continue, which answer would you circle for "separatism"? Embarrassingly, I'd have to circle no. 2. (I've since looked it up on Wikipedia, so I feel a little better, but that still doesn't get me to no. 5 on this scale.) You can see how quickly this question helps an instructor categorize a learner's level of sophistication on a topic. My own lack of sophistication would be a lesson to myself and the instructor that I have some serious work to do in this course.

Why is this approach more valuable than simply asking students to define separatism? First, you're looking for a quick way to assess students' background knowledge, and as you probably just experienced, it takes students surprisingly little time to judge their own knowledge. A student can quickly circle "never heard of it" but might labor long and hard to generate a bogus answer if asked, "What is separatism?" There is a time savings for you as well—it takes very little time for you to score a background knowledge probe, whereas it would take two evenings to read all those bad essays on separatism. If you're still learning the material yourself, a quiz is also a bad idea the first week because you may not even know all the terms yet. It's disconcerting if you don't know whether a student's definition of separatism is insightful prose or well-crafted hogwash.

To get the most candid feedback, ask students to complete the probe anonymously so they can be upfront about how little they actually know without any fear that their lack of knowledge will affect their grade or your perceptions of them. Besides, you're not trying to measure the performance of individuals; you're trying to identify which concepts you'll need to explain in more depth and detail to the entire class.

How do you create a background knowledge probe? A reasonable strategy is to select one to three terms from each chapter or week, resulting in a list of about twenty to twenty-five terms or phrases. Include some common concepts—something that seems like common knowledge to you may not be common to someone five to thirty years younger. It's also a good idea to include some very common concepts so that everyone can rank at least one item with a (4) or a (5). (Students find it discouraging to have an entire list of terms they can't even pronounce.)

When I'm clueless about a chapter later in the book and I honestly don't know any of the terms yet, I simply pick two or three words in bold from the text or chapter headings that seem to be used repeatedly. It's fine to include terms that you don't know very well. I usually do. The students won't ask you to define any of those terms on Day 1, and if someone does, you can simply say, "Glad to hear you're interested. That term will make more sense if we cover it in context. Mind if we wait on it?" I know it seems risky, but by including some terms you don't know very well on the background knowledge probe, you can gauge where your students have expertise that you can harness. If your students know more about a topic than you do, it's better to know upfront. Make a note on your syllabus so that when you get to those areas of student expertise, you can take the spotlight off your lecture—it sounds like the perfect day to have a student-led discussion or one of the active learning activities I described last chapter.

Meetings with Students

Talking face-to-face is still one of the best ways to get to know a person, so ask students to meet with you briefly during the first few weeks of classes. You can provide a sign-up sheet divided into ten- to fifteen-minute blocks so that students sign up for a time during your regular office hours (faculty office hours typically go unused for the first few weeks of classes anyway). If you have a larger class, take a tip from Derek Bruff, a senior lecturer of mathematics at Vanderbilt University, and design the sign-up sheet so that two or three students are scheduled for each meeting time. Group meetings have a number of advantages according to Derek, who uses this strategy in a statistics course with fifty-five to sixty students. It's more time-efficient for you, obviously, but students often find it easier to say something because they aren't the only one in the scary professor's office. Plus, each student gets to know at least one other student in the course right from the start.

Faculty who conduct these meetings often, as Derek does, recommend asking three types of questions:

1. *Personal questions.* "Where are you from? What kinds of things do you like to do in your free time? Is anything significant

happening in your life this term?" These questions probably won't affect how you teach, but they help establish rapport, plus they give students a chance to tell you what's competing for their attention—maybe they are getting married, scheduled for surgery, or participating in an ultimate frisbee tournament.

2. *Motivation questions.* "What's your major? Why did you pick that major? What are your career goals?" Students' answers to these questions help shape your teaching because you can pick examples from the text and assignment topics that tap into their intrinsic interests. The year Derek had more electrical engineering students in his statistics class than mechanical engineers, he chose more electrical examples.

3. *Questions about experience and sticking points.* "What courses have you taken in *XX?* [Insert the name of your field.] What did you get out of those courses? What was hard about those courses, and how did you study for them?" If you can predict which concepts and topics are sticking points for students, you can plan to spend more time on those topics and offer some explicit study strategies for working through the hardest material. Students also appreciate your concern about the topics that are hardest for them.

Student Syllabus Review

You're probably already planning to review the syllabus on the first day of class. If you're like me, that overview involves a ten- to thirty-minute lecture during which you point out sections of the syllabus that students could realistically read for themselves, all the while using up their rapidly dwindling attention span. If I'm lucky, someone will break the student silence with a question or two. On a really lucky day, I won't discover any typos.

There is a better way, and I thank my colleagues in chemistry for teaching me how to do a student syllabus review (see Appendix C). In this activity, students still receive an overview of the course and the syllabus, but you also receive something helpful from them. The basic idea is that you divide students into small groups, pass out the syllabus (one per person) plus a sheet of questions (one sheet per group), and ask students to answer the questions as they read and discuss the syllabus. In other words, you don't lecture to them about the syllabus—they read it for themselves in their small groups. After the groups have worked together for fifteen to twenty-five minutes—depending on the length of your syllabus—the class comes back together to discuss a few select questions. Students get a chance to ask you anything that's unresolved, and you learn a bit about their priorities and concerns. You collect their sheets to read later, but the most important issues will probably be raised and addressed in the class discussion.

At the end of this chapter, I provide a generic version of questions that you can adapt. Rest assured: students will be searching the syllabus for the section that explains how they will be graded and when things are due; those are the first things students look for when they are handed a syllabus.[21]

You might be thinking, "But I need to review X because X is so important." Create a question about X if you're concerned that students won't read about it on the syllabus. If, for example, you want students to pay extra attention to your newly revamped plagiarism policy, you could ask, "Which parts of the plagiarism policy seem pretty standard and which parts seem unique?"

The beauty of this interactive exercise is that you've established a good rapport and energy in class; the students have had a chance to ask you their initial burning questions; and you have valuable information about the students who fill up your roster.

You'll learn a lot from them during the discussion. Some concerns you can predict, but in my experience, each class has its own unique worries. I've had some neuropsychology classes that were concerned about having enough time for group work; others were worried that the videos we'd be watching about the brain would be too gross. The exercise gave me a chance to ask about previous bad experiences with group work or graphic videos, and then we worked as a class to generate mutually agreeable solutions. (Actually, I always give ample warning about the unpleasant videos because I'm squeamish myself, but they don't know that.)

The most important question in this activity is the last one: "List three questions that you have about the course that aren't answered in the syllabus." Students will effectively vet and answer most of the obvious questions in their small groups. One student will say to her group members, "I don't see anything about make-up exams in the syllabus," and someone else will say, "It's on the bottom of page 3," saving you from that tedious hunt-and-peck activity. The questions that make it to the large group discussion are either important details that you've overlooked in the syllabus (which happens to all of us when we're teaching a course for the first time) or questions that tell you where students need genuine help.

"Take a Stand" Activity

I learned about this activity from Sylvia Hurtado, who is an expert on student differences. Her classes are discussion classes, and like the rest of us, she has some students who are talkers and some who are not. She does an activity on the first day so that students can identify how they contribute to the dynamics of the discussion. She assigns a label to each of the four corners in the classroom and asks students to get up out of their chairs and move to the corner of the room that best describes how they typically participate in a class discussion. If a student is someone who "talks a lot," she goes to one corner. If a student is someone who "waits until I have something important to say," he goes to a different corner. The third corner is for students who "mostly listen," and the last corner is for students "who tend to criticize or challenge what's being said" (also known as the "Devil's Advocate").

Once students have taken a stand, the entire class engages in a discussion about these four different roles that students play almost automatically. (When I do this, I sometimes ask students to move to tables or clusters of desks that are closest to their corner—the discussion can be lengthy and once they've taken a stand, they may as well sit down.) Begin by asking students who "talk a lot" about their reasons for doing so. Typically such people are uncomfortable with silences, want the class to be interesting, or process their ideas out loud. As Sylvia explains, "They might not even have their thoughts totally formulated but they go ahead and raise their hands and use the opportunity to think out loud. So they talk a lot as a result." Students who don't say much in class might find it liberating to learn that it's OK to raise their hand before their answer is perfectly crafted. Sylvia then turns to the students who mostly listen and asks them for their reasons. Some of them need more time to process their answers; by the time they are ready, the discussion has often already moved on. The class can agree that they might need to slow down the discussion from time to time to ensure that everyone has a chance to contribute.

By the end of the activity, all four groups get a chance to share why they take certain positions and when they experience anxiety in a discussion. The diversity of learning styles in the room is validated, and when a discussion is lagging, you can refer back to these four positions and ask, "I wonder if anyone has been waiting for something really important to contribute," or "It would seem as though we're reaching consensus pretty quickly. Would anyone like to challenge what's been said so far?" Standing in one of these four corners on Day 1 doesn't mean that students are locked into their roles, but it makes the dynamics of a discussion transparent. Moreover, in my experience, the people who "mostly listen" and "wait until they have something important to say" speak up a little more often when they've participated in this activity. My sense is that people who are ordinarily quiet feel more supported because the instructor has created a learning environment where their thoughtfulness is recognized and they feel genuinely invited, rather than pressured, into the conversation.

"What Do You Do?" Activity

A relatively quick, easy, and common activity is to use 3 x 5" cards to gather information about your students: you simply pass out cards on the first day of class and ask students to write down their names, contact information, major/minor, and answers to basic questions, such as, "Why are you taking this course?" or "What other *XXX* courses have you taken?" (where *XXX* is the academic discipline, such as physics or history). When you get back to your office, you can read through the cards to get a better picture of your students; you can also review an individual's card before that student meets with you for the first time.

You may already use 3 x 5" cards on the first day of class— I have for years—but I recently saw a simple but powerful variation of this activity. Sven Arvidson is a philosophy professor who teaches soul-searching courses like "The Philosophy of the Person." He does something a little more interesting with his cards on the first day. After he asks the two standard questions about names and contact information, he asks, "What do you do?" He writes that on the board and then he waits. You can imagine what happens next—students push back, "What do you mean? Do you want us to describe our jobs or something?" But Sven doesn't take the bait. He repeats the question and leaves it wide open. "What do you do?" The answers he receives are illuminating. Some students respond with a one-line answer ("I swim every morning at 6:00 a.m.," or "I survive"), but most students give him a quick glimpse of the complexity of their lives. They talk about spending time on Facebook, singing in their church choir, making the decision to come back to school, taking care of their mother with Alzheimer's, working two jobs— you name it.[22]

Sven then uses this information to connect the course material to students' interests and background knowledge, a key principle for creating a good learning environment. When he talks about music, he can call on the student who mentioned her church choir. If he's trying to decide between using a skiing analogy or a swimming analogy and he knows that several students are training for triathlons, he'll go with swimming. He may personally know more about skiing, but he can invite students to help him build the swimming analogy, encouraging their deep learning every step of the way.

"The Average Student" Activity

If you like numbers, and some of us do, here's an alternative to the "What do you do?" activity. Begin by tracking down some data about your students through your school's Institutional Research office. The website probably has an easy-to-read report that will give you a quick picture of the students on campus, including the number of African-American students, the median SAT score of incoming freshmen, or the average age of graduate students in your program. Your institution may participate in the National Survey of Student Engagement (or NSSE)

or the Cooperative Institutional Research Program (CIRP) Freshmen Survey. If so, you have access to some very enlightening
and often surprising information, such as how much time students spend preparing for class each week. (Brace yourself for
some discouraging statistics. As we saw earlier, the numbers
are low.)

Of course, these statistics about SAT scores or hours spent
partying each week are just averages and don't describe every
person in your class. They don't even necessarily describe any
one person in your class. That's another way these data are useful to you. You can ask your students how they differ from the
average student on campus (or the average student nationally, if
those are the only data available). Compile a quick fact sheet
with five or six statistics, then present the list to the class for
consideration. By doing this the first week of classes, you can
gather some background information about your students while
publicly recognizing that they are a diverse group. You might
begin, "I recently learned that the average undergraduate student here at Midwestern State University

- is twenty-two years old;
- is white;
- is attending school in-state;
- spends typically ten hours a week studying outside of
  class;
- frequently does volunteer work;
- has never written a paper longer than twenty pages; and
- is planning to study abroad."

The interesting part of this exercise comes when you ask, "Is
this you?" You can reassure students that of course these numbers don't capture them entirely; they are much more than just
a few statistics. "But in what ways *is* this like you? And in what

ways are you completely different from this fictional, averaged person?" Pass out 3 x 5" note cards and ask students to write their name on their card along with an explanation of how they are similar or dissimilar to this "average student." You may have some students who match all these categories and thus are, by this definition at least, truly average. Encourage those students to describe something about themselves that isn't captured by this list. Or they can explain the story behind one of these facts —why would they like to study abroad, or how do they feel about never having written a twenty-page paper?[23]

How Do You Respond to What You've Learned?

With both the background knowledge probe and the average student activity, it's important that you report back to students on what you've learned to close the feedback loop. Plan to take three to five minutes in class to give them a few highlights, preferably within a class or two of completing the activity. You're demonstrating that you learned something you can use and that you value their feedback, which makes them more inclined to cooperate when you ask for their input again down the road.

What might you learn? On the one hand, perhaps students have more mastery of a topic than you expected. Your students might also have aspirations that you didn't share as a twenty-year-old. If so, how can you keep them challenged? Might they bring research findings to class as part of their participation grade? On the other hand, you may be disappointed by what you learn. Perhaps you'll discover that students aren't used to working as hard as you had hoped, or that they're not able to coordinate meetings for out-of-class group work because they commute long distances to school.

Even if you're feeling disappointed, find a way to encourage students when you return to class the next day. Keep in mind that in most classes, students are still on your side during that magical first week, and you want to keep them there. Let them know that you have high expectations for them. They will probably have to work a little harder than in some of their previous courses, but you believe they can rise to the challenge. Reassure them that you will support them in learning the material, and that you know the extra effort will be highly rewarding. As we learned in Chapter 2, high expectations are vital to students' success. Even if your first reaction is disappointment, you want to say to yourself, "I have a chance to make a difference. I have a chance to create a learning environment in which my students exceed their own expectations."

If students aren't coming into your course with the strengths or background that you expected, you may also need to adjust your teaching plans. If you have a class of commuters and group work is an essential part of the course, perhaps you should build some time in class for teamwork (or at least time for them to coordinate future meetings). Admittedly, it's not easy to rearrange class time to make room for group work if you hadn't originally planned for it, but if it's essential to students' success in the course, you're wise to make that adjustment. If you were expecting students to produce two twenty-page papers and most of them have never written a paper that long, you haven't necessarily set an impossible goal. But you need to decide how you will help students acquire the skills they need to accomplish that goal. What will you need to teach them about organizing a twenty-page paper or using lengthy quotes? (As you may know, cutting and pasting long quotes can be a common beginner's mistake on the first long paper.) What kinds of practice will give students a chance to make mistakes early in the course, learn from those mistakes and your feedback, and then produce their best possible work when it's time for you to assign a grade?

The Hard Part: Teaching These Students

So you've gathered some information about your students. You're halfway toward your goal of effectively teaching students you don't understand. Perhaps you're even more than halfway because you've established a rapport with them and a supportive learning environment, in which case students will give you more leeway because they see that you're on their side.

This last section provides a variety of teaching strategies that take into account students' concrete active learning styles, the fact that they are a diverse group, and the reality that today's students are probably not inclined to put in the kind of hours you once spent on your homework. (I'm not promising a miracle, but we'll do our best.) I've also tried to pick strategies that will work well when you're teaching as a content novice. In part, that means that these techniques don't rely on years of accumulated examples. These strategies should also help save you time rather than adding to the work you're doing for this course.

But as appealing as some of these strategies may be, don't try them all at once. Small changes are often more effective than large, sweeping ones; you'll run the risk of looking disorganized or insecure if you try too many new things at once. Pick two, maybe three strategies this term. Next term, you can add two more.

Clarify Your Expectations

Take time in class on a regular basis to clarify your expectations. This is a common-sense practice in any classroom, but it's vital when you're teaching students who differ from you in some fundamental way. Those differences open the door to misinterpretation.

It's particularly important to be clear when it comes to grading. Give written instructions, not just verbal ones, for each assignment to ensure that everyone (including you) has the same information. Written instructions let students review exactly what you expect without relying on their own sketchy notes. Sometimes instructors rationalize that it's fine to skip written instructions on a short homework assignment because they don't want to make too big a deal of it. I understand this line of reasoning, but you're doing certain students a disservice if you expect them to rely on their imperfect notes. Freshmen capture fewer important details in their notes than more experienced college students; one study shows that freshmen write down only half the critical points that juniors capture in their notes.[24] Students with learning disabilities are also at a disadvantage if you don't provide written instructions. In lecture classes, they often record 30 to 40 percent less information than their peers.[25] Lastly, if you have written instructions, the assignment will be clearer to you and to your students, which means you'll probably spend less time grading misguided work and haggling over points.

If possible, make your expectations clear by giving students a grading rubric for one or more of your assignments. A rubric itemizes the criteria by which you'll be judging students' work and describes different levels of performance for those criteria.[26] For a writing assignment, for example, students will probably need clear "Structure and Organization," so you'd make that one of the criteria on your rubric. The rubric would list how an "A" paper would be structured and organized, compared with how a "B" paper would be organized, and so on. If you haven't created a rubric before and you're teaching a new course, the prospect of specifying how an "A" paper differs from a "B" paper can be daunting; fortunately, many good rubrics are available on the web. How can you tell a good rubric from a bad one? A good rubric uses clear, concrete language that means the same thing to different people, so students can use it to guide their research and writing and you can use it to guide your feedback and grading.

Make It Normal to Seek Help

We've established that most college classrooms are more racially and ethnically diverse than they used to be, which means we're teaching in a crossracial environment. But the student body is typically more diverse than the faculty, roughly 85 percent of whom are white.[27] Certain dynamics arise in classes with majority teachers and minority students that make faculty less effective teachers and students less effective learners, despite everyone's best intentions.

One of the issues facing minority students (as well as female students in male-dominated disciplines) is "stereotype threat." This is the discomfort and performance anxiety that members of a group feel "when they are at risk of fulfilling a negative stereotype about their group."[28] A student who belongs to a group that has been stereotyped in an academic discipline where that student wants to succeed will often feel constrained and self-conscious. For example, if you're a Latino student and you know there's a widely held belief that Latino students tend to have lower test scores than their white peers, you may be burdened by that belief. You may internalize it and use it as an excuse, if only in your own mind, not to prepare thoroughly for an exam. Or it may mean that you work extra hard to prove that the stereotype isn't true. If you're a female who likes math but you know there's a widely held belief that women don't get very far in math or engineering, you may give up more easily when you run into a hard calculus class. Or you may try twice as hard to prove that you can do just as well as the men in your study group. Working extra hard on one's own might sound like a good thing, but not when it prevents a student from attending review sessions or showing up for office hours when she needs help.

How does that performance anxiety affect behavior in class, and what can you as the professor do to reduce students' stress? In my interview with Beverly Daniel Tatum, author of *Why Are All the Black Kids Sitting Together in the Cafeteria?* and an expert on race in the classroom, she noted, "If you're a student who has that awareness of the stereotype, it influences how you interact with faculty. Even though you know in your heart-of-hearts that you are well prepared, you're concerned that the professor will see you as another instance of an underprepared African-American student." Say, for example, that the student is taking "Introduction to Philosophy" and finds Descartes or Marx confusing (as many of us would). Beverly points out that "he may not ask his question in class or come to office hours because he doesn't want to reveal a vulnerability that confirms the stereotype." As a result, minority students who are burdened by this stereotype, such as African-American and Latino students, often don't ask for help.[29] Unfortunately, this way of thinking often leads to a self-fulfilling downward spiral, Beverly cautions. If a student doesn't seek help when he needs it, he won't do well in class.

Fortunately, there are teaching strategies you can employ to minimize stereotype threat. As Beverly observed, "These strategies are relatively straightforward, but if you're not thinking about this issue, you won't think of this mechanism. So, for example, if you know that students may be hesitant to reveal confusion, you can have a policy that requires all students to meet with you." By requiring all students to meet with you in the first few weeks or after the first exam, you take away the stigma of seeking help.[30] The meetings can be brief—students can sign up for ten-minute slots. If a student is doing well in the course, you can use the meeting to gather background information, as suggested earlier in the chapter. Emphasize to students that seeking help is a good thing. You might include a statement in your syllabus explaining that students who earn an "A" in the course usually come to all the review sessions. Or you could share a personal story in class about how meeting with a professor to talk about a paper that you bombed helped you decide on your major. One professor I know ends every class, and I mean *every* class, by reminding students of when he has office hours and how eager he is to meet with them.[31]

The goal is to normalize help-seeking behaviors so that all students ask for assistance when they need it. Otherwise, some students may be prevented from doing so by their concerns about what asking for help signifies. All students benefit from such a policy because everyone is more likely to get the help they need.

In addition to encouraging everyone to ask for help, you can also reduce stereotype threat by establishing high but attainable standards for all students, as we discussed in Chapter 2, and by letting students know that you genuinely believe they can meet those standards.[32]

Vary How You Teach and Assess Student Learning

Diverse students call for diverse teaching practices. That doesn't mean you have to do something radically different each week of the term, but if you have a preferred and standard way of teaching, try experimenting with a different instructional strategy occasionally. Pick a strategy that will help you reach one of your other goals for the course, one of the goals on the syllabus that's important to you but that might not occur given your typical teaching style. If you normally lecture but told students they would have a chance to practice critical thinking skills, try introducing a case study and allowing students to critique the choices made in the case. If you normally teach by discussion but you had promised that "by the end of the course, you'll be familiar with the three reasons Bill Gates chose to build his empire from Seattle," try weaving in some mini-lectures to provide that context. You'll have to be the judge as to how you want to diversify your teaching, but let your syllabus and your learning objectives be your guide.

A diverse group of students also calls for variety in how you assess student learning. Chances are you're inclined to grade students on the same kinds of assignments that you liked as a student. (Or you're inclined to grade students on the basis of painful traditions that you once thought were tedious but have now come to appreciate.) Keep in mind that some students are good test-takers while others shine on research papers. Some students struggle with writing assignments but can show what they know in oral presentations. Clearly, it's important that students learn to adapt and work outside their comfort zone, just as they will be expected to adapt to different demands in their future careers. But if you're interested in seeing how well students have mastered the concepts in your course, give them multiple ways to show that mastery. Otherwise, you may just be measuring how good they are at taking tests.

A word to the wise: this advice about diversifying your assessment strategies is for people who are designing a *future* course, not for those who are in the middle of the semester or quarter. If the term has already started, my advice would be to keep looking for ways to diversity your teaching strategies, but leave the grading system and assignments alone. Most students' lives, just like yours, are heavily scheduled and ridiculously constrained.

If you announce three-quarters of the way through the course that you've decided to give a final exam instead of a final paper (or vice versa), chances are you will not be treated as a hero in most classes.

Use Clickers

One difficulty in teaching students you don't understand is that it's hard to gauge what they do and don't comprehend on the basis of their outward behavior. You may be expecting students to ask questions when they don't understand something, but, as we learned earlier, some students may fear that revealing confusion only confirms a stereotype. Other students might believe it's insulting to question something the professor just explained. Students' behavior might be hard to interpret in other areas as well: perhaps when you were a student, you took a steady stream of notes when a concept excited you, but your first-year students barely pick up their pens.

Here too, clarify your expectations. If you expect students to ask questions, explain why questions are important. If you expect students to take notes and no one does, talk to them about it at the start or end of a class to find out what it means when students don't take notes.

Another clever strategy at your disposal is to use "clickers," or Classroom Response Systems. We discussed clickers in Chapter 5 as part of the Peer Instruction activity. The basic idea is that you ask a question and students can answer anonymously and simultaneously, giving you an immediate picture of how well the class understands a concept. Ideally, you want to ask a multiple-choice question where their incorrect answers clarify how much or how little they know. For example, in a political science course, you might ask, "Who was Great Britain's prime minister when the United States invaded Iraq in 2003?" then give the correct answer, Tony Blair, as well as three strategic incorrect answers, such as Margaret Thatcher, John Kerry, and Robert Mugabe. If most students select "Margaret Thatcher," you'll know that their timeline is off, but that at least they associate the right people with British leadership. If half the class chooses "John Kerry" or "Robert Mugabe," it means they have very little knowledge of foreign (or domestic) governance and you have to cover some more basic issues. Derek Bruff, the mathematics instructor who teaches engineering students, often uses clickers at the start of class as a way to find out where he needs to begin explaining the concepts for the day.[33]

You could also use clickers as a way to collect demographic information that students might not want to reveal publicly but that relates to the point you're trying to make. For example, when you're discussing the role of cash in a finance course, you could ask, "How much cash do you estimate you have in your wallet at this moment?" and give students several ranges ($0–$10, $11–$25, and so on). I've seen a finance professor do this exercise and was surprised to learn how many of her MBA students had more than $50 within reach. If you're reading a novel about racism in an English course, you could ask, "How many of you have family members who make racist jokes at big family gatherings?" By getting a chance to weigh in anonymously first, most students discover that they're not alone in their experience and feel more confident asking questions from those lived experiences. In the process, you understand them a little better and can hook the material to something real in their lives.

Have Students Collect the Data

When you're teaching students who differ from you in some fundamental way, you may run into some resistance when you try to teach certain concepts, particularly concepts that challenge a popular, mainstream view. In a sports management course, students may not want to hear that certain rules in the National Football League (NFL) are less about the fairness of the game and more about what's best for commercial advertisers. In a sociology course, students may not believe that the goods and services at a grocery store in low-income minority communities are often more expensive or of poorer quality than the goods and services in wealthier white communities. Beverly Daniel Tatum, who enjoyed a teaching career as a clinical psychology professor, explained to me that she used to encounter this problem in her "Psychology of Racism" course: "You could give students a lecture or an article explaining these racial and social inequities, but the nature of the subject is such that students could respond, 'I don't believe that,' or 'You're just exaggerating.'" They might question whether you're capable of being objective, particularly if you're an African-American instructor critiquing a race issue or a former football player who is critiquing the NFL. That skepticism shields them from the hard work of real change. It means they don't have to re-evaluate their world view—they can just regurgitate what you want to hear when they sit down for an exam and then return to their comfortable old ways of thinking when they log in to Facebook that night or when a homeless person asks them for money.

Beverly learned that students were more receptive to these uncomfortable truths when they were given an opportunity to discover them for themselves. She would ask students to go out and collect data on a question (in the K–12 school system this activity is known as "inquiry-based learning"). Each week, they were given field assignments. For example, rather than simply telling students that grocery stores in communities of color had lower-quality goods and services, she would go into class and say, "For this week, your field assignment is to visit some grocery stores in this part of Santa Barbara and a few stores in that part," directing them to lower-income communities of color and higher-income white communities. The assignment was to take notes on the level of service and the quality of the goods at these stores. Students would return to class the next week and say, "I couldn't believe it—certain foods were actually more expensive in the lower-income Latino neighborhood than they were in the wealthy white neighborhood," or "In the African-American part of town, there were barriers so you can't take the shopping cart back to your car." As they discussed their firsthand observations, students came to the very same conclusions that they might have challenged a week earlier. Recall that, on average, at least half our students are concrete active learners, so they trust direct experience. And when you're asking students to rethink an entrenched view of how the world works, they will trust their own direct experience more than your authority. It's much harder to say, "That's just a liberal bias" when you've personally documented the problem in your own handwriting.

The instructor's role in this kind of self-generated learning isn't an easy one. You need to identify controversial issues in which students would be inclined to challenge or resist the data, and then construct an opportunity for them to collect data for themselves. Creating an inquiry-based learning activity will probably take more time than simply typing up some lecture notes, so this is one instance where you won't save on preparation time, but the outcome can be much more significant. You can effect attitude change and stir students to take action. At the very least, students will want to be in your class because this is how they want to learn. When Beverly taught this way at the University of California at Santa Barbara, the course was so popular that she had to offer it three times a year.

Give Autonomy, Sweet Autonomy

A general strategy for reaching students whose interests and motivations differ from your own is to provide opportunities for choice and autonomy whenever it's reasonable to do so. If you can give students a choice about how they will engage with the material in class, even if it's only a choice between two options, then they can select the option that best aligns with their priorities. Perhaps one of your goals for the course is for students to "collect data on mainstream views about a controversial concept and evaluate those views." Instead of automatically assigning a traditional research paper on that concept, try offering some creative (and active) alternatives, such as giving students the choice between doing a content analysis of CNN.com or conducting interviews with family and friends. Chances are, their sense of ownership will translate into a better, richer experience, and a higher-quality product.

The final project for a course is one area where instructors traditionally allow students some latitude. Students can often choose from a few predetermined topics or problems, or they can generate their own topic. In my conversations with faculty, I learned about a brilliant strategy for giving students autonomy while maintaining a manageable workload.

This idea comes from Derek Bruff, the Vanderbilt mathematician. Let's first look at the problem Derek faced with his final projects, which was basically the universal problem of balancing motivation, quality, and time. He assigns a very work-intensive final statistics project for which students collect their own data, and he knows students will put more into the project if they care about the data they have to collect and analyze. Some topics are obviously nonstarters: his class of sixty engineers, mostly men, won't care about the number of shoes purchased at Macy's every Christmas. But Derek is a mathematician teaching non-math majors, so it's hard for him to predict what students will find compelling in any given year.

When he first started teaching this course, he let students generate their own research questions. This increased their motivation but created two problems: (1) some projects were fantastic while others were misguided (many projects were too big for the scope of the course or the data were impossible to collect); and (2) the course ended with an avalanche of work because he was grading twenty-seven to thirty lengthy projects, each with a unique research question, a different set of variables, and an original cocktail of statistical tests.

Most recently, he tried to achieve the best of all possible worlds. He had each student submit a two-page research proposal about halfway into the course. Each student could propose his or her own research question, then explain why that question was worth studying and what kind of data would be collected to test the question. He received fifty-seven one-to-two-page proposals, all submitted electronically. He then read through them all, setting aside the proposals that were unfeasible, unethical, or poorly designed, and he narrowed the pool to about thirty workable proposals. He made these proposals available on the course webpage and invited students to vote for their top choices. He then selected the four most popular research proposals and announced that these proposals had won. Students could then choose one of the four topics for their research project.

His assessment of the experience? A win for everyone involved. The resulting projects were of much higher quality because many students were working on better topics than they had originally proposed. Students were motivated because they had ample input in picking the topics. His grading experience was also more manageable—he was able to prepare rubrics for each of the four topics because he knew them well in advance, plus his teaching assistants could help with the grading, which wouldn't have been the case if he had fifty different projects coming in.

Derek told me afterward that he couldn't have predicted the most popular topics. If he had chosen the topics, he would have proposed subjects related to engineering, such as the probability that a bridge in New York City might collapse (since he has so many civil engineers in the course). But most students voted for topics they could relate to in their everyday lives, such as the relationship between one's GPA and the number of hours one sleeps each night. After all, they are students first, engineers second.

Ask Students to Generate the Examples

When you're teaching students you don't understand, it's also hard to pick good examples. You might know which examples are exquisite demonstrations of a concept, but the fact that an example makes sense to you doesn't mean it will make sense to them. And if the topic is outside of your expertise, it's harder to know the best examples anyway.

One solution is to have students help you generate the examples. In a biology class, you might have students generate examples of a symbiotic relationship and examples of a parasitic relationship. (If you're like me and it's been a while since you've opened a basic biology textbook, a symbiotic relationship is one in which both parties benefit from the relationship, whereas only one party benefits at the cost of the other in a parasitic relationship.) If left to your own devices, you might generate a brilliant example of a symbiotic relationship, such as the bacteria living in the human stomach, but students might not relate to something they've never seen. The examples that students propose are likely to be more concrete and easier to visualize, such as the relationship between a bumblebee and a flower (remember that at least half of your students are probably concrete active learners). Often students will generate an example that is slightly off the mark, but this simply gives you an opportunity to clarify the concept. For example, if students suggest that termites and wood have a parasitic relationship because the termites benefit by eating the wood, you can clarify that both organisms need to be alive and growing in such a relationship: "wood" could refer to the plywood in someone's house, which hopefully wouldn't be alive and growing.

An added bonus to this approach is that you now have a new batch of accessible, student-generated examples at your disposal, which can be very helpful if you're teaching outside of your expertise. You can use the good examples to introduce key concepts and the not-quite-right examples to clarify common misconceptions. You could even use some of the incorrect student-generated examples on an exam, asking why this might be a common misunderstanding (you would, of course, graciously omit the name of the student who first suggested it).

You might be thinking that when you chose the professor's life, you just wanted to be in a classroom with people who shared your outlook when you were a student and who simply love to learn. You want to be with people who are excited by big ideas. That's a perfectly legitimate desire. But to be honest, it's more likely to happen when you go to a faculty meeting than when you step into a classroom. And even in a faculty meeting, it's not guaranteed.

As Eric Mazur, the physicist, observed in our interview, "Very few students are going to end up in the same career path as the professor. We have maybe one student in a lifetime who is going to become our successor." Given that so few students will follow in our footsteps, maybe our role isn't to teach them all the facts and equations that we, as professional knowledge collectors, wish we had known sooner. Eric continues, "Maybe our biggest role is to be someone who motivates rather than someone who is just a source of knowledge." If that's our primary role, and that role fits nicely with our vision of teaching as creating a learning environment, it takes away the burden of our having to be the expert in the room. That might be frustrating if you view the classroom as a place where you can tell the world what you know to be true, but it might be a relief if you're not an expert on the topic in the first place.

7 Getting Better

almost titled this chapter "Getting Feedback," but then I thought you'd skip it. Everyone wants to get better, but let's be honest—not everyone wants feedback. Chances are, if you're like me, you don't want to inspect your teaching too closely, let alone invite someone else to do so. At least not yet. Some faculty members happily seek feedback in their more established, familiar courses, but they understandably want to get through a new course at least once before scrutinizing what is or isn't working.

When we teach outside our comfort zone, we are less likely to do informal assessments of students' learning. Sure, we still do problem sets, exams, and papers, but we are less likely to ask, "What's the muddiest point from today's class?" or collect ungraded information about what students do and don't understand.

Why? At the most basic level, we spend so much time learning the material and preparing for class that we don't have the time to think about formative teaching evaluations. I often see this with new faculty. They have every intention of collecting feedback from students and eagerly grab all the handouts and sample midterm evaluations at new faculty orientation, but once they get in the classroom, they are too busy. I also suspect that they don't want to add to their sense of feeling overwhelmed. They promise to collect feedback next year, when they have things under control.

With more experienced faculty, time may not be so much of an issue (in part because senior faculty are typically teaching only one new course). But more experienced faculty are often concerned that asking for student input will make them appear less competent. After all, these professors are acutely aware of how much they *don't* know in this periphery course, and they'd rather not look too insecure. Just like their junior colleagues, they would rather ask if everything is going well once they are pretty sure that yes, everything is going well.

These positions are understandable. There is only so much you can do, and no one wants to increase their sense of vulnerability. But getting some feedback from your students is one of the best things you can do when you're teaching something new. It helps you become a better teacher more quickly. In this chapter I present two kinds of assessment activities—activities to evaluate how students are experiencing the course and activities to assess what your students do and do not understand.[1] I also suggest language for framing the feedback process so students see it as evidence of your credibility, not your fallibility.

Why It's So Important to Assess Your Teaching The First Time

Given that most instructors want to wait until they teach a course a second or third time before they assess it, I know I'm in for a hard sell. (If you're already convinced, you can skip ahead to the next section.)

The best argument for doing assessments the first time you teach a course is that a higher percentage of students will succeed. Some students will be successful learners regardless of what you do in class, and we all love those students, but it's the other students you need to hear from. John Bean, a professor of English at Seattle University, explained: "What you're really trying to do is figure out what works for some students and what works for others and which students you're missing entirely." Because it's your first time through the course, you don't have a reference point for which students you might be missing. Are students asking too few questions? Is it normal for half the class to do poorly on the first exam?

Then there's the issue of student misconceptions. As faculty, we often assume that once we've taught the correct information, it automatically replaces any incorrect or naïve knowledge that students have been harboring. Sometimes it does, but often those misconceptions can coexist quite peacefully with the correct knowledge.[2] To replace misconceptions, we actually have to draw attention to them. But it can take years of teaching a topic before faculty realize which misconceptions are interfering with students' understanding. Rather than grading two hundred exams to discover the most confusing concepts, ask students about them the first time you teach the course.

If you do some small assessments, it's easier to gauge when students are bored or lost. When you're teaching something you know well, you can multitask: you can derive an equation on the board or lead a case study discussion and still notice that students are staring back with blank faces. When you're teaching something you don't know well, your attention is focused more on what you're doing than on what your students are doing. You're relying more heavily on your notes than you ordinarily would, or you're paying more attention to the time. All of this self-monitoring diverts your attention from subtle student cues you might ordinarily notice. (Of course, if a student falls asleep you're going to notice, but there were probably more subtle cues twenty minutes ago that you were losing that student.)

If you can find out which concepts or authors are most confusing to students, you can also alleviate some of your own anxiety about office hours. I interviewed faculty who dreaded office hours for their periphery courses. One engineering professor said that those one-on-one conversations were especially difficult because he couldn't anticipate which questions students were going to bring to him, and he couldn't postpone an answer with the student sitting right there. But if you do assessments periodically, you'll have a better sense of which topics students are likely to bring to your door, and you can prepare beforehand. (Incidentally, when a student stumps you in office hours, it's also reasonable to say, "Good question—let's go back and take a look at the book." You're showing him how you go about figuring out the answer.)

One last reason to do periodic assessments is that it can be hard on faculty when students fail. And it may be even harder on you when students fail one of your periphery courses. This may sound counterintuitive because you might care more about students' success in topics that are near and dear to your heart. But in courses where you know the material well, you can probably find evidence that a failing student didn't try hard enough or didn't use the right resources. As Codrina Popescu, the chemistry professor from Ursinus College, explains, she knows what she needs to do in chemistry to ensure students' success. She knows which concepts and skills will be essential later, and if a student is struggling with these critical issues, she can make an effort to steer that student back on track. But if a student fails her general education course, she feels guilty. It's harder to be sure that she did enough: "If I'd been the expert, I would have done a better job. I would have detected the problems students were having, and those students would have done better."

Admittedly, a midterm course evaluation or a few "muddiest point" exercises won't prevent determined students from failing your course. But if you have been taking the class's temperature periodically, you'll be able to make regular course corrections and rest easier knowing, in the end, that you did all you could to support your students' success.

Collecting Feedback You Can Use

Your priority is to collect feedback that you'll be able to use. Usable feedback comes in reasonable amounts; it's neither too much nor too little, and it focuses on changes that are within your control. I have three pieces of advice for soliciting usable feedback.

1. Plan Your Feedback Strategy Early in the Course

When you're teaching a course outside of your expertise, the workload keeps increasing as you march steadily toward the end of the term. If you tell yourself that you'll figure out an assessment strategy in week five or six, it's very unlikely to happen. If you're planning to do a midterm evaluation, find an evaluation form you'd like to use early in the term (preferably before the course begins) and make a note on your calendar as to when you plan to administer it. If you're thinking of doing regular small assessments, begin them early in the course—in week one or two so that you establish a culture of feedback for you and your students. Once you see how helpful the process can be, you're more likely to seek feedback again.

2. Don't Collect More Feedback Than You Can Handle

A new business instructor once came to my office, harried and flushed, and pulled out a dog-eared, two-inch stack of evaluations from his briefcase. He had distributed a four-page midterm evaluation to a class of around one hundred students, and he wanted to know what to do with it all. I just sat there looking at the tattered stack for a few awkward seconds. Almost two weeks had passed since the students had completed the evaluations, and he'd been carrying the stack around with him; he had been too overwhelmed preparing class each day to read them (plus I'm sure he was just as daunted as I was by the towering stack of student handwriting).

Be modest. Undershoot when you ask for feedback. You can always ask again later.

3. Report Back to Students on What You've Changed

Remember to close the feedback loop by letting students know what you've learned from their comments and what changes, if any, you plan to make in response. If you don't say anything, students will wonder whether you've read their feedback.[3] They may decide that the whole feedback activity was pointless, which makes it difficult to solicit constructive input from them again. Some faculty rationalize that as long as they implement some of the changes that students request, they don't need to make any announcements or draw attention to those changes. An announcement somehow seems over the top. I'm not suggesting that you need to wear a crown for the day, but if you don't say anything, students might not notice that anything has changed. Or some students will notice the changes but won't realize that they were prompted by someone's feedback. You may as well get credit for being the responsive and receptive teacher that you actually are. And students will learn that constructive feedback is worth giving.

Classroom Assessment Activities

I'm including two kinds of assessments here: strategies for assessing students' experience in the course, and strategies for assessing what students do and don't understand. In all these activities, but especially when students are describing their experiences in the course, let students respond anonymously. You're probably not the type to let a negative comment sway your grading, but your students can't be sure of that.

Assessing Students' Experience in the Course

The One-Point Raise

I learned this assessment technique from a friend who is a clinical psychologist. She uses a similar technique with her clients. In the first part of the activity, you ask each student to rate an experience on a scale of 1 to 10, and in the second part, you ask them what would raise their score by 1 point. You collect their written feedback and read it outside of class. It's very simple but surprisingly powerful.

Begin by asking students to get out a blank sheet of paper. If you've prepared for this ahead of time, you can distribute a handout with the question written at the top. Pick an aspect of the course for which you would like some feedback—maybe it's the clarity of today's class or maybe it's the interest level in a topic—and ask students to rate the course on that dimension. "Rate how interesting today's class was for you on a scale of 1 to 10." Next, define the two endpoints of the scale so that students have a common understanding of what a 1 means compared with a 10. Use extremes in defining these endpoints so that students see them as widely different and are encouraged to use the full range. Don't forget your sense of humor: "So a '1' would mean that today's class was so painfully boring that you wish you had gone to the dentist's instead of coming to class, and a '10' would mean that today's class was so fascinating that you would choose to re-watch it, in its entirety, on YouTube." Some students will smile and others will roll their eyes, but you've got their attention. Chances are you won't get many 1s or 10s in your ratings, but you'll know that a 9 is very high praise indeed. (I once had a small evening course in which two students gave the class a 10. Both of them said that they would stay in class a full hour longer because it was so valuable. I was delighted, but one of them later admitted that her ride wasn't coming for an hour anyway.)

Once students have jotted down a number, ask them, "Now, what would raise your score by 1 point?" Some students will identify something that was under your control—they wish you had written more on the board, spent more time discussing a video, and so on. But some students will identify something that was entirely their responsibility. I've had students indicate that their score would have gone from a 5 to a 6 if they had simply gotten more sleep the night before, or from an 8 to a 9 if they had finished the reading. Because the survey is anonymous, students generally have nothing to lose by being honest. I once did this activity in a freshman seminar and a student wrote that his score would have gone up a point "if I had ended the phone call with my girlfriend earlier last night."

In five minutes, you've quickly and effectively gathered information that offers insight into the classroom dynamics for that day. Best of all, you can see how much or how little was within your control.

Early or Midterm Course Evaluation

Handing out a final course evaluation form that's tailored to your course at the end of the term can provide invaluable feedback on what did and didn't work. Handing out an adapted version of that same evaluation form during the first few weeks of your course, when there is still ample time to make changes based on students' input, is pretty close to brilliant. In one fell swoop, you can find ways to improve the learning environment. You can ask for feedback on some part of the course that's requiring a lot of work for you (maybe you don't need to invest that much effort after all), and you can show students that you care about their learning. In many cases, you can improve the course or your teaching before it's over.

When you begin to search for or develop a midterm evaluation for a course that's outside your expertise, you want a form that

- provides some positive feedback (you deserve some reassurance on what's going well);
- ensures you receive some suggestions for improvement;
- focuses on dimensions of the course that you're willing to change; and
- is easy to summarize or tabulate (after all, you're still short on time).

I know many faculty who use an open-ended course evaluation with three or four simple questions, such as "What strengthens your learning in this course?" or "What hinders your learning in this course?" One advantage of open-ended questions is that they can be prepared quickly: you can type up a few questions and create a midterm evaluation in five minutes. The time you save in creating the form, however, can come back to haunt you when you have to identify the themes in students' feedback. The twenty-five students in your class may go in twenty-five different directions. And many of their comments may concern things that you're not willing or even able to change, such as the time the course is offered, the amount of reading you've required, or the monotony of your voice. (I know at least one very tall, senior male professor who would strongly disagree that one has control over the timbre of one's voice.)

To avoid these problems, use a midterm evaluation that focuses student feedback. If you use an evaluation form with close-ended questions (that is, questions that limit students' responses to predetermined categories), the feedback is easier to tabulate, plus you've directed students' attention to those parts of the course where you genuinely want their input.

You can find a variety of good forms online, but my favorite approach, particularly when you're teaching a course for the first time and you want to be sure you receive *some* encouraging feedback, is to use a two-column form. (See the sample in Appendix D.) The heading of the first column reads, "I like the way the instructor . . ." and is then followed by a list of different practices, such as "encourages students to ask questions," "uses visual aids effectively," and so on. The heading at the top of the second column reads, "I would like the instructor to . . ." followed by a list of the same practices from column one with suggestions for how they might be improved. So this list might become "I would like the instructor to encourage students to ask more/fewer questions (Circle one)" or "use visual aids more often."

The two-column form is quick to administer in class or online, and it's wonderfully easy to tabulate. You can make direct decisions about what to keep and what to change based on the balance of checkmarks in the two columns. If 80 percent of the students in the class say they would like to spend more time on discussion and only 10 percent say they want less time on discussion (and 10 percent skip the question altogether), the decision is simple: more time on discussion. But in almost every course, the students are split on at least one issue. Half the students want more discussion and half want more lecture. When that happens, I follow my preference, which is typically to keep the status quo if I think it's working.

In addition to the time savings and clarity that this two-column form provides, it also shows students how to give constructive feedback on teaching. Such modeling will help them when it comes time to fill out their final course evaluations. Instead of simply writing, "I loved/hated this class" on the final evaluation (which might stir your emotions but doesn't help you make pedagogical decisions), students can draw on some of the language from the midterm evaluation and write, "I loved this class because the instructor encouraged students to ask lots of questions; we covered new topics that weren't in the readings; and she showed the cutest slides of her dog." Or the disgruntled student might write, "I hated this class because the instructor allowed too many questions that had nothing to do with the reading. Ditch the dog." You may not want to receive that last comment from the disgruntled student, but it lets you know what to consider changing. It's much more informative than just "Screw this course," a comment a dear colleague recently received.

If you do use the two-column form, be sure to include only questions about practices you're willing to modify. It can be misleading to ask students for feedback on an aspect of the course that would be very difficult for you to change. (Remember my friend with the baritone voice.)

I have to admit that I usually include a few open-ended questions on the back of the two-column form. Partly this is because I'm a sucker for feedback. But there's a more strategic reason for asking those open-ended questions. There may be a problem with the course that you don't realize. Once students have offered feedback on the issues you prioritize, they can raise a new issue in the open-ended questions.

You may be thinking, "Ah, but that defeats the purpose—I was trying to save time by excluding the open-ended questions." In my experience, and I've seen this form used in dozens of classes, students write much less on the open-ended questions once they have had a chance to check off some behaviors they like or dislike. When students make comments at the end, they typically explain why they checked something on the first side of the sheet (which is fine because you were seeking feedback on that practice anyway) or, less often, they inform you of something you didn't realize was an issue. Either way, the feedback is more directed and efficient than if you gave them only the open-ended questions.

"Five-Year" Question

I learned about a clever assessment strategy from Myra Strober, the labor economist from Stanford University. Myra's a professor at both the Graduate School of Business and the School of Education, so she's taught a wide range of classes, everything from "Women's Employment" to "Economics of Education." In all her courses, she asks the same question on the last day of class: "Five years from now, what will you remember from this course?" She asks the class as a group because she wants to hear students' answers, and she wants to be sure the students hear one another. Some students comment on the process: "I'll remember that this is the course where I got to know what my classmates really think." Others comment on what this course means for their real lives: "I learned the kinds of questions to ask before I take a job." Their answers are meaningful, often personal. And the activity is a powerful way to end the course.

Assessing Students' Understanding

If you like to stand in front of the ice cream counter and have thirty or forty different flavors of ice cream to choose from, then you'll love the book *Classroom Assessment Techniques* by Thomas Angelo and Patricia Cross.[4] It features fifty creative techniques for assessing student learning. If you're satisfied to have someone else narrow down the menu, then this next section is for you. I've selected a few favorite strategies from Angelo and Cross's popular book, and I also include a few of my own. I've picked assessment strategies that require the least amount of preparation and the least amount of expertise in the subject matter.

Muddiest Point

This is one of the simplest and quickest assessments you can do to determine where students are running into comprehension problems. Ask students to get out a sheet of paper and write down their answer to the following question: "What is the muddiest point in today's class?" (or the muddiest point in today's discussion, the readings for this week, the lab due Friday, and so on). You can read the feedback during break or after class and then address students' sticking points. Students may be confused by a concept that's relatively rudimentary, which tells you that they're probably missing more complex concepts as well. They may be confused by an example that's not important, in which case you can reassure them not to worry. Either way, you'll now see which concepts require extra review. You'll often discover that students need more help with the basic concepts, concepts that you probably understand well, rather than the slippery nuances of an advanced concept that you're still learning. It's not that students understand the advanced concepts either, but they often need more help securing the basic concepts than you realize. The muddiest point exercise can be wonderfully reassuring if you're feeling out of your league as the instructor.

Clarity Grid

This activity is essentially a more elaborate version of the muddiest point exercise in which you ask students to tell you which parts of a concept make sense and which parts are still causing trouble. Give students a sheet of paper with three labeled columns. At the top of the page, name a concept or term that students have recently learned. For a class in neuropsychology, I might use "prosopagnosia," an inability to recognize faces. Label the first column "What makes sense to me about this concept," the second, "Why it makes sense to me," and the third, "What I'm still working to understand." The students' task is to complete the sheet on the basis of what they can recall about the concept.

Each column reveals something important about students' understanding. The first column reveals a potential disconnect between what you taught and what students learned. What "makes sense" to your students may be accurate and complete—in which case students successfully learned what you taught—but in some cases, what makes sense to your students may be incorrect or incomplete, revealing what they have either missed or misunderstood. In my example on prosopagnosia, the student might write, "It means people can see faces but they can't recognize faces. It's pretty rare and results from brain damage on the right side of the brain." This is generally correct but lacks necessary details, such as the exact area of the brain affected.

The second column, "Why it makes sense to me" usually reveals the assumptions behind students' reasoning. Students may make accurate statements in the first ("What") column but offer incorrect or misleading reasons in the second ("Why") column. In my example, the student might note, "It makes sense to me that people can see something but not understand what they see. It's like when I look at Chinese characters and can't make sense of them." He is comparing an inability to recognize faces to an inability to read Chinese. This is faulty reasoning—presumably the student could learn to read Mandarin (with dedicated time and effort), but most people with prosopagnosia can never learn to recognize faces again once they've lost the ability, despite years of trying and often to the dismay of their husbands or wives whom they no longer recognize.

The last column is a modified version of the muddiest point. By framing it as "What you're still working to understand," you convey a sense of hope that students can still master the issue. It also conveys the subtle but meaningful message that concepts in the course will take work and effort to understand. For example, the student writing about prosopagnosia might wonder if a person with this disorder is upset by the fact that he can't recognize anyone, or if he avoids crowds. The activity also offers insight into how students are engaging with the concept. I once had a student write, "So what does he see when he looks at someone? Just a smiley face?" I had never thought of it that way. His response prompted a fantastic discussion of how we might experience the world differently if we had this impairment.

Another nice thing about this activity is that you can create the three-column sheet long before the course begins. When you pass out the form in class, simply tell students which concept to write at the top. Because you can prepare the activity in advance, it can be part of your "Emergency Assessment Kit," discussed in Chapter 4.

"Survey Says"

Although this activity is named after the popular phrase from the 1970s game show *Family Feud,* you don't have to survey anyone (or listen to any hokey game show music). In this activity, offer a popular view on an issue and ask students to comment on this view in writing. In an ecology class, you might offer a commonly held view about farming, such as, "Eating organic food is one of the best things you can do for the environment because it supports low-impact farming." Or in an education class, you might offer the widespread belief "The No Child Left Behind Act is an unfair extension of federal laws over schools."[5] Whatever statement you make, follow it with a question: "Given what you know now, what do you think of this view?"

Since you're not an expert in the field, you may only be familiar with popular views of some topics—you might even have shared some of those views just a few weeks earlier. Or you might find it hard to generate "commonly held views" because you're so overwhelmed. A quick web search on Google can yield a wealth of ideas. Try combining the topic of interest, such as "organic food," with phrases like "widespread belief," "popular misunderstanding," "common concern," or, and this might seem strange, "five myths." (For some reason, journalists like to offer myths in herds of five.) Whatever the popular view, have it written out so that students can refer back to it as they write.

Once again, you can also prepare copies of this activity before teaching the course and keep them in your Emergency Assessment Kit (see Chapter 4). Simply pick a commonly held view that students could address at any point in the course. If you do this activity before you address an issue in class, it can help you identify common misunderstandings.

Directed Paraphrasing

This activity is taken from Angelo and Cross's book *Classroom Assessment Techniques,* and it's ideal for faculty who are teaching outside of their expertise. If you've ever had to write for a nontechnical audience, you know that the ability to paraphrase a complex or technical concept into layman's terms is a valuable skill. It's also a skill that students don't often practice because they are typically writing for you, the professor, whom they know (or at least believe) is an expert.

In this activity, students are asked to restate a concept as if they were explaining it to a specific audience with a defined set of interests. In an accounting course, you might set up the following scenario: "Imagine that you work for a large accounting firm. A national conference of forensic investigators and detectives is being held downtown this year, and you've been invited to be part of an expert panel on fraud and financial misconduct. Your job is to prepare a four- to five-minute explanation of how accountants can determine whether someone has 'cooked the books' in language that will make sense to detectives and FBI agents."

You're probably thinking, "That's lovely, but I'm pressed for time." You can always do a quick search online to find some directed paraphrasing activities. They already exist for many academic disciplines and courses. If you'd like to create your own but are having trouble thinking of opening scenarios, here are two that can easily be adapted to different courses and disciplines:

You've applied for a job as a _____ for the next
_____ movie. They liked your application and have
called you for an interview. The person doing the hiring says, "I
see that you've taken a course in _____. How will a
background in that make you a better member of our crew?"
[Fill in the blanks to suit your needs. In an English course, a student could be applying for a job as a scriptwriter and need to
explain how postmodernism will help him write a better script
for the next *Batman* movie. A robotics student could be asked
to be a technical consultant for the next Pixar film.]

You've been asked to help write part of a web-page advertise-
ment for a week-long retreat. The retreat is titled
"_____" and is aimed at well-paid, well-educated
business professionals who don't have a background in
_____. Write a one-paragraph description that intro-
duces the concept of _____ to this audience and will
motivate them to sign up for this retreat. [Music students could
explain "eurhythmics" for a "Find the Musician Within" retreat.
Agriculture students could explain "principles of crop rotation"
for "A Farmer's Way: Growing Your Best Life."

I know this seems a bit like Mad Libs, but these templates are
surprisingly flexible.

Why did I claim that this activity is ideal for non-experts?
You're asking students to write to a non-expert audience, so this
is one instance where your lack of expertise can offer a rich
range of experiences. What questions might a non-expert, like
yourself, have about the topics in your course? Why should a
non-expert care? You might be delighted and persuaded by students' answers.

Although I've featured several activities here, assessment

strategies are sprinkled throughout this book. You may have already seen the activities in Chapter 6 under "The Easy Part: Learning about Your Students." In addition, several of the active learning strategies in Chapter 5 are designed to indicate where students are getting stuck in the material (activities such as "Sequence Reconstruction," "Peer Instruction," and "Category Building").

Bringing in a Colleague to Assess Your Teaching

I know the title of this section might make you shudder. You want me to invite someone into a class where I don't know what I'm doing? I don't have a sadistic streak, I promise. I'm writing this section because most faculty do not take this route, but as I was doing my interviews, the faculty who *did* voluntarily invite supportive colleagues into their periphery classrooms found it extremely helpful. Without any prompting from me, they said it was a piece of advice they would offer other content novices.

Whom should you invite? Go with the person who will create the least amount of stress for you. (When I asked junior faculty in my interviews, they said they wouldn't invite a department chair or a tenured member of their own department. That would make them much too nervous, and they wouldn't want that person judging their teaching abilities on the basis of this early snapshot.) If you found a supportive ally outside of your department, as suggested in Chapter 3, that person would be a great choice because they have already been supporting you behind the scenes. They know some of the challenges you face. A colleague from your teaching center may be another nonthreatening option; most centers have policies to ensure that your teaching conversations remain confidential. That can be a relief when you want to confide that you're nervous about the next part of the course—the topic never made sense to you when you were a student, and you're not sure you can do it justice now, either.

A friendly face in the classroom can help assess your teaching in two ways: the colleague can do a classroom observation or, if trained, conduct a Small Group Instructional Diagnosis (SGID). I'll describe how to do each of these in a way that maximizes the benefits for you and minimizes the stress.

Classroom Observation

A classroom observation can be extremely helpful because your colleague can look for things that you're probably too preoccupied to notice. When are students taking notes and when do they stop? Is there someone in the class who looks ready to participate but needs some encouragement? Do you look at your watch too often? To increase your comfort level and ensure that you and your colleague are on the same page, I suggest doing the classroom observation in three steps.

Step 1: Meet with your colleague a few days before class to discuss the skills you're working on as a teacher. If you can tell her what to prioritize—whether it's your pacing, handling of students' questions, use of PowerPoint, ability to talk over a loud radiator, whatever—your colleague will be able to focus her attention and provide more useful feedback. You can also let your colleague know if you'll be explaining a particularly difficult concept so she can help you assess your explanation. (Surprisingly, faculty often skip this first step of setting priorities for the observation. But I find that it makes the observation much less stressful for you because you and your colleague are working together on your priorities.)

Step 2: Your colleague visits your classroom.

Step 3: You and your colleague sit down to discuss your respective observations of the class. You can assess whether this was a representative class and what did and didn't go as expected. Your colleague can let you know what she observed with respect to your priorities. She might also ask about other observations that weren't necessarily on the agenda but that she found interesting. She might want to know why you made certain choices and how often you do certain things. Do you usually break students into small groups or tell stories about graduate school? Remember that she may be looking for new ideas to improve her own teaching. Just be sure that this conversation occurs within a few days of the class itself. That can be difficult when you're so busy preparing for class, but if you wait too long, you'll find it harder to reconstruct the details of what happened on a particular class day (for example, what exactly did you say that agitated that one student?) and the process will be less useful.

Small Group Instructional Diagnosis (SGID)

This is simpler than it sounds. And it's so helpful. If a campus offered this to every newly hired instructor, it should be listed as a faculty benefit, right up there with free photocopying.

The SGID, or "Midterm Class Interview," as it's sometimes known, is a structured group interview process that's usually offered midway through a course. The basic idea is that a facilitator helps students identify those aspects of the course that support their learning and those aspects that could be improved. Students collaboratively create feedback that helps you, the instructor, see the course from their perspective.

You'll need a facilitator for this activity because you have to leave the room for fifteen to twenty minutes. Students will be more open during the SGID if their feedback is anonymous. If you're in the room when students are offering suggestions, they will hesitate to say that you talk too fast or that your examples are outdated. They certainly won't tell you that they only do half the readings. A person needs some training to facilitate an SGID smoothly, so contact the teaching center or professional development office on your campus to learn if anyone is trained in conducting these interviews.

If you've never done an SGID, you might be thinking that this activity is essentially the same as conducting a written midterm evaluation. There are definitely similarities. But the advantage of the SGID is that students have a facilitated conversation about the course, and they get a chance to correct one another. I've conducted about three dozen SGIDs, and in more than half of them, a student discovers that he is alone in his negative view. For example, the student who loudly complains that the readings are boring discovers that he's the only one who feels that way. Or a student who says that the feedback on the first draft of her paper was cryptic might learn that the instructor provided a handout explaining the codes he used. Students can be surprisingly quick to correct one another.

Some faculty cringe at the thought of this activity, so I know it may not be for you. Fair enough. But let me address the most common concerns I hear. Instructors are often worried that students will say cruel things or that having a conversation will unify the students against the instructor. But I've been conducting SGIDS for eight years in two different institutions, and in my experience, just the opposite occurs. Students are rarely cruel in an SGID—they typically word their comments carefully and sensitively, unless they are looking for a laugh. Moreover, a skilled facilitator will help students reword complaints into constructive suggestions. As for unifying the students against you, in most cases, students find that the SGID is a positive experience that endears them to their instructor because that instructor cared enough to get their feedback. In small classes, instructors often tell me later that discussions were more animated immediately following the SGID activity. In large classes, as long as the instructor responds to the feedback, a few students will usually comment on the final course evaluation that the "midterm activity" was proof that the instructor truly cares. It always surprises me that students don't realize that you care sooner, but somehow this activity sends the message home.

Students' Perspective: Enhancing Your Credibility Rather Than Detracting from It

Some faculty members are concerned that asking for feedback will make them appear less competent. They worry that it will be like wearing a sign around their neck announcing, "I don't know what I'm doing."

Instructors who regularly conduct assessments in their classes will tell you that a good assessment only adds to their credibility rather than detracting from it. If you show your commitment to improving students' learning and the environment in which they learn, you will see positive results. The research shows that faculty who collect midterm feedback and who make changes to improve their teaching on the basis of that feedback see increases in their ratings on the end-of-course evaluations. An instructor's sensitivity and responsiveness to students' progress correlate strongly with students' final ratings of the instructor— in fact, they rated fifth of seventeen factors in one literature review. Students also reported liking the subject matter more after their instructors had responded to midterm feedback. Clearly, students are receptive to assessments when they're done well.[6]

So, how do you do an assessment well? I have six suggestions.

1. Frame the activity as your commitment to offering the best course possible. When you introduce the activity, emphasize several key points:

- Your goal is to improve the course and your teaching while the students are still taking the course. The concrete and constructive feedback students provide *during* the course allows you to achieve that goal, whereas the final course evaluations help next year's students.
- You want to hear what's working well and what could be improved. If you know what's working for most students, you can be sure to preserve those successful components as you consider other possible changes.
- Promise to report back to students on what you learn.

2. Explain why you won't be making certain changes. Some faculty hesitate to ask students how to improve a course because they are concerned that students will ask for unreasonable things. It's true. Students do ask for unreasonable things. And you retain the right to decide which proposed changes are good changes and which proposed changes conflict with the learning outcomes for the course. Rest assured, you don't give up those rights simply by asking students for their perspective and suggestions.

To maintain your credibility, however, you need to address the proposed changes you *are* making as well as the changes you're *not* making. You don't have to respond to every bizarre request—

one student may suggest that you bring bagels to class because it's too early for them to get breakfast on their own. (I'd probably make a joke about the convenience of Pop Tarts, but you could always just let this one drop.) But when you receive a cluster of legitimate requests around a practice that you're not willing to change, you need to let students know why.

Let's consider the students' workload, the inevitable complaint in most classes. As you may recall from Chapter 6, students spend on average only thirteen to fourteen hours a week doing the work for all their classes combined, so chances are that whatever you've assigned, it's more than they want to do. When you ask for student feedback, they ask for a lighter reading load. Maybe you are willing to cut one of the readings—particularly if you're having trouble keeping up with the readings yourself. But most instructors are reluctant to do so. You've sought the advice of experts on the topic (at least you've looked at some syllabi online), and you've chosen each reading to address your big questions. When you respond to students' feedback, you can explain why you're staying with what's on the syllabus. But you can also let students know that you've heard them, and if possible, you want to work with them to find other ways to make the workload manageable. Could you reduce the number of homework assignments instead? Could you discuss reading strategies, explaining when to skim and when to read every word?[7] By explaining why a change is unreasonable (and offering alternative solutions when possible) you show respect for the students and clarify that the choices for the course were carefully made.

3. Don't ask for feedback every class. I know some people can do this and make it work, but it's not the strategy I would recommend for everyone. It's particularly problematic if you're struggling with time or confidence. Collecting written feedback every day creates a time problem because you've got to read and think about that feedback after each class. If you collect feedback every day but don't get around to reading it, suddenly two weeks have slipped by and students haven't seen any changes based on the last three times you asked for feedback. It's like crying wolf. The next time you ask for students' input on something, their comments are likely to be apathetic or insulting, which is no help at all.

Collecting feedback in every class, particularly feedback on students' experience in the course, is also a mistake if your confidence is wavering. As Myra Strober observed, "You need a strong stomach when you ask students to evaluate your teaching. Students' comments will be contradictory. Some will be just plain nasty. And some will be off-topic—they might say something about your clothes." Most of us can handle a smattering of contradictory advice or the occasional random comment about our clothes, but few of us want to deal with it every week.

4. Don't ask for feedback in the last five minutes of class. The default for most of us is to do an assessment in the last five minutes of class. It makes sense—you've managed to get through as much material as you can and students can comment on the full class session they just sat through. That's exactly the problem. Chances are the students don't want to sit anymore. They want to pack up and get to their next class or get their next espresso at Starbucks. You'll receive more thoughtful feedback with more thorough comments if you ask for feedback at a time when the only other alternative is more teaching from you. I usually ask for feedback in the first ten minutes or midway through class.

5. Get all students' input on major changes that are proposed. Let's say that on a midterm evaluation students tell you that the number one thing you could do to improve the course is to eliminate the final exam. To make up for the lost points, they ask you to increase how much the last paper is worth. They make a good argument—most courses in the department offered at the 400-level don't have final exams—and you were dreading the long stint of exam-grading right before the holiday break anyway.

Before you make any decisions, discuss the issue with the entire class to find out what problems might arise if you make this major change. Ideally, take a vote. Some students may be stronger at test-taking than at paper-writing, so they may have been counting on the final exam for weeks to keep their grade afloat. It would be unfair to them to change the plan midstream. If you take a vote, know what options you're willing to consider: does the vote need to be unanimous for you to cancel the final exam? If three or four students still want to take the exam but most students want to increase their grade on the last paper, would you be willing to create an exam for that small group of holdouts?

6. *Don't reissue the syllabus five times.* Revising and reissuing the course calendar once on the basis of something important you learn from your students (and preferably after the vote you just took in class) is a fine strategy. And if you have a good rapport with your class, you can probably revise and reissue the syllabus a second time without too much discord. But don't reissue the syllabus every other week. Too many changes make you appear disorganized and make students nervous.

Asking students for their feedback can make faculty feel vulnerable. We tend to fear the worst. But we also tend to work harder than necessary when we teach outside of our expertise. Other people can see that, but it's not as obvious to us because all we can see is how much more work there is to do. Having a trusted colleague visit your class or asking students to do a quick assessment exercise can reassure you that things are going better than you realized. Well-structured feedback can help you relax about the parts of the class where your preparations are just fine and help you focus your energy where students need it most.

8   Advice for Administrators

Akira Watanabe is an assistant professor who just finished his first year of teaching.[1] He is a materials science engineer who designs high-performance fabrics. And by high-performance, I mean more sophisticated than the most expensive Gore-Tex jacket at REI. For his Ph.D., he developed a self-cleaning fabric for military and biological textiles. Most of us associate "self-cleaning" with our ovens, but a "self-cleaning fabric" requires even less work: you simply put the fabric in water, then dirt, bacteria, and even harmful chemicals rinse away. No need for detergents—water alone does the trick. You can imagine why his research would garner attention from government and private agencies, and why the textiles department at a major research university quickly hired him.

But Akira's first year of teaching was disastrous. He expected to be teaching topics he knew well, courses on the engineering and product development of high-tech materials or what are known in the industry as "smart textiles." Instead, he was assigned to teach courses in fashion. That's not a misprint. Akira was assigned to teach 300- and 400-level courses on fashion design and marketing. He wasn't teaching how to use polymers in a lab or any related courses. Instead, he was doing all he could to teach students how to make and market products that might someday make the cover of *Vogue* magazine. If his story wasn't so sad, it would be funny.

The toll of teaching these courses was tremendous. For two semesters, Akira averaged four hours of sleep a night. The week I spoke with him, he had slept fifty minutes on Monday, two hours on Tuesday, and two and a half hours on Wednesday. His all-consuming teaching load had suffocated his research. The only day of the week that he would do research was Sunday, usually after 5:00 p.m. The tests on his samples kept failing, in part because he would start a test, let it sit for a week, and then need to start all over again the next Sunday. He had received an enviable grant of more than $200,000 to develop a new product, but eight months later, he still couldn't provide a proof of concept. The company cancelled the grant. Everyone lost—he lost his money to fund graduate students, the university, college, and department lost the indirect costs he was bringing in, and everyone involved probably lost a longer-term relationship with a lucrative sponsor.

How did this happen? You might be thinking that Akira must teach in a tiny department where no one else is available to teach these fashion courses; on the contrary, he teaches in a department of more than twenty faculty members. But the relatively large size of the department might also contribute to the communication and mentoring gap. Perhaps in a department that large, the operating assumption is that someone else must be helping the new person; thus no one felt a pressing need to take Akira to lunch to ask how his courses were going. This was also a case of very bad timing. The person who had most recently taught Akira's courses was on leave and had left no teaching materials. To make matters worse, the department chair who had hired Akira was away on sabbatical when he started. That chair, the one who had offered him the job, had promised to support him during his first year of teaching, but the interim chair wasn't sure how to help. The new chair tried his best but was stuck in a bind—the course assignments were already set. Students were registered and the courses needed to be taught.

I haven't spoken with his department chair, but I can imagine that Akira's colleagues might not have realized how much he was struggling. It's taboo for junior faculty to talk about the fact that a course is beyond their expertise. Heaven only knows what your colleagues will remember about your first few years in the department when they discuss your case for tenure; you certainly don't want them to remember you as complaining or incompetent. When junior faculty are given inappropriate course assignments, they do their best to get through the course and preserve their credibility. New faculty who do ask for help often do so too late or without an obvious sense of urgency. As Akira looked back over his first year, he explained, "I know now that I made many mistakes. I used to think, 'I cannot strongly ask for the lecture notes.' I have to be more polite and hope that they will help. I cannot be arrogant and say, 'You promised you would help,' even though they had. They had promised."

Did the original department chair really expect a product engineer working on cutting-edge technology to be ready to teach courses on how to predict fashion trends? Why didn't this come up in the interview process? Perhaps it did come up but each side misunderstood the other's needs and concerns. English is not Akira's native language. He was expecting to teach courses in "product design and development," which to the department chair might have meant something very different from self-cleaning jackets.

In my twenty-eight interviews with faculty and administrators, this was the hardest story to hear. Akira's experience is near one end of the continuum, I suspect, though perhaps you can top it with a story of your own. I tell his story here not because it's representative but because I want to show how easy it can be for misunderstandings and bad timing to make a new teacher's experience miserable, despite everyone's good intentions. I'm also writing this chapter because these issues go beyond the individual level to the institutional level as well. When faculty have to teach as content novices, what can administrators realistically do to minimize the negative impacts for faculty and students? We know that faculty at our own institutions face challenges on a regular basis, perhaps not as difficult as Akira's, but people are uncomfortably stretched all the time, sometimes willingly at first. This chapter looks at practical strategies for administrators to improve the support and culture for this kind of exhaustive teaching. You want your faculty to be challenged in manageable, fulfilling ways. You don't want them overwhelmed, demoralized, and determined to pack their bookshelves and look for better jobs elsewhere.

What's at Stake

That last sentence might seem like a bit of an overstatement. People don't really leave an institution simply because they were given a terrible teaching assignment when they started, do they? Obviously, not everyone does. But some do. Many researchers have studied how to boost faculty morale and hold onto good people. Despite the volumes of research, there is no secret formula. (Then again, maybe journals are the wrong place to look for secrets.) But researchers have shown us that when faculty voluntarily leave an institution, it's a pretty safe bet that two predictable things were happening at that institution, and at least one thing wasn't happening.

The first predictable issue is that faculty who leave are overburdened and pressed for time. When researchers have crunched the numbers, time commitment was the single best predictor of faculty intent to leave.[2] The time-commitment problem includes both "the need to subordinate one's life to one's work" and also inadequate time to give one's work the attention it deserves.[3] What strikes me about this research finding is that it mirrors the language I heard from many faculty teaching outside of their expertise. Every person with whom I spoke, even faculty who loved to teach unfamiliar topics, said the drain on their time was unmatched. Several mentioned that even when they worked as hard as they could, it still wasn't enough—the class and the students deserved more attention. This concerns me, and it should concern you as an administrator. We all know what it's like to be busy, but teaching as a content novice can mean subordinating everything to one's teaching.

Does everyone leave when they have insufficient time to do their job well and still have a life outside the classroom? Of course not. If we all left on those grounds, there would be no faculty left anywhere. So what forces the issue?

In addition to having too little time, a second key factor that drives people to leave is poor leadership by their department chair. In one study, researchers tracked down and interviewed faculty after they had left an institution to ask what they liked and didn't like about their former academic home. In 39 percent of the interviews, faculty cited poor departmental leadership as a key source of dissatisfaction.[4] Poor departmental leadership was defined as poor communication and management skills and a failure to "protect" junior faculty from difficult teaching assignments and committee work. Sometimes instructors are stuck teaching unfamiliar courses because the department chair doesn't understand their areas of expertise or didn't ask about which courses they are comfortable teaching. As a result, and perhaps entirely inadvertently, the chair schedules junior instructors for courses that overwhelm them.

Although poor departmental leadership can be insufferable, another factor is even more disheartening, and it's the component that is most often missing when faculty leave or plan to leave. (And no, it's not a competitive salary.) The primary element that is missing is collegiality. Some faculty call it a lack of community. Study after study demonstrates that faculty who leave or who plan to leave usually feel discouraged or angry that no one supports them in meaningful ways, or, worse yet, that people promise to support them but withdraw that support when it's needed most.[5]

Incidentally, administrators often think that salary is the main reason people leave. It's certainly a source of dissatisfaction for many faculty, but it may also be the easiest answer that a departing instructor can give when her department chair or dean presses for an explanation. It takes a bold and perhaps incensed individual to say, "It was the absence of effective leadership" to the very person who led ineffectively. Salary does make the list of important variables, but in most studies, it ranks after issues like lack of collegiality, poor departmental leadership, and unreasonable time commitments.

Why have I included this research about faculty morale and retention? My hope is that if you're an administrator and you weren't sure if you needed to do something about junior faculty who are teaching outside of their expertise, you're more certain now. Two of the primary risk factors that send faculty packing—time commitment and poor departmental leadership—are serious concerns for faculty who are unhappily teaching what they don't know. I would argue that the third risk factor, lack of collegiality, is also a concern. First, let's picture the ideal scenario. If an instructor feels supported by a collegial department, perhaps even recognized as someone who is "taking one for the team" by teaching an undesirable course, this person is more likely to stay. But an instructor who is never offered any support (or who is promised support but then discovers it's unavailable when he needs it, as was the case for Akira) probably experiences his department as highly uncollegial. It doesn't matter that people are jovial in the hallway if those same people don't come through when it really counts.

Strategies for Deans and Provosts

As described in Chapter 1, though it's commonplace for faculty to teach outside of their expertise, few instructors openly discuss it in these terms. It's a new and risky way of talking about what we do. Not something one wants to admit to the provost or dean. And compared with outdated classrooms or evaporating grant money, it probably isn't the top item that members of your faculty are going to raise in the precious thirty-minute meeting they secure with you.

But faculty workload *is* a huge issue on most campuses. And with good reason. Class sizes are growing, more underprepared students are entering college and graduate school, and taxpayers in many states are demanding that faculty spend more hours on their teaching.[6] (I won't even mention the growing pressures on research.) With no obvious release valve in sight, many administrators are looking for innovative ways to approach the workload problem. You may not be able to do much about student preparation or taxpayer demands (and resolving the issue of class size may take some time). But you can offer some direct and immediate support for faculty teaching beyond their comfort zone.

Set the Tone

Faculty look to you, as provost or dean, for many things, but on this particular issue, they'll want you to set the tone for what is and isn't valued on campus. At the very least, they'll appreciate hearing the administration acknowledge that an intellectual sprawl is occurring in many disciplines, and teaching in the twenty-first century means keeping up with that sprawl. Textbooks keep getting longer, professors are expected to learn and use new technologies in their classes, and students want their examples to be applied and up-to-date. (For a more detailed examination of why instructors are increasingly teaching outside of their expertise, see Chapter 2.) If you discuss periphery teaching as a legitimate issue with department chairs, they can more easily discuss it with faculty. If you mention it in your speech at new faculty orientation, you show that you're attuned to the changing demands of teaching, and new hires will feel more comfortable asking their chairs for support.

Seek the Input of Faculty Committees

If teaching is a high priority in the tenure process, raise this issue with the dean's council or the faculty senate. There are some predictable places on campus where people are most frequently burdened by teaching outside of their expertise. Which departments are in academic fields that are experiencing the most rapid growth in new research? If hiring isn't keeping up with that growth, then existing faculty are probably scrambling to stay on top of the literature. Do some departments have a high level of turnover? Departments that are trying to fill holes in the dam probably have more content novices at the front of the room, and unwillingly so.

Some individuals are also more likely than others to shoulder the burden of teaching outside their expertise. When you look at the faculty of color across your campus, are most of them teaching the diversity courses in their departments? If so, are they actually content experts on diversity? Christine Stanley, an associate dean at Texas A&M, points out that department chairs often "ask a Latina or African American faculty member to teach the only diversity course in the department. It's not their area of expertise because not every person of color is an expert in diversity issues, but we ask this person to teach the course anyway, and then students evaluate it really hard." The research literature shows that this is a common frustration for untenured faculty of color.[7] If your campus wants to increase the retention rate of faculty of color, this is one area to improve their experience.

In addition to identifying who might be pressed to teach as a content novice, provide leadership on how faculty can document these experiences. Your tenure and promotion guidelines may already mandate that factors which increase teaching workloads, such as class size and the number of new course preparations, should be taken into account when evaluating teaching effectiveness.[8] Teaching as a content novice dramatically increases workload, so what kind of information would a reappointment, promotion, and tenure committee (RPT) need to determine that a tenure candidate had taught several courses outside of his or her expertise? You may not find instant agreement on this issue, but the conversation has to begin somewhere.

Fund Professional Development Programs

I know this is probably the section you would prefer to skip. Budgets are always tight, even in a good enrollment year. But the choices you make about distributing resources send a strong message to faculty. In my interviews with administrators, two types of professional development programs were recommended, and both can be done on a relatively small scale.

One suggestion was to offer incentives to faculty who teach outside of their expertise. Faculty could be given $500–$1,500 for taking on such a course. This could be a competitive program—just as some campuses have programs where faculty can apply for money to develop an innovative course, your campus could have a small microgrant program where faculty apply for money to develop and teach a course in an unfamiliar area. If you need to justify the expense in concrete terms, the money could be used to buy books or attend a local conference on the topic. Or instead of having a competitive system, the money could be awarded to faculty in their first year of teaching at your institution. Departments or colleges could have a pool of funds to be awarded to faculty teaching outside of their expertise in Year 1, and the award could either be a set amount or be adjusted on the basis of the number of periphery courses a person taught that year.

Mary Deane Sorcinelli, the associate provost for faculty development at the University of Massachusetts–Amherst, suggested another kind of microgrant program based on mutual mentoring. U-Mass has launched an innovative microgrant program to support mentoring in research, and she suggested that the same kind of mentoring model could be applied to teaching. She first described how their program supports faculty research: "When you're a junior faculty member, you know what you need to move forward in your research career, where the gaps are in your knowledge." Junior faculty on her campus can apply for microgrants (up to $1,200) to receive some mentoring from other faculty members. "I'll give you an example of an assistant professor in biology who needs to gain training in some lab techniques that she will be using. She needs to learn how to do a specific procedure to move her research forward. A senior female faculty member at a major research university in Texas is skilled in this area. So with this small grant, the assistant professor will visit the lab in Texas, spend two days with her senior colleague to learn everything she can, and then take that knowledge back, teach it to her grad students, and share it with her colleagues. As well, she will establish a working collaboration with an expert in her field." The mentoring model has been successful with faculty beyond the sciences; instructors in English, art, philosophy, and public health, to name just a few, have received these grants and used them in exciting ways.

Mary Deane Sorcinelli proposed that a similar mentoring program could be developed for faculty seeking mentoring for a course they will be teaching. Faculty could partner with someone on another campus who is a content expert in the field and who teaches the class regularly and teaches it well. The instructor could visit this experienced person to sit in on their class for a day or two, to talk about their best and worst teaching decisions, and to see which audio-visual materials are worth the investment. A microgrant could be offered to cover the person's travel expenses. A new collaboration is formed, and the faculty member comes back to campus invigorated with ideas and feeling supported by his institution. Students also get much better teaching.

Train Department Chairs

If the provost's office does any mentoring or training seminars for department chairs, add this to your list of training topics. As

Mary Deane Sorcinelli points out, "Department chairs are just sort of surviving; they often aren't trained to be managers," so management training, when it's done well, can be invaluable. Mentor department chairs on how to discuss this issue with junior faculty one-on-one. You can use Akira's story at the start of the chapter as a case study. Teach department chairs about some of the common but faulty assumptions that could lead to bad course assignments, such as the mistaken assumption that a new colleague from Italy is automatically an expert on "international" approaches to a topic, simply because she dresses better than most instructors and was trained abroad. Department chairs might not remember what it's like to spend a year or two scrambling to learn the material they've been assigned to teach, so you'd be doing them and their faculty a service by discussing the problem and some possible solutions. Even if they do remember, they may not realize what a difference their support could make.

Strategies for Department Chairs

As a department chair, you're probably not sitting on a pile of money to hand out for new course development, and you certainly don't have a lot of time. But you (or the department chairs before you) have invested a lot of time and resources in hiring the people in your department. If you have faculty teaching outside of their expertise, you want them to see that the department is a good place to be. Your two priorities in this regard are to protect your junior faculty and promote a department culture that talks about teaching.

Protect Your Junior Faculty

I'll first focus on junior faculty, particularly new hires. Perhaps some of your mid-career and senior colleagues are teaching outside of their expertise, but chances are they are doing so voluntarily. There's an additional reason to focus on junior faculty in your department—the first few years have a lasting impact on how the person views the department. Research shows that a bad experience that goes unsupported in a junior faculty member's first few years can leave that person feeling bitter with the department or the institution for years.[9] Many of the people who have "negative transformational experiences" will leave to find new work elsewhere. Even if the frustrated person doesn't leave, he or she can contribute to an uncollegial atmosphere for years to come. Junior faculty, particularly new faculty, should be a priority for you if you want to foster a supportive community (not to mention keep your sanity).

Don't Put New Faculty in This Situation

If at all possible, you'd like to avoid putting brand new hires in the precarious position of teaching outside of their expertise in Year 1. They are figuring out genuinely important things like what they need to do to get tenure and ordinary conveniences like where to get a vegetarian meal when they're done teaching at 2:00 p.m. As Christine Stanley observes, "What a lot of people don't realize is that these individuals, these really junior folks, are a little bit like new students. They are going through their own development and acculturation, and they're already anxious, just like students, about expectations of the institution and the department. . . . I realize there are extenuating circumstances, but I would never want to put a junior faculty member in that position of teaching what they don't know. If it happens one time, it shouldn't happen again."

Your department may already have a tradition of protecting junior faculty from certain courses during their first few years. If so, that's fantastic—you're just adding another dimension to that conversation. If your department doesn't have this tradition, there are a few basic ways you can protect your colleagues in their first, and probably most impressionable, year on campus.

1. Ask. The first step is to know which topics are within a new hire's knowledge base and which topics would require extensive homework on their part. You can look at someone's CV and make your best guess, but if the person isn't in your area, it's probably a poor guess. I'd venture to say it's a terrible guess. We all make naïve assumptions about someone else's field—it's hard to know what's standard training for a graphic designer or a policy analyst unless you're one yourself. And some people don't have "standard" training. Your best bet is to have a conversation with your junior colleagues to find out which courses they consider within their expertise. Even if you think you covered this issue during the interview process, be sure to have this important conversation again after this person has accepted the job. Some faculty have said that the only conversation they had with their chairs about course assignments was a quick verbal review of potential courses during their campus visit, when they were eager to say yes to just about anything to get the job.

Look for ways to talk with new and junior faculty about teaching so they have room to be honest about courses that will be an uncomfortable stretch for them. Think about how to frame the conversation so they can discuss something potentially embarrassing with dignity instead of anxiety. You could remind them that the department wants their first year to be as successful as possible. Acknowledge that it's hard to prepare new courses in a new environment. (I'm sure there's a story you can tell about something you found impossible when you first landed on campus—anything from getting your parking permit to submitting your grades online.) You can let them know that you want to minimize the number of courses that will require them to learn or relearn the material if it's been years since they've studied it. Let's be honest—you won't be able to shield them from that learning experience entirely. But you could review a list of possible courses together and ask where they would have the most and least to learn.

2. *Approach a senior colleague about covering the course.* You probably won't have the luxury of tailoring the fall lineup of courses to the new person's interests. Perhaps you discover too late that you've scheduled your new colleague to teach a course he has no idea how to teach. Ask a senior colleague in your department to teach that course instead. Even if she isn't a content expert, she'll probably find it less difficult to learn and teach a new course than would her junior colleague.

If you can persuade a senior colleague to teach the class, the new hire can sit in on it. Melissa Pasquinelli had this opportunity her first year of teaching chemistry at North Carolina State. She was going to be teaching engineering students how to solve engineering problems, but Melissa is a chemist, not an engineer. Her specialty is physical chemistry, and she does her research through computer simulations rather than traditional experiments. As a graduate student, she had little reason to enter the engineering building, but now she needed to think like an engineer every day. For starters, she had to teach students to use microscopes to characterize different kinds of fibers: "I really don't know anything about fibers, and I don't do experiments. I haven't used microscopes since I was in high school." It could have been a miserable beginning to her career at North Carolina State, but the department chair arranged for a senior colleague to teach the course one last time, while Melissa sat in the back row, taking notes and writing down questions to ask the professor later. When she taught the course on her own the next se-mester, it was still challenging, but she felt much more prepared. And she felt grateful to be in a supportive, collegial department.

3. Postpone the course. This may not be an option, but if you have a course on the books for fall term that will be a stretch for your new colleague and students haven't registered yet, perhaps you can postpone it a year, or at least until spring term, when your new colleague will be more acclimated. Delaying the course and moving it away from a new hire's start date can make the experience much more manageable. Kevin Otos, our friend from the drama department at Elon University, was able to wait until his second year before teaching a course completely out of his professional element. He used that time to talk to plenty of people, compare syllabi, get a sense of what was really expected for the course, and read as much as he could.

If It's Unavoidable, Support Them

Despite your best efforts, you may find yourself caught in a bind. When you have to assign a new colleague to a course outside his expertise, you can support him in several ways. Here I list seven strategies, from things you can do right away to things you can do long after the course is over.

1. Offer as much notice as possible. Obviously, faculty will do a better job teaching any course if they've had more time to prepare, but for content novices, it's crucial to have as much time as possible. It may not be a matter of life and death, but it's certainly a matter of control and competency. Instructors who are teaching outside of their comfort zone will want to learn all they can before they begin. Remember, new and junior faculty are, at some level, trying to impress you and the rest of the department.

It's hard to impress anyone if you feel consistently underprepared.

Understandably, you might have learned at the last minute that you have a course you need to fill—perhaps someone in the department suddenly goes on sick leave. These things happen. But many times faculty members feel as though a cone of silence has been lowered around the department chair. Instructors feel blind-sided when given an unexpected teaching assignment, and department chairs feel defensive because they're sure they told the instructor. Faculty would rather have you be the annoying chair who has double-checked that everyone knows their teaching assignments than the despised chair who somehow overlooked someone.

2. *Find a mentor for the new person.* Preferably, you're looking for a mentor who has taught the course in question and who is willing to provide teaching resources and advice. If that content expert will be away on sabbatical when the new person teaches the course, ask the content expert to take his or her new colleague out for coffee before leaving town.

If there is no content expert in the department or if people in your department are prickly, look more broadly for a mentor. Pick someone in your college who is politically savvy and has strong teaching skills, someone who will help the junior colleague brainstorm teaching solutions and who appreciates the frustrations of new faculty. You could also put your junior colleague in touch with the teaching center on your campus for support and advice.

You may not be a fan of assigned mentoring. You may have the philosophy that mentors and "mentees" should find each other because you personally have better memories of the mentor you found than of the mentor who found you. The "kismet" approach to mentoring works for long-term mentors who help junior faculty navigate tenure, build research agendas, and even nurse political wounds, but the timeline is more urgent for specific course assignments. The clock is ticking, and your junior colleague might feel more supported to know that he already has someone to whom he can turn. You also have an insider's knowledge of who has taught that course before or who might have the best teaching advice.

3. Don't just tell new faculty, "Do whatever you want." When I asked Akira what department chairs could do to help faculty who are stuck teaching a course outside of their expertise, he gave this surprising answer, "Don't say, 'Do whatever you want.'" This might be exciting or even expected advice for a course that's within your comfort zone. For most courses, professors want the autonomy to teach whatever they want. As experts, they know what students need to learn to be successful. But therein lies the problem. If the instructor is a content novice, he doesn't know what the students need to know. Akira emphasized that "the advice 'Do whatever you want' doesn't help me or my students. *Why* does this course have to be taught? Why is there a lab? At least tell me why students are required to take it their third year but aren't ready for it their second year."

Kevin Otos voiced a similar concern about his desire for a bit more guidance. He said that he was given a lot of freedom in how to teach his "Global Experience" course: "Freedom is nice, but a good course requires a lot of structure and form." He found himself investing too much energy into simply creating the structure for the course. A mentor who could help him think through the advantages and disadvantages of different course structures would have been ideal.

4. Offer a course release. When a new or junior instructor will be teaching an entire course or two outside her expertise, can you give that instructor a course release that term or that year? You probably don't have many course releases to spare, but this is an excellent place to use one. Additional time to prepare for class or get at least a little research done will make that heavy teaching load much more bearable.

5. Don't burn that person again. Try to avoid assigning the same person to courses outside of his or her comfort zone semester after semester (or year after year). It's an easy mistake to make—after all, they survived it once, right? But if the instructor couldn't get any research done or gave up his personal life the first time it happened, that person needs a breather to catch up.

You might be thinking, but if they've taught the course once, it's much less work the second time around. Not necessarily so. As Michael Bérubé from Penn State explained, and as many faculty agreed, you have to teach a course three times before you're really comfortable with it: "The second time is almost as much work as the first. I change everything. I mean, c'mon, I can't make the same mistakes. Students deserve new mistakes, better mistakes in Year 2."

If your junior colleague has told you that she is completely overwhelmed by the prep work, it's especially important to give her a break to show her that you have heard her and that you want her to succeed. When an instructor is immediately thrown back into a frustrating course, she can't help feeling as though no one in the department cares.

6. Raise the issue in Reappointment, Promotion, and Tenure meetings. As Christine Stanley noted, department chairs also need to support junior faculty when they aren't in the room—namely, in discussions about a person's teaching for reappointment and tenure. Department chairs need to remember those times when they've asked a junior faculty member to teach something outside of their expertise and the junior person has come through. By drawing attention to these circumstances, you are providing two kinds of invaluable support: you are showing that the person under review is a cooperative team player in the department, and you are encouraging the RPT committee members to keep these less-than-ideal circumstances in mind as they read the student course evaluations for that term. If the course evaluation numbers are lower than average, the committee will know why, and if the numbers are higher than average, they can be appropriately impressed (though something tells me RPT committees are hard to impress). And if the junior faculty member accomplished little research that year, there is an obvious professional reason.

7. *Communicate your commitments to your replacement.* This piece of advice won't apply to every department chair who picks up this book, at least not immediately. If you're going on sabbatical or you're stepping down from your role as department chair, keep track of the commitments and agreements you make with new hires and junior faculty and communicate them to the new chair. Everyone is put in a difficult position when it's discovered that a chair promised an instructor help that his successor cannot provide, as we saw in Akira's story. Understandably, if you're about to go on leave, it's not your first priority to review the teaching agreements you made. But block off twenty minutes of your week, find the file of your new hire, and write down a few notes. You just invested a lot of time in this faculty search. A little more time upfront could save you and your colleagues another search down the road.

Promote a Departmental Culture That Talks about Teaching

I've been a member of departments that almost never talked about teaching, and I know many faculty in the same boat. Sure, we swapped horror stories about impossible students, and we figured out how to meet the latest assessment standards that had been handed down from on high. Those were important topics, certainly, but we rarely talked about the choices we made or the choices we regretted once we'd closed the doors to our classrooms.

You might expect an absence of teaching talk at large research-focused universities, but it's often missing from teaching institutions as well. I asked Sylvia Hurtado from UCLA what she hears as she visits campuses to talk with faculty about their freshmen. "Faculty actually do want to talk about their teaching and they enjoy talking about their teaching, but it happens less than you'd expect," she admitted. "I'll be doing a workshop at a school known for great teaching, and faculty have said, 'We haven't talked about teaching in ten years.'"

There may be days when it seems you have little in common with the members of your department, but departments are a great place to talk about teaching. We teach the same basic set of students. We struggle to help students understand the same conceptual stumbling blocks in our field (also known as threshold concepts, as we discussed in Chapter 4). We teach in the same poorly designed classrooms.

Or perhaps your department does talk about teaching, but you never discuss the day-to-day issues that matter to individual faculty members. I've heard stories about departments that have become so focused on program assessment and learning outcomes that their conversations about teaching consist of little else. But there are so many other important topics about teaching that we need to discuss. In my interview with Parker Palmer, he said, "I would love to see more departments having generative conversations about the question, 'How can we expand the degrees of freedom for all of us?' Let's agree on what minimally has to be taught or transmitted in order for the 101 students to become 201 students to become 301 students. But at the same time, how do we do that in a way that liberates everyone to pursue their own genius as a teacher, the pieces of the field that are most alive for each of us?"

This may sound too touchy-feely for your department. You know your colleagues better than I do, and if you personally tried to open such a conversation about teaching at your next department meeting, you might be met with icy stares and silence. That doesn't necessarily mean your colleagues have nothing to say about teaching—it just goes against the norm to discuss it. If there are unspoken "house rules" (and what department doesn't have them?), it may help to use a facilitator who brings his or her own set of rules. This person could be a chair from another department. The campus teaching center is also an inexpensive place to start, provided your institution has one. Or your faculty may be more willing to talk with an outside expert. However you approach it, your goal is to set a precedent for supporting authentic talk about teaching.

Strategies for Faculty Developers and Teaching Center Professionals

If you work at a teaching center or in a faculty development office, you're accustomed to raising issues that aren't publicly discussed by other administrators on your campus, such as how faculty of color are treated differently on campus or how to handle the move toward larger class sizes. The issue of teaching what you don't know is another important topic to add to your list.

The good news is that if you're a faculty developer, you probably have a lot of experience learning something so that you can turn around and teach it. One of my inspirations for this book was that I found myself agreeing to give teaching and learning workshops on topics on which I had very little expertise, knowing full well that I would be spending the two weeks before that workshop reading as much as I could on the topic. Perhaps that's irresponsible of me, and once this book is published I'll learn that I'm the only faculty developer who learns as she goes. But I think this line of work draws people who like to be generalists, who don't want to be limited to the findings in just their home discipline, but who want an excuse to keep reaching into the best teaching ideas in other fields. Mary Deane Sorcinelli summed it up nicely in our interview: "Faculty developers, because of their work with faculty from a range of departments, are very aware of disciplinary differences. They like to cross the borders and boundaries, get a little messy, keep it loose." So let's look at some ways to get a little messy.

Raise the Topic of Teaching What You Don't Know at Faculty Orientation

If your office coordinates the new faculty orientation on your campus, do new hires a favor and raise this taboo topic right from the start. One of the big stresses of teaching outside of your comfort zone is that faculty feel they cannot talk about it. Just by raising the issue, you've given them at least one place where it's safe to discuss it. Normalize the experience of being a content novice by letting them know it's not just an issue for new faculty. You can quote some of the famous people in this book as a way to reassure them that they aren't alone, or you can share some of your own stories. Chances are you've had to teach outside of your expertise at least once, and people often feel relieved to hear that you, "the teaching expert," has experienced the same day-to-day frustrations as everyone else.

Another reason to raise this topic during orientation is that you're trying to help new faculty, particularly people who have just completed their Ph.D.s, to have realistic expectations about the professoriate. As Mary Deane Sorcinelli observed, "This is one aspect of the curricular program that doesn't seem fair, but you can expect it to happen." It's not a liability of the institution or a weakness of their department; it's simply a growing reality in higher education.

Get Information about the Student Body into the Hands of Faculty

Although your Institutional Research office probably creates an annual report about your student body, I'll bet most instructors have never seen it once, let alone perused it every year for updates. Find ways to inform faculty about student demographics and behaviors that they might not expect. As Sylvia Hurtado from the Higher Education Research Institute observes, "When faculty see the information about the students they are actually teaching, they are usually surprised that the assumptions they've been holding are not true." You could provide a one-page summary sheet that begins, "You may be surprised to learn that . . ." or "Students aren't like they used to be." On that one-page list, you can provide some honest data about your students. If you're concerned that it will send a negative public relations message about your institution, you can provide data for your campus alongside the national data so that faculty can see that studying fewer than fifteen hours a week is the norm nationwide.

Some schools circulate the Beloit College "Mindset List" to their faculty by email.[10] A new list comes out each fall and aims to provide a worldview of the average eighteen-year-old by listing events that happened before the freshman class was born or circumstances that have been true throughout their lives. For the fall 2008 list, the statements included, "Rap music has always been mainstream"; "Russia has always had a multiparty political system"; and "What Berlin Wall?" If you're frustrated that students keep asking for more "real-world" examples, it helps to see that the examples you've been using in class were part of your real world, not theirs.

This list is most useful for faculty who teach undergraduates, but with some simple math and a little research, you could also provide a mindset list for faculty teaching graduate students. The Beloit College website archives the lists for the past ten years, so if you learn the age of the average graduate student on your campus, your office can provide the "mindset" list for when the average student started college.

Offer Targeted Workshops

My guess is that your office already offers seminar and workshop topics that will help faculty who are teaching outside of their comfort zone. If you are toying with the idea of offering a workshop directly titled "Teaching What You Don't Know," it might help to know that in my interviews, some faculty loved this phrase but others backed away from it. Some instructors preferred phrases like "teaching on the edge of my expertise," or the all-purpose "teaching outside of my comfort zone." (I tend to think that the main reason faculty come to *any* workshop is that they find themselves teaching outside of their comfort zone.)

Then again, faculty who are teaching outside of their expertise are particularly short on time and are spending many evenings, weekends, and lunches learning as they go. They may not attend a workshop, appealing though the title may be, because they finally managed to close their office door and are learning the material for later in the week. Realistically, you might catch them the next term, when they are making sense of what happened and trying to devise a better plan of attack for the next time.

Provide Small Grants

If your center has funds to support faculty doing innovative teaching, you could also provide stipends or small grants for those teaching courses outside of their expertise. Several programs are described in the earlier section for provosts and deans that might be well suited to your center.

Offer to Facilitate Departmental and College-Level Conversations

Even the most skilled department chair may not be able to get his faculty to have an honest conversation with one another about what they don't know. But you might be able to. When I asked Parker Palmer what administrators could do to support faculty teaching outside of his expertise, he immediately spoke to this delicate issue: "Common sense tells us that people need to sit down and talk about a shared practice, which means thinking out loud about professional work in front of other people who do that same work. It means creating the conditions that allow people to make themselves vulnerable, and that's why you need facilitators—because we both know faculty are so great at showing off in front of one another. They can get snotty about how 'I'm better than you at this.' It's very, very hard for faculty to acknowledge mistakes in front of each other."

Let's say that a department chair invites you in to help her department have this conversation. Where do you begin? In most settings, you probably wouldn't want to walk in and start with the blunt and unsettling statement, "We're going to talk about how little we actually know in some of our classes." I'd suggest approaching this sensitive issue indirectly, more academically. One safe approach is to talk in terms of problems, assumptions, and hypotheses. Faculty can always point to problems that recur in the classroom, even if they can't agree on which problem is most important. Most instructors have also developed assumptions and hypotheses as to why a particular problem is occurring. They have ideas about which teaching strategies address the problem and which strategies fail to do so or potentially even exacerbate it.

Parker Palmer thought this was where a facilitator could begin. Start with a commonly recognized problem that's important to the department, perhaps grade inflation: "One of the best ways to frame this would be, 'Let's have a conversation about teaching that allows us to conduct an experiment on the assumptions we've developed together as faculty.'" For example, most faculty have some assumptions as to why grade inflation is such a problem. The facilitator can help faculty identify those teaching and assessment practices that the instructors think contribute to grade inflation and practices that they think discourage it. Ideally the conversation would move into practices that faculty wonder about but that no one has the courage to try. There are bound to be disagreements, and that's fine. As a department, faculty members can identify a hypothesis or assumption about grade inflation that they want to test; maybe they want to test the hypothesis that instructors who have a sobering discussion with students about the problem of grade inflation will have a higher number of students complaining to the department chair but will also receive a greater number of high-quality rough drafts for the final paper. Once the department has targeted their strategy, they can ask for a volunteer to try that strategy in class. As Palmer suggests, "Then somebody can go back to the classroom with the blessing of his or her colleagues who have said, 'Yeah, this hypothesis, this risk you're about to take, it may end you up flat on your ass, but it's a risk worth taking.' As a group, you've considered a problem that needs to be solved and you're trying a solution in a careful, knowing way."

The department can then make a commitment to bring you, the facilitator, back in a few weeks to discuss the progress or outcome of the teaching experiment. People will want to know what happened. Parker Palmer imagined how that second conversation might go: "If it works, great, we all learn. If it doesn't work, great, we all learn! And nobody's feeling like, 'Oh what an idiot I was for trying that.' Instead, we're participating in a collegial conversation where we all learn from failure." Depending on the egos in the room, you may want to remind everyone that we all learn as much, if not more, from failure as we do from success. Once a department has had that conversation with you once or twice, they might be willing to have the same progressive conversation without you in the room. The point is to get faculty first to talk about the risks they take in the classroom and then to support one another in that risk-taking.

Propose Faculty Learning Communities

Several of the administrators I interviewed mentioned the value of forming small groups of four to five faculty members who could meet on a regular basis to support and learn from one another around the theme of "teaching outside of your expertise." These semiformal groups are often referred to as "faculty learning communities."[11] Maybe your office already sponsors some learning communities, or maybe this is a good way to start. A learning community could bring together first-year faculty (people who are teaching outside of their expertise for the first time) or faculty teaching in the general education program, people who are teaching outside of their comfortable disciplinary boundaries. Alternatively, a learning community could bring together faculty who are teaching students they don't understand. Although learning communities can serve many purposes, at their core, they provide a much-needed sense of camaraderie and a sanity check. Instructors in a learning community can celebrate the brilliant comment they made in class or laugh over the equally disastrous one.

Whether you're a department chair or a provost, an associate dean or the director of a teaching center, some experienced faculty may be surprised if you raise the issue of teaching what you don't know. After all, it hasn't been discussed in the past. Disgruntled, a senior professor may raise his hand and ask, "Does this mean that you think the quality of the faculty is going down?" You can thank him for the question (aren't you polite and gracious?) and explain that some faculty have been teaching outside of their expertise for years, but it hasn't been labeled as such. This is a relatively new way of thinking about teaching, and just a few years ago, no one was talking this way.

But college and university teaching is changing. It's probably even more accurate to say that college and university teaching has been changing for years and the conversation is finally catching up. People have begun to come out of the woodwork at all kinds of institutions to embrace this idea of teaching what you don't know and teaching students you don't understand. If people are beginning to talk about it on your campus, it certainly isn't a weakness in the faculty or in the education you offer your students, but a sure sign of progress. People are looking for honest ways to become better teachers. They're facing reality.

Appendixes

Ten Solid Books on Teaching Strategies

There are many good books on teaching, and this is by no means an exhaustive list. But you can turn to any one of these books to find organized, honest, and practical advice.

Bain, Ken. *What the Best College Teachers Do.* Cambridge, Mass.: Harvard University Press, 2004.

Bean, John. *Engaging Ideas: The Professor's Guide to Integrating Writing, Critical Thinking, and Active Learning in the Classroom.* San Francisco, Calif.: Jossey-Bass, 1996.

Bligh, Donald L. *What's the Use of Lectures?* San Francisco, Calif.: Jossey-Bass, 2000.

Brookfield, Stephen D. *Discussion as a Way of Teaching: Tools and Techniques for Democratic Classrooms.* San Francisco, Calif.: Jossey-Bass, 2005.

Gross-Davis, Barbara. *Tools for Teaching,* 2nd ed. San Francisco, Calif.: Jossey-Bass, 2009.

Lang, James M. *On Course: A Week-by-Week Guide to Your First Semester of College Teaching.* Cambridge, Mass.: Harvard University Press, 2008.

Lieberg, Carolyn. *Teaching Your First College Class.* Sterling, Va.: Stylus, 2008.

McKeachie, Wilbert, and Marilla Svinicki. *McKeachie's Teaching Tips:*

Strategies, Research, and Theory for College and University Teachers, 12th ed. Boston, Mass.: Houghton Mifflin, 2006.

Nilson, Linda. *Teaching at Its Best: A Research-Based Resource for College Instructors,* 2nd ed. San Francisco, Calif.: Jossey-Bass, 2007.

Race, Phil. *The Lecturer's Toolkit: A Resource for Developing Assessment, Learning and Teaching,* 3rd ed. London: Routledge Press, 2007.

B Case Study Collections and Resources

These case study repositories provide complete cases as well as strategies for using them effectively. Check them out online. Cases in the sciences and social sciences are typically available free of charge, whereas cases in business, public policy, and the health professions are available for a fee.

Business

- Harvard Business School Cases
- Problem-Based Learning Clearinghouse, University of Delaware

Government, Public Policy, and Public Affairs

- Electronic Hallway, Evans School of Public Affairs, University of Washington
- Kennedy School of Government Case Program, Harvard University

Medicine and Dentistry

- Center for Teaching Excellence, University of Medicine and Dentistry of New Jersey (Resources on active learning)

Sciences and Social Sciences

- National Center for Case Study Teaching in Science, University of Buffalo
- Problem-Based Learning Clearinghouse, University of Delaware

Student Group Syllabus Review

Goals
- To explore how the course is designed
- To clarify expectations and what you and the professor can do to meet them
- To answer your questions about the course

Step 1: Introduce yourselves.

Step 2: Please take 5–10 minutes to read over the syllabus and calendar.

Step 3: Discuss each of the questions below with your group members. One person in your group should keep notes on the group's discussion.

1. Looking at the course objectives, what other classes have you had that will be helpful?
2. Looking at the course calendar, which topics interest you most? The least?
3. What do you want or expect from the professor?
4. Identify two or three things in the syllabus that concern you.
   a.
   b.
   c.

5. What strategies could you use to address these concerns?

6. Identify two or three things in the syllabus that you're glad to see.

    a.

    b.

    c.

7. When do you plan to submit your first project for a grade? What do you think it will cover?

8. List three questions you have about the course that aren't answered in the syllabus.

    a.

    b.

    c.

D Midterm Course Evaluation

Instructor_____Course_____

The purpose of this evaluation is to improve how the course is taught, and therefore improve your learning. I will report back to you on the feedback I receive.

For the first section, please check all items that apply. If you like the way I do something but would like me to do it even more often, you can check both columns.

I like the way the instructor:	I would like the instructor to:
____ gives an introduction at the start of class.	____ give more/less introduction at the start of class (circle one).
____ balances lectures and group work.	____ lecture less/do more group work.
	____ lecture more/do less group work.
____ clarifies the objective of each class.	____ clarify the objective of each class more.
____ explains the relationships between concepts.	____ explain more of the relationships between concepts.
____ summarizes the main points.	____ summarize the main points more often.
____ utilizes the board effectively.	____ utilize the board more effectively.
____ utilizes visual aids effectively.	____ utilize visual aids more effectively.
____ discusses concrete/real-life examples.	____ discuss more real-life examples.
____ encourages students to ask questions.	____ encourage more questions.
____ responds effectively to questions.	____ respond more effectively to questions.
____ incorporates students' questions into lectures.	____ incorporate students' questions into lecture.
____ is open to different points of view.	____ be more open to different points of view.
____ shows respect toward all students.	____ show more respect toward all students.
____ grades fairly.	____ grade more fairly.
____ provides feedback on exams.	____ provide more feedback on exams.
____ varies the pace according to the difficulty of the material.	____ vary the pace more according to the difficulty of the material.

(Page 2 of 2)

For the second section, please provide your thoughts and opinions on the following questions. Please make your feedback as concrete, constructive, and specific as possible. By being specific, you can help me change the course to meet your needs.

1. What are the strongest features of this course and of the instructor? In other words, what contributes most to your learning?
2. What specific suggestions do you have for improving your learning in the course?
3. Is the pace of the course typically:
   too fast, just right, or too slow
   Please explain how it's too fast or too slow in the space below.

Notes

Introduction

1. The four faculty members discussed in this introduction—Zach, Andy, Susan, and Cheryl—are all real people. I have, however, changed their names and some identifying details to ensure their anonymity.

2. *Survey of Earned Doctorates, 2006,* table 18. The SED is a federal agency survey conducted by the National Opinion Research Agency (NORC) for the National Science Foundation, National Institutes of Health, U.S. Department of Education, National Endowment for the Humanities, U.S. Department of Agriculture, and the National Aeronautics and Space Administration. This statement is based on the length of time it took to complete a doctoral degree in 1981 compared with 2006. The average amount of time spent in graduate school increased in five of the six academic disciplines that were examined (life sciences, physical sciences, engineering, social sciences, and education). Graduates in education saw the greatest increase, from 10.9 years in 1981 to 12.7 years in 2006 (a 17 percent increase). The average time to degree completion in the four other fields increased 1–12 percent. The one exception was the humanities: students in the humanities saw no increase in the average time spent to complete a doctorate—the figure was 9.7 years in both 1981 and 2006. Of course, we could argue that a student who

spends more years in school is not necessarily better educated than someone who spends fewer years. It is the case, however, that recent Ph.D. recipients spent as much if not more time in school earning their degrees than colleagues twenty years their senior.

3. An important caveat: this book focuses on strategies for teaching what you don't know. If you're looking for general teaching advice —such as a step-by-step plan for creating your syllabus or guidelines for preventing plagiarism—you'll want to look elsewhere. There are some fantastic books on college teaching, and I've listed ten of my favorites in Appendix A. These are the books I turn to when I have teaching and assessment questions. I hope you'll find them useful, too.

1. The Growing Challenge

1. U.S. Department of Education, National Center for Education Statistics, *National Study of Postsecondary Faculty (NSOPF:04), 2004*, table 233. The number of hours that faculty spend teaching varies widely by type of institution: whereas at research-intensive universities, 48.9–52.2 percent of faculty teach fewer than four hours a week, at liberal arts colleges 47.6 percent of faculty teach ten hours a week or more.

2. Dan Simons is known for his research on unexpected visual events and our inability to notice them. I highly recommend his lab's website. The vanishing-construction-worker study and the gorilla-by-the-elevator study are both classics: http://viscog.beckman.uiuc.edu/ (accessed December 30, 2008).

3. Jennifer Rowley, "Developing Constructive Tension between Teaching and Research," *International Journal of Educational Management* 10, no. 2 (1996): 6–10. See also Fred Antczak, "Learning and the Public Research University: Twenty-two Suggestions for Reducing the Tension between Teaching and Research." Paper presented at the Conference on College, Composition, and Communication, Nashville, Tenn. Many authors have suggested ways that instructors can minimize the divide between teaching and research. Some, like Rowley, write for faculty at "teaching institutions" who need

help meeting the pressures of increased research demands. Others, like Antczak, offer strategies for faculty at "research institutions" who are being required to meet higher teaching standards. Professors are finding many ways to integrate their research and teaching; the challenge can be frustrating, but it's not insurmountable. My point is that there is an inherent tension between teaching and research and they tug in opposite directions: research requires a faculty member to tunnel into more and more details, and teaching requires that same faculty member to make broader connections.

4. Ken Bain, *What the Best College Teachers Do* (Cambridge, Mass.: Harvard University Press, 2004). For a summary of several studies that demonstrate the importance of addressing students' misconceptions, see National Research Council, *How People Learn: Brain, Mind, Experience and School* (Washington, D.C.: National Academy of Sciences, 2000).

5. See, for example, Elliott Vichinsky et al., "The Diagnosis of Iron-Deficiency Anemia in Sickle Cell Disease," *Blood* 58 (1981): 963–968.

6. My colleagues in medical school may not agree, but in many ways, medical school professors have an easier time than the rest of us in terms of the teaching-research divide. Courses in the health professions are often team-taught, so the pathology professor specializing in sickle-cell anemia may only teach the three weeks of the course focused on blood disorders. In most academic disciplines, professors teach an entire course alone.

7. Philip Lewis, "The Publishing Crisis and Tenure Criteria: An Issue for Research Universities?" *Profession* 11 (2004): 14–24. See also Philip Wankat and Frank Oreovicz, "Tenure and Teaching," *Journal of Professional Issues in Engineering Education and Practice* 129, no. 1 (2003): 2–5. Of course, faculty at large research institutions may be experiencing more pressure to teach effectively rather than an increasing pressure to publish more articles in top-tier journals. But these demands for better teaching and learning at research-intensive schools aren't typically accompanied by a free pass on one's research. On the contrary—professors are expected to maintain a

world-class research program while becoming better teachers. The time and energy have to come from somewhere, so I suspect that a good number of faculty at research-intensive schools feel pressured to narrow their research to maintain their publication rate. Or perhaps they've moved cots into their offices to save time on their commutes.

8. Charles L. Outcalt, "Eric Review: Community College Teaching—Toward Collegiality and Community," *Community College Review* 28, no. 2 (2000): 57–70.

9. Benjamin F. Jones, "The Burden of Knowledge and the 'Death of the Renaissance Man': Is Innovation Getting Harder?" *Review of Economic Studies* 76, no. 1 (2009): 283–317.

10. The sixth edition of the classic *Norton Anthology of English Literature,* Volume 1, was published in 1993, and the eighth edition was published in 2005.

11. Therese A. Huston et al., "Expanding the Discussion of Faculty Vitality to Include Productive yet Disengaged Senior Faculty," *Journal of Higher Education* 78, no. 5 (2007): 493–522. Other studies show that faculty who experience reduced autonomy in their teaching options and poor collegiality within their departments tend to be more dissatisfied with their careers: E. A. Pollicino, "Faculty Satisfaction with Institutional Support as a Complex Concept: Collegiality, Workload, Autonomy." Paper presented at the Annual Meeting of the American Educational Research Association, New York, N.Y., 1996. Also see "New Study Indicates Faculty Treatment Matters More Than Compensation," *Collaborative on Academic Careers in Higher Education:* http://www.gse.harvard.edu/news_events/features/2006/09/26_faculty_treatment.html (accessed February 8, 2008).

12. National Center for Education Statistics, "Number of Instructional Faculty in Degree-Granting Institutions, by Employment Status and Control and Type of Institution: Selected Years, Fall 1970 through Fall 2005," *Digest of Education Statistics,* 2008, table 248: http://nces.ed.gov/pubsearch/pubsinfo.asp?pubid=2009020.

13. The published statistics from the National Center for Educational Statistics show that the number of faculty increased from 1,174,000

in 2003 to 1,290,000 in 2005, or 116,000 faculty over two years. Although most institutions have different titles and classifications for different kinds of non–tenure-track instructors, I refer to them all as "adjuncts" for simplicity's sake. Data for 2003 come from Laura G. Knapp et al., *Staff in Postsecondary Institutions, Fall 2003, and Salaries of Full-Time Instructional Faculty, 2003–04* (Washington, D.C.: U.S. Department of Education, National Center for Education Statistics, 2005), table 7.

14. All the statistics cited in this paragraph were derived from table 248 in NCES, "Number of Instructional Faculty in Degree-Granting Institutions," and from table 7 in Knapp et al., "Staff in Postsecondary Institutions." Some educational analysts have predicted that this trend of accelerated adjunct hiring has reached its peak, such as the Center for the Education of Women, *Non Tenure Track Faculty: The Landscape of US Institutions of Higher Education* (Ann Arbor: University of Michigan Press, 2006), http://www.cew.umich.edu/PDFs/NTTlandscape06.pdf. Others speculate that the economy will dictate whether the proportion of adjunct faculty will continue to grow.

15. Ronald G. Ehrenberg et al., "Who Bears the Growing Cost of Science at Universities?" *NBER Working Paper 9627* (2003). The cost of conducting searches and hiring new tenure-track faculty is considerable. With start-up packages at research-intensive universities approaching a half million dollars in some science and engineering programs, department chairs have very strong incentives to hold onto their new faculty and keep them happy.

16. National Center for Education Statistics, "Doctor's Degrees Conferred by the Sixty Institutions Conferring the Most Doctor's Degrees: 1995–96 through 2004–05," *Digest of Education Statistics* (Washington, D.C.: Department of Education, 2006), table 311: http://nces.ed.gov/programs/digest/d06/tables/dt06_311.asp. This figure of 52,000 reflects the approximate number of doctorates that are awarded annually (based on statistics for 2004–05), so this would be an upper limit to the number of new faculty who just completed their Ph.D.s. Admittedly, not all Ph.D. graduates seek academic careers, and many Ph.D. recipients complete postdocs

before their first faculty position. Nonetheless, there were a total of 80,070 new part-time and full-time positions in 2004–05, and over 52,000 new Ph.D. candidates on the market that year. Presumably, there were also several thousand all-but-dissertation (ABD) candidates who were looking for a paycheck as they finished their degrees. Although I cannot give an exact number, I believe it's reasonable to argue that a fair number of new hires are fresh from their Ph.D. experience.

17. J. Douglas Toma, "Expanding Peripheral Activities, Increasing Accountability Demands, and Reconsidering Governance in U.S. Higher Education," *Higher Education Research and Development* 26 (2007): 57–72.

18. Stephen L. Daigle and Patricia Cuocco, "Public Accountability and Higher Education: Soul Mates or Strange Bedfellows?" *Educause Research Bulletin* 9 (2002): 1–14. See also National Commission on Accountability in Higher Education, *Accountability for Better Results: A National Imperative for Higher Education National Commission* (Washington, D.C.: State Higher Education Officers, 2005): http://www.sheeo.org/Account/accountability.pdf (accessed March 23, 2009). This commission released a report in 2005 with an extensive list of recommendations to ensure that colleges and universities are "meeting the needs of the American people." No funding, however, was offered to colleges and universities to make these changes. The commission did recommend that the federal and state governments work together to allocate their education budgets to support higher graduation rates and offered a list of guidelines for "budgeting for improved performance."

19. At the time I write this, 318 institutions have joined the Voluntary System of Accountability, and membership has climbed over 35 percent in ten months: http://www.voluntarysystem.org (accessed March 23, 2009).

20. National Survey of Student Engagement (NSSE), *Experiences That Matter: Enhancing Student Learning and Success* (Bloomington, Ind.: Center for Postsecondary Research, 2007).

21. Toma, "Expanding Peripheral Activities." See also Mary Burgan, *What Ever Happened to the Faculty: Drift and Decision in Higher Edu-*

cation (Baltimore, Md.: The Johns Hopkins University Press, 2006); and Jack H. Schuster and Martin J. Finkelstein, *The American Faculty: The Restructuring of Academic Work and Careers* (Baltimore, Md.: The Johns Hopkins University Press, 2006).

22. "Tuition Inflation," FinAid, The SmartStudent Guide to Financial Aid: http://www.finaid.org/savings/tuition-inflation.phtml (accessed December 29, 2008).

23. For information on undergraduate education, see Congressional Budget Office, *Private and Public Contributions to Financing College Education,* 2004: http://www.cbo.gov/doc.cfm?index=4984 (accessed December 3, 2007). For graduate education, see Kristin Davis, "The Hunt for Money," *U.S. News & World Report:* http://education.yahoo.com/college/essentials/articles/grad/hunt-money.html.

24. Bain, *What the Best College Teachers Do.*

25. Huston, "Expanding the Discussion."

2. Why It's Better Than It Seems

1. I don't actually have any advice on getting more restful sleep, but if you feel more confident and prepared going into class, sleep will, I hope, come more easily. As I conducted my interviews, it was a small but strange comfort to learn that other people have teaching nightmares, too.

2. The phrase "content expert" appears most often in the higher education literature in discussions of distance, blended, or e-learning. In some distance education programs, a "content expert" researches and creates the content for the website and a "faculty facilitator" delivers it. When I use the phrase "content expert," however, I am not referring to someone who only prepares the content; I am referring more broadly to any college or university instructor who is teaching in their specialty. To the best of my knowledge, the phrase "content novice" is not commonly used in any literature.

3. I appreciate that faculty most likely move along a continuum between content novice and content expert. My hope is that a future study will investigate the stages between the two.

4. "Penelope" is a pseudonym. Until "teaching what you don't know" is a more commonly discussed phenomenon, she asked to have identifying details removed from her story.

5. Before you turn to Google or poll your colleagues, "Phylzpytt" is just a nonsense word meant to capture the fact that some concepts are so mysterious they seem downright unpronounceable the first time you encounter them. But when you have to teach such concepts, you suddenly realize that you're more equipped to make sense of them than you realized.

6. Faculty who discuss teaching practices with colleagues in other departments on campus find that it improves their teaching because it forces them to inquire more deeply into their own instructional choices and motivations. They are encouraged to see their common purpose. See William M. Sullivan et al., *A New Agenda for Higher Education: Shaping a Life of the Mind for Practice* (San Francisco: Jossey-Bass, 2008). A mentor or close colleague outside your department can also give advice on navigating intradepartmental tensions. Warring subgroups and cliques within a department can become a source of faculty dissatisfaction, and when these tensions arise, it can be difficult to find a neutral source of advice within the department. See Susan Ambrose et al., "A Qualitative Method for Assessing Faculty Satisfaction," *Research in Higher Education* 46, no. 7 (2005): 803–830. Lastly, forming friendly relationships outside of your department enhances your sense of community on campus. New faculty are often disappointed by the lack of community and collegiality in their first few years of teaching at small colleges as well as at big universities, and institutional structures for supporting those faculty friendships and conversation, such as faculty lounges, are in many cases being eliminated to make space for new offices or programs. The responsibility for creating communities falls increasingly on the individual instructor. See Judith M. Gappa et al., *Rethinking Faculty Work: Higher Education's Strategic Imperative* (San Francisco, Calif.: Jossey-Bass, 2007).

7. In my sample of 28 faculty, I interviewed individuals from different academic disciplines (7 instructors in math, science, and engineering; 6 in the social sciences; 5 in the humanities and fine arts; 3 in

education; 3 in business; 2 in law; and 2 in the health professions) and an equal number of men and women (14 men, 14 women). Twenty-five institutions were represented in the sample; roughly half were public and half were private (11 and 14 institutions, respectively), and they varied in size (6 small schools with fewer than 4,000 students; 12 medium-sized schools with 4,000–10,000 students; and 7 large schools with more than 10,000 students). Despite having done quota sampling with respect to academic discipline, gender, and type of institution, I realize that the sample is small, and the quantitative psychologist in me knows that it's quite possible that one of these variables is related to a person's comfort level teaching as a content novice. What the field really needs is a larger empirical study, perhaps a survey, to determine whether there is a statistical relationship between these variables. These interviews are the preliminary qualitative research that could open the door to future quantitative research.

8. For this part of the book, I'll omit the instructors' names. Everyone was generous in sharing their stories, and I'm especially grateful to the Strained and Anxious faculty who took the time to talk with me. I don't think I'd be helping them if I attached their names to their stories.

9. "Imposter syndrome" is a concept from the research literature that refers to people's "feelings of not being as capable or adequate as others perceive or evaluate them to be." Christiane Brems et al., "The Imposter Syndrome as Related to Teaching Evaluations and Advising Relationships of University Faculty Members," *Journal of Higher Education* 65 (1994): 183–193, quote on pp. 183–184. Brems and her colleagues found that instructors who showed few signs of imposter feelings were likely to have higher teaching evaluations and were successful in encouraging more questions from students. I'm not describing the Strained and Anxious faculty as having an imposter syndrome because I did not administer the "Imposter Phenomenon Questionnaire" that is used to assess such a problem. To learn more about the questionnaire, see Pauline R. Clance, *The Imposter Phenomenon: When Success Makes You Feel Like a Fake* (Toronto: Bantam, 1985).

10. Maryellen Weimer, *Learner-Centered Teaching: Five Key Changes to Practice* (San Francisco, Calif.: Jossey-Bass, 2002), p. 46.

11. Suzy Braye, "Radical Teaching: An Introduction," *Teaching Professor,* 9, no. 8 (1995): 1–2. I thank Maryellen Weimer, who uses this quote effectively in her book *Learner-Centered Teaching,* p. 25, as she examines the balance of power in the learner-centered classroom.

12. Donald L. Bligh, *What's the Use of Lectures?* (San Francisco, Calif.: Jossey-Bass, 2000).

13. Carolyn Lieberg describes active learning this way in her book *Teaching Your First College Class* (Sterling, Va.: Stylus, 2008).

14. Bligh, *What's the Use of Lectures?* See also Michael Watts and William E. Becker, "A Little More Than Chalk and Talk: Results from a Third National Survey of Teaching Methods in Undergraduate Economics Courses," *Journal of Economic Education* 39, no. 3 (2008): 273–286. A national survey of undergraduate economics professors reveals that in 2005 an estimated 83 percent of class time was spent lecturing. Unfortunately, that number hasn't changed much since 1995, even though active learning strategies are more widely publicized and researched.

15. Weimer, *Learner-Centered Teaching,* p. 46.

16. No one is a blank slate—we build on what we already know—and a good learning environment brings out that knowledge, challenges what's incorrect, and builds on the rest. For more on students' preexisting knowledge and the way incorrect knowledge can interfere with learning, see National Research Council, *How People Learn: Brain, Mind, Experience and School* (Washington, D.C.: National Academy of Sciences, 2000).

17. National Research Council, *How People Learn.*

18. We could define a learning environment in many legitimate ways. In the book *How People Learn,* John Bransford and colleagues at the National Research Council write about the importance of designing learning environments that are learner-centered, knowledge-centered, assessment-centered, and community-centered. Maryellen Weimer focuses on the learner-centered dimension and explores how faculty should give students some control over what they learn; look for ways to focus more on the process than on the

content; and create more evaluation activities that allow students to learn something while we assess their skills.

19. Robert B. Barr and John Tagg, "From Teaching to Learning—A New Paradigm for Undergraduate Education," *Change Magazine,* 27, no. 6 (November/December 1995): 12–25. For other thought-provoking discussions of learning environments in the United States, see National Research Council, *How People Learn;* John Tagg, *The Learning Paradigm College* (San Francisco, Calif.: Jossey-Bass, 2007); Dee Fink, *Creating Significant Learning Experiences: An Integrated Approach to Designing College Courses* (San Francisco, Calif.: Jossey-Bass, 2003); and Ken Bain, *What the Best College Teachers Do* (Cambridge, Mass.: Harvard University Press, 2004). In the United Kingdom, see John Biggs, *Teaching for Quality Learning at University,* 2nd ed. (Berkshire, England: Open University Press, 2003). There is even a journal titled *Learning Environments Research,* published by Springer Link.

20. Suzanne Hidi and K. Ann Renninger, "Interest, a Motivational Variable That Combines Affective and Cognitive Functioning," in *Motivation, Emotion, and Cognition: Integrative Perspectives on Intellectual Functioning and Development,* ed. D. Y. Dai and R. J. Sternberg (Mahwah, N.J.: Erlbaum, 2004), pp. 89–115; see also Albert Bandura, "Self-Regulation of Motivation and Action through Internal Standards and Goal Systems," in *Goal Concepts in Personality and Social Psychology,* ed. L. A. Pervin (Hillsdale, N.J.: Erlbaum, 1989), pp. 19–85.

21. Jillian Kinzie, "Promoting Student Success: What Faculty Members Can Do," Occasional Paper No. 6 (Bloomington, Ind.: Indiana University Center for Postsecondary Research, 2005).

22. Marilla Svinicki, *Learning and Motivation in the Postsecondary Classroom* (Bolton, Mass.: Anker Publishing, 2004). Faculty who simply pile on the work are not students' favorite teachers. To see some of the differences between teachers who motivate their students with high expectations and teachers who discourage their students with unrealistic ones, see Bain, *What the Best College Teachers Do.* See also Barbara Gross Davis, *Tools for Teaching,* 2nd ed. (San Francisco, Calif.: Jossey-Bass, 2009).

23. Roger Buehler et al., "Exploring the 'Planning Fallacy': Why People Underestimate Their Task Completion Times," *Journal of Personality and Social Psychology* 67 (1994): 366–381. See also Daniel Kahneman and Amos Tversky, "Intuitive Prediction: Biases and Corrective Procedures," *TIMS Studies in Management Science* 12 (1979): 313–327.

24. Pamela J. Hinds, "The Curse of Expertise: The Effects of Expertise and Debiasing Methods on Predictions of Novice Performance," *Journal of Experimental Psychology: Applied* 5 (1999): 205–221, Experiment 1.

25. Ibid., Experiment 2.

26. George Loewenstein et al., "Misperceiving the Value of Information in Predicting the Performance of Others," *Experimental Economics* 9 (2006): 281–295.

27. Pamela J. Hinds et al., "Bothered by Abstraction: The Effect of Expertise on Knowledge Transfer and Subsequent Novice Performance," *Journal of Applied Psychology* 86 (2001): 1232–1243.

28. Ibid. Hinds did not call participants in this research study "content novices" and "content experts"; she simply called them "beginners" and "experts.

29. Ibid.

30. Ibid.

31. George Kuh and the group at Indiana University who are working on the National Survey of Student Engagement, or NSSE, have been raising awareness of the concept of deep learning in the United States. Kuh also talks about the DEEP project, which is quite different from deep learning and thus potentially confusing. DEEP is an acronym for Documenting Effective Educational Practices and refers to a kind of academic institution, whereas "deep" refers to a student's learning style. The DEEP project was a two-year study of twenty institutions (known as DEEP institutions) that had particularly high rates of student success as reflected in their graduation rates and their NSSE scores. The DEEP project identified the distinctive features of these highly successful learning environments. Presumably the students at these schools were engaged in deep learning, but deep and surface approaches to learning, as defined

by researchers in the United Kingdom, weren't directly measured in the DEEP project.

32. Ference Marton and Roger Säljö, "On Qualitative Differences in Learning I: Outcome and Process," *British Journal of Educational Psychology* 46 (1976): 4–11.

33. Ference Marton et al., *The Experience of Learning*, 2nd ed. (Edinburgh, Scotland: Scottish Academic Press, 1997).

34. Graham Gibbs, *Improving the Quality of Student Learning* (Bristol, England: Technical and Educational Services, Ltd., 1992).

35. Paul Ramsden, *Learning to Teach in Higher Education* (London: Routledge, 1992). See also Biggs, *Teaching for Quality Learning at University*.

3. Getting Ready

1. Grant Wiggins and Jay McTighe, *Understanding by Design*, 2nd ed. (Alexandria, Va.: Association for Supervision and Curriculum Development, 2005), pp. 1, 34. See also Dee Fink, *Creating Significant Learning Experiences: An Integrated Approach to Designing College Courses* (San Francisco: Jossey-Bass, 2003). For a similar approach that emphasizes the importance of context in course design, see Donald H. Wulff et al., eds., *Aligning for Learning: Strategies for Teaching Effectiveness* (San Francisco, Calif.: Jossey-Bass, 2005).

2. John Bean and other experts in the Writing across the Curriculum movement offer clear advice on how to create writing assignments that you'll enjoy grading and that your students will enjoy writing. John C. Bean, "Theory and Praxis in *The Allyn and Bacon Guide to Writing*, 4th Edition." Workshop presented August 16, 2006, at the University of New Mexico, Albuquerque. See http://www.unm.edu/~wac/CurriculumResources/BeanAgenda.pdf (accessed December 22, 2008).

3. Wiggins and McTighe, *Understanding by Design*.

4. John Biggs, *Teaching for Quality Learning at University*, 2nd ed. (Berkshire, England: Open University Press, 2003).

5. Lynn M. Kelting-Gibson, "Comparison of Curriculum Development Practices," *Educational Research Quarterly*, 29 (2005): 26–36. This re-

search was done with K–12 teachers rather than with college faculty; there appears to be little empirical research at the college level directly comparing courses developed through backward design with courses developed through more traditional means.

6. The research on student-generated questions has primarily been done with K–12 students, but there are a few empirical studies with college students. See, for example, Mohammed Aliakbari and Jamshid Mashhadialvar, "Does It Matter Who Makes Comprehension Questions? A Comparison between the Levels of Comprehension Obtained from Author-Generated Questions and Student-Generated Questions." Presentation at the Eleventh Annual Meeting of the Pan-Pacific Association of Applied Linguistics, Chuncheon, South Korea, July 28–30, 2006. See also Peggy Cole, "Learner-Generated Questions and Comments: Tools for Improving Instruction," *Proceedings of Selected Research and Development Presentations of the Association of Educational Communications and Technology,* New Orleans, La., January 13–17, 1993. For work with K–12 students in the sciences, see Christine Chin et al., "Student-Generated Questions: A Meaningful Aspect of Learning in Science," *International Journal of Science Education* 24, no. 5 (2002): 521–549. For research on students' text comprehension and the best ways to teach students how to generate their own questions, see Barak Rosenshine et al., "Teaching Students to Generate Questions: A Review of the Intervention Studies," *Review of Educational Research* 66, no. 2 (1996): 181–221.

7. Some instructors allow graduate students to shape the questions for a course, but it appears to depend on the program and the students. Masters degree programs for students coming directly out of college often have highly structured courses in which students only get a chance to drive the questions on their own individual or group projects. Doctorate programs for students who are a little older often have smaller, seminar-style classes where students can help drive the questions from Day 1.

8. The observation that junior faculty seemed to feel better after they talked to me, while I felt important and valued, might have a scientific basis. Research shows that it's very helpful to confide in others

about a stressful experience. People undergo less stress and have better physical health if they unburden something that is bothering them to another person. If there's no one on campus you trust, at least discuss the fact that you're teaching outside of your expertise with a family member or personal friend. James W. Pennebaker, *Opening Up: The Healing Power of Confiding in Others* (New York: William Morrow and Co., 1990).

9. Michael Bérubé explained that his teaching read, the one he does right before class, involves making a page-by-page list of key passages in the novel that he's teaching. This kind of "close reading" is appropriate for humanities classes when you want to draw students' attention to an author's word choice, but in the social sciences or sciences, a teaching read might be very different. It would involve the information that would be most relevant to you in class, the information that would help you answer key questions. In experimental psychology and neuroscience courses, for example, my teaching read typically involves jotting down key terms and examples, researchers' names, relevant brain areas, the methods and results of an experiment, and why a particular finding is worth knowing.

10. I know this isn't possible in some fields, such as nursing, medicine, and law, where there are board exams and many parts of the curriculum absolutely must be taught. I would hope that the later advice about using case studies to cover dreaded, unfamiliar topics in these kinds of courses is useful.

11. To be honest, I don't know how Codrina organized her course "Common Intellectual Experience" when she taught it. We discussed many aspects of her teaching experience but not the details of her course design. I'd like to think she'd enjoy this approach.

12. Barbara Gross Davis, *Tools for Teaching,* 2nd ed. (San Francisco: Jossey-Bass, 2009).

13. I thank Kevin Otos of Elon University for the first example. It's a standard clause that he includes in his syllabi.

14. Geoffrey R. Norman and Henk G. Schmidt, "The Psychological Basis of Problem-Based Learning," *Academic Medicine* 67, no. 9 (1992): 557–565. See also S. Mamede et al., "Innovations in Problem-Based

Learning: What Can We Learn from Recent Studies? *Advances in Health Sciences Education* 11, no. 4 (2006): 403–422.

15. Karl A. Smith, "Characteristics of an Effective Case Study." Paper presented at the Southeast Advanced Technology Education Consortium Case Study Forum, Nashville, Tenn., 1999.

16. John C. Bean, *Engaging Ideas: The Professor's Guide to Integrating Writing, Critical Thinking, and Active Learning in the Classroom* (San Francisco, Calif.: Jossey-Bass, 1996).

4. Teaching and Surviving

1. James Eison, "Confidence in the Classroom: Ten Maxims for New Teachers," *College Teaching* 38, no. 1 (1990): 21–25; quote p. 23.

2. John S. Cook, "Undergraduate Teaching Assistants: The Relationship between Credibility and Learning in the Basic Communication Course." Paper presented at the Eighty-Eighth Annual Meeting of National Communication Association, November 21–24, 2002, New Orleans, La. I should note that this research looked at the credibility of graduate teaching assistants (TAs) rather than that of full instructors, but for the majority of the classes included in this study, the teaching assistants were the primary instructors in the classroom. In some ways, it is helpful for our purposes that the study focuses on teaching assistants rather than on full professors. The students are more likely to come to the course knowing little about their TA, so that credibility would just be based on the TA's behaviors and communications, which is what we're interested in, whereas a full-time instructor is more likely to have a reputation that could enhance or reduce students' perception of credibility.

3. Philip Wankat, *The Effective Efficient Professor: Teaching, Scholarship and Service* (Boston, Mass.: Allyn and Bacon, 2002). See also Joan Middendorf and Alan Kalish, "The 'Change-up' in Lectures," *The National Teaching and Learning Forum* 5, no. 2 (1996): 1–5.

4. Jan H. F. Meyer and Ray Land, eds., *Overcoming Barriers to Student Understanding: Threshold Concepts and Troublesome Knowledge* (London: Routledge, 2006).

5. David R. Henderson, "Opportunity Cost," in *The Library of Econom-*

ics and Liberty: The Concise Encyclopedia of Economics: http://www.
econlib.org/library/Enc/OpportunityCost.html (accessed August 6,
2008).

6. Jenny Booth, "On the Mastery of Philosophical Concepts: Socratic
Discourse and the Unexpected 'Affect.'" In Meyer and Land, eds.,
Overcoming Barriers to Student Understanding, p. 176.

7. See Raymond S. Nickerson, "Confirmation Bias: A Ubiquitous Phenomenon in Many Guises," *Review of General Psychology* 2 (1998):
175–220, for a comprehensive overview of the research literature
on confirmation bias.

8. Lorraine Hope et al., "Understanding Pretrial Publicity: Predeci-
sional Distortion of Evidence by Mock Jurors," *Journal of Experimental Psychology: Applied* 10 (2004): 111–119.

9. Ibid.

10. Nalini Ambady and Robert Rosenthal, "Half a Minute: Predicting
Teacher Evaluations from Thin Slices of Nonverbal Behavior and
Physical Attractiveness," *Journal of Personality and Social Psychology*
64 (1993): 431–441.

11. Carolyn Lieberg, *Teaching Your First College Course: A Practical
Guide for New Faculty and Graduate Student Instructors* (Sterling, Va.:
Stylus Publishing, 2008).

12. Several scholarly articles document the ways students challenge
the authority of faculty of color. For example, see Christine A. Stanley et al., "A Case Study of the Teaching Experiences of African American Faculty at Two Predominantly White Research Universities," *Journal on Excellence in College Teaching* 14, no. 1 (2003):
151–178. See also Juanita M. McGowan, "Multicultural Teaching:
African-American Faculty Classroom Teaching Experiences in Predominantly White Colleges and Universities," *Multicultural Education* 8 (2000): 19–22.

13. McGowan, "Multicultural Teaching."

14. K. Denise Bane, "Free to Be the Me You See: Discovering the Joy of
Teaching," in *Faculty of Color: Teaching in Predominantly White Colleges and Universities,* ed. C. A. Stanley (Bolton, Mass.: Anker Publishing, 2006), pp. 54–67.

15. For example, see Katherine Grace Hendrix, "Student Perceptions of

the Influence of Race on Professor Credibility," *Journal of Black Studies* 28 (1998): 738–763. See also Katherine Grace Hendrix, "She Must Be Trippin': The Secret of Disrespect from Students of Color toward Faculty of Color," in *Neither White nor Male: Female Faculty of Color*, New Directions for Teaching and Learning 110, ed. Katherine Grace Hendrix (San Francisco, Calif.: Jossey-Bass, 2007), 85–96.

16. A word of caution, passed along by faculty of color who run into this dilemma: if you go by "Professor" and dress formally but work in a department where most of your white colleagues use first names and dress casually, you risk appearing aloof and conceited. It can be the catch-22 of formalities in the classroom: you'll achieve more respect, but students might find you less approachable.

17. Frank A. Bonner II, "The Temple of My Unfamiliar," in *Faculty of Color*, ed. Stanley, pp. 80–99.

18. James F. Bonilla, "'Are You Here to Move the Piano?' A Latino Reflects on Twenty Years in the Academy," in *Faculty of Color*, ed. Stanley, pp. 68–77.

19. Ken Bain, *What the Best College Teachers Do* (Cambridge, Mass.: Harvard University Press, 2004).

20. This phrase "discretion in disclosing the details" comes from a helpful book by Douglas Reimondo Robertson, *Making Time, Making Change: Avoiding Overload in College Teaching* (Stillwater, Okla.: New Forums Press, 2003), p. 27.

21. Amos Tversky and Daniel Kahneman, "The Framing of Decisions and the Psychology of Choice," *Science* 211 (1981): 453–458.

22. John R. Anderson, "Acquisition of a Cognitive Skill," *Psychological Review* 89 (1982): 369–406.

23. I've recently learned that this flavorology work is a published area of research: Alan Hirsch, *What Flavor Is Your Personality? Discover Who You Are by Looking at What You Eat* (Naperville, Ill.: Sourcebooks, 2001).

24. I have mixed feelings about this "concrete" analogy. I like it because we can probably all picture fresh concrete and the mess we'd make if we built something as complex as a house on top of it. But I hesitate to use it because teaching is not an act of simply pouring knowledge into students' waiting minds. Students have to actively

integrate the information to learn it. Every analogy falls apart at some point, and I just want to be sure you see the limits of this one.

25. I thank David Green, my colleague at Seattle University, and Bob Farmer, a colleague in the U.K., for this brilliant example of teaching a difficult concept.

26. Bain, *What the Best College Teachers Do*, p. 125.

27. Richard M. Felder and Linda K. Silverman present the argument that inductive reasoning is a more natural approach to learning. See Felder and Silverman, "Learning and Teaching Styles in Engineering Education," *Engineering Education* 78, no. 7 (1988): 674–681. On the issue of whether students want to begin with theory or observable evidence, a good resource is Charles C. Schroeder, "New Students—New Learning Styles," *Change* 25, no. 5 (1993): 21–27.

28. National Research Council, *How People Learn: Brain, Mind, Experience and School* (Washington, D.C.: National Academy of Sciences, 2000).

29. Allan Paivio, *Mental Representations: A Dual Coding Approach* (Oxford, England: Oxford University Press, 1986).

30. Although many books advise faculty to acknowledge the student in their reply, I found this clever and simple framework of first replying to the student and then answering the question in *Learning to Teach, Teaching to Learn: A Handbook for NUS Teachers*. NUS is the National University of Singapore, which has a fantastic online handbook for university teachers that I believe would have international appeal. It's well organized and offers specific examples of most instructional suggestions: http://www.cdtl.nus.edu.sg/Handbook/default.htm (accessed March 27, 2008).

31. Robert Boice, "Classroom Incivilities," *Research in Higher Education* 37 (1996): 453–486.

32. Robert Boice, *Advice for New Faculty Members: Nihil Nimus* (Needham Heights, Mass.: Allyn and Bacon, 2000).

33. See, for example, Dee Fink, *Creating Significant Learning Experiences: An Integrated Approach to Designing College Courses* (San Francisco, Calif.: Jossey-Bass, 2003).

34. I know one education instructor who simply brings blank 3 x 5" cards with her to every class so that she can make up an assessment

activity if she has extra time. Two other great sources for in-class assessment activities are John C. Bean, *Engaging Ideas: A Professor's Guide to Integrating Writing, Critical Thinking, and Active Learning in the Classroom* (San Francisco, Calif.: Jossey-Bass, 1996); and Elizabeth F. Barkley et al., *Classroom Assessment Techniques: A Handbook for College Faculty* (San Francisco, Calif.: Jossey-Bass, 2005).

35. Michael Prince, "Does Active Learning Work? A Review of the Research," *Journal of Engineering Education* 93, no. 3 (2004): 223–231.

5. Thinking in Class

1. Mark S. Cracolice, "How Students Learn: Knowledge Construction in College Chemistry Courses," in *Chemists' Guide to Effective Teaching,* ed. N. J. Pienta et al. (Upper Saddle River, N.J.: Pearson Prentice Hall, 2005), pp. 12–27. Cracolice shared the clever bowling analogy with me when he came to do a workshop on my campus. He often uses his bowling metaphor in talks about active learning, but he hasn't had a chance to write it up yet. To read more about his work on active learning in chemistry, see D. K. Gosser, V. S. Strozak, and Marc S. Cracolice, *Peer-Led Team Learning: General Chemistry* (Upper Saddle River, N.J.: Pearson Prentice Hall, 2006).

2. Michael Prince, "Does Active Learning Work? A Review of the Research," *Journal of Engineering Education* 93, no. 3 (2004): 223–231.

3. See, for example, Richard Hake, "Interactive-Engagement vs. Traditional Methods: A Six-Thousand-Student Survey of Mechanics Test Data for Introductory Physics Courses," *American Journal of Physics* 66, no. 1 (1998): 64; National Research Council, *How People Learn: Brain, Mind, Experience and School* (Washington, D.C.: National Academy of Sciences, 2000). For a review of both the strengths and the limitations of active learning, see J. Michael, "Where's the Evidence That Active Learning Works?" *Advances in Physiological Education* 30 (2006): 159–167.

4. Kathy L. Ruhl et al., "Using the Pause Procedure to Enhance Lecture Recall," *Teacher Education and Special Education* 10 (1987): 14–18.

5. Prince, "Does Active Learning Work?" p. 1.

6. I certainly haven't exhausted the possibilities. You can find other clever activities in John Bean, *Engaging Ideas: The Professor's Guide to Integrating Writing, Critical Thinking, and Active Learning in the Classroom* (San Francisco, Calif.: Jossey-Bass, 1996); or Elizabeth F. Barkley et al., *Collaborative Learning Techniques: A Handbook for College Faculty* (San Francisco, Calif.: Jossey-Bass, 2004).

7. Several of these activities were developed by other educators and are discussed extensively in the active learning literature; other activities are my own. Peer Instruction and ConcepTests were developed and popularized by Eric Mazur; see his book *Peer Instruction: A User's Manual* (Upper Saddle River, N.J.: Prentice Hall, 1996). The Think-Pair-Share activity was first introduced by Frank Lyman but has been popularized by many; see Frank Lyman, "The Responsive Classroom Discussion," in *Mainstreaming Digest*, ed. A. S. Anderson (College Park, Md.: University of Maryland College of Education, 1981). The Three-Step Interview and the Fishbowl have been popularized by faculty across many disciplines and are summarized nicely in Barkley et al., *Collaborative Learning Techniques.* Comparative Note-Taking is a less structured version of the Note-Taking Pairs in that same book. Category Building is a collaborative and hands-on adaptation of the Categorizing Grid described by Thomas Angelo and K. Patricia Cross in *Classroom Assessment Techniques,* 2nd ed. (San Francisco: Jossey-Bass, 1993).

8. If you are interested in longer activities, see Barkley et al., *Collaborative Learning Techniques.*

9. The claim that students' attention span occurs in waves of roughly fifteen to twenty minutes has been documented using different testing methods. Bonwell and Eison looked at note-taking behaviors: Charles C. Bonwell and James A. Eison, *Active Learning: Creating Excitement in the Classroom* (Washington, D.C.: George Washington University, 1991). Burns studied students' recall of a lecture after it was over and then analyzed the students' summaries in half-minute increments. Students remembered the most from the first five minutes, and then their recall dipped sharply approximately eighteen to twenty minutes into class. Ralph A. Burns, "Information Impact and Factors Affecting Recall." Paper presented at the Annual Na-

tional Conference on Teaching Excellence and Conference of Administrators, Austin, Tex., 1985 (ERIC Document Reproduction Service No. ED 258 639).

10. Christopher J. Lucas and John W. Murray, Jr., "Teaching: Lecture and Discussion," in *New Faculty: A Practical Guide for Academic Beginners* (New York: Palgrave, 2002), pp. 39–70.

11. James M. Lang, *On Course: A Week-by-Week Guide to Your First Semester of College Teaching* (Cambridge, Mass.: Harvard University Press, 2008).

12. See Mazur, *Peer Instruction.*

13. Derek Bruff has written a book on using clickers in the classroom titled *Teaching with Classroom Response Systems: Creating an Active Learning Environment* (San Francisco: Jossey-Bass, 2009).

14. For Mazur's own work, see Mazur, *Peer Instruction.* See also Bruff, *Teaching with Classroom Response Systems.*

15. I have found that it works best to explain the entire activity upfront, because once the interviews have begun, it can be hard to get students to quiet down enough to hear additional instructions.

16. Shannon F. Harp and Amy A. Maslich, "The Consequences of Including Seductive Details During Lecture," *Teaching of Psychology* 32, no. 2 (2005): 100–103.

17. I didn't want to distract you with this seductive detail in the text, so I reserved it for the dedicated reader. According to the National Oceanic and Atmospheric Administration data for 2001, lightning kills, on average, seventy-three people in the United States each year: http://www.publicaffairs.noaa.gov/grounders/lightningsafety.html (accessed April 13, 2009). Martin Uman reports that approximately 19 percent of people killed by lightning each year are golfers. Putting those numbers together, that's approximately 14 golfing deaths on average annually. Unfortunately, Uman reports these figures in a rather outdated book from 1971, so the number of lightning-related deaths on the golf course could be different today. Martin Uman, *Understanding Lightning* (Pittsburgh, Penn.: Bek Technical Publications, 1971).

18. Prince, "Does Active Learning Work?"

19. This line of reasoning is explored in more detail in John Biggs,

"What the Student Does: Teaching for Enhanced Learning," *Higher Education Research and Development* 18 (1999): 57–75.

6. Teaching Students You Don't Understand

1. Charles C. Schroeder, "New Students—New Learning Styles," *Change* 25, no. 5 (1993): 21–27.
2. Ibid. "Concrete active" and "abstract reflective" come from David Kolb, *The Learning Styles Inventory: Technical Manual* (Boston, Mass.: McBer).
3. These proportions most likely vary by academic discipline—some fields, such as philosophy, probably attract a lower percentage of people who prefer concrete active approaches to the material, and other fields, such as engineering, probably attract a higher percentage of these learners.
4. Schroeder, "New Students."
5. These numbers reflect the averages for comprehensive universities. Data are also available for large research institutions, liberal arts colleges, and community colleges. For the 1980s and 1990s data, see George D. Kuh, "How Are We Doing? Tracking the Quality of the Undergraduate Experience, 1960 to the Present," *Review of Higher Education* 22 (1999): 99–119. For the 2007 data, see the National Survey of Student Engagement, *Experiences That Matter: Enhancing Student Learning and Success* (Bloomington, Ind.: Center for Postsecondary Research, 2007). For the 2008 data, see the National Survey of Student Engagement, *Promoting Engagement for All Students: The Imperative to Look Within—2008 Results* (Bloomington, Ind.: Center for Postsecondary Research, 2008). Note that it's difficult to make an exact comparison of the numbers over a thirty-year span of time because the survey questions and instruments change, as do the classifications for institutions. Type of institution is also an important variable: the amount of time students spend on their homework differs widely. At small liberal arts colleges, for example, 85 percent of students put in at least sixteen hours a week on class preparation in the 1980s, but even that number has dropped dramatically, to only 45 percent in 2008.

6. National Survey of Student Engagement, *Experiences That Matter.*
7. National Survey of Student Engagement, *Promoting Engagement for All Students.*
8. Michael Planty et al., *The Condition of Education 2008* (Washington, D.C.: U.S. Department of Education, National Center for Education Statistics, NCES 2008–031), p. 68.
9. Susan Choy, *Findings from the Condition of Education 2002: Nontraditional Undergraduates* (Washington, D.C.: U.S. Department of Education, National Center for Education Statistics, NCES 2002–012), p. 4.
10. Thomas D. Snyder et al., *Digest of Education Statistics: 2008* (Washington, D.C.: U.S. Department of Education, National Center for Education Statistics, NCES 2009–020), table 271.
11. Ibid. To offer a frame of reference, the total number of students earning bachelor's degrees increased 30 percent between 1997 and 2007. Social sciences and history (excluding psychology) grew at basically the same rate, 31 percent, from 124,891 bachelor's degrees in 1997 to 164,183 in 2007. The physical sciences and science technologies have grown a dismal 8 percent, from 19,496 to 21,073. English language and literature departments did slightly better, graduating 13 percent more students in 2007 than in 1997, from 48,641 to 55,122. But none of these areas compare with business, which grew by 45 percent, or communications and journalism, which grew by 58 percent. Relatively new applied fields like "parks, leisure, and fitness studies" have almost doubled, growing from 14,246 students to 27,430. Maybe our students are out reading Thoreau in a cabin in the woods, but I suspect not.
12. Snyder et al., *Digest of Education Statistics: 2008,* table 271. The one exception to this statement is the growing number of students in the visual and performing arts. Between 1997 and 2007, there was a 70.0 percent increase in the number of students graduating with degrees in the arts. Of course, there were still roughly 85,000 students graduating with visual or performing arts degrees in 2007, compared with 327,000 with business degrees, but it's still an exciting trend.
13. Thomas D. Snyder et al., *Digest of Education Statistics: 2008,* table 226.

14. Planty et al., *The Condition of Education 2008,* table 26.2, p. 147.
15. *Open Doors 2007: Report on International Educational Exchange* (New York: Institute of International Education, 2007). Report highlights are available online: http://opendoors.iienetwork.org/.
16. Angela P. McGlynn, *Teaching Today's College Students: Widening the Circle of Success* (Madison, Wis.: Atwood Publishing, 2007). California, Texas, Florida, New York, and Illinois are the states with the most ethnically diverse student bodies.
17. Different sources have been credited with the phrase "helicopter parents." Foster W. Cline and Jim Fay are credited with introducing the term in a book on parenting techniques, but college administrators have applied the phrase in new ways to describe the interfering nature of parents on college and university campuses; see Cline and Fay, *Parenting with Love and Logic: Teaching Children Responsibility* (Colorado Springs, Colo.: Pinon Press, 1990). For use of the term in higher education, see Lydia Lum, "Handling Helicopter Parents," *Diverse: Issues in Higher Education* 23, no. 20 (2006): 40–43.
18. McGlynn, *Teaching Today's College Students,* p. 54.
19. Mary Ann Mason et al., "Why Graduate Students Reject the Fast Track," *Academe* 95 (January–February 2009). Available online: http://www.aaup.org/AAUP/pubsres/academe/2009/JF/Feat/maso.htm.
20. Ibid., p. 56.
21. Angela H. Becker and Sharon K. Calhoon, "What Introductory Psychology Students Attend to on a Course Syllabus," *Teaching of Psychology,* 26 (1999): 6–11.
22. P. Sven Arvidson, *Teaching NonMajors: Advice for Liberal Arts Professors* (Albany, N.Y.: State University of New York Press, 2008), p. 74. See also P. Sven Arvidson, "Students 101: How to Tailor Your Teaching to the Interrupter, the Hijacker, and Other Familiar Types," *Chronicle of Higher Education,* vol. 55, issue 6, October 3, 2008, p. A10.
23. If you've never taught freshmen before, I highly recommend that you take a quick look at a recent national report on first-year students, either the NSSE or the CIRP annual reports. Perhaps you

have teenagers at home or maybe you write for *Rolling Stone* magazine, but most college faculty are out of touch with the mindset of eighteen-year-olds. These reports won't tell you everything about your students, and thankfully so, but they will tell you a lot about students' work habits. The NSSE, for example, will tell you what students expect to do in their classes, which might help you decide what you can reasonably expect from them.

24. J. Hartley and A. Cameron, "Some Observations on the Efficiency of Lecturing," *Educational Review* 20 (1967): 30–37.

25. Sharon K. Suritsky, "Notetaking Difficulties and Approaches Reported by University Students with Learning Disabilities," *Journal of Postsecondary Education and Disability* 10, no. 1 (1992): 3–10.

26. Mary Huba and Jan Freed, *Learner-Centered Assessment on College Campuses: Shifting the Focus from Teaching to Learning* (Boston, Mass.: Allyn and Bacon, 2000); H. G. Andrade, "Teaching with Rubrics: The Good, the Bad, and the Ugly," *College Teaching* 53, no. 1 (2005): 27–30.

27. *Digest of Education Statistics: 2005* (Washington, D.C.: U.S. Department of Education, National Center for Education Statistics, NCES 2006–030), table 224.

28. Joshua Aronson et al., "Stereotype Threat and the Academic Underperformance of Minorities and Women," in J. K. Swim and C. Strangor, eds., *Prejudice: The Target's Perspective* (San Diego, Calif.: Academic Press, 1998), pp. 83–103; quote p. 85.

29. Ibid.

30. Beverly Daniel Tatum also makes this suggestion in her book *Can We Talk about Race?: And Other Conversations in an Era of School Resegregation* (Boston, Mass.: Beacon Press, 2007).

31. Just be careful not to complain that "no one comes to office hours." Instructors often make this comment, hoping, perhaps, that their lament will encourage some students to show up at their door. But if a student already perceives that there's a stigma attached to asking for help and he doesn't want to reinforce your negative stereotype, your innocuous comment just sealed the deal. That student won't single himself out as the only one needing help. It's much

better simply to say, "I'm eager and available to help you make sense of the material." I know one management instructor who fibs to his students and tells them how fantastic it is that he has so many students coming to his office hours, even when no one has bothered to come. After he makes that announcement, he always gets more students seeking help.

32. Geoffrey L. Cohen et al., "The Mentor's Dilemma: Providing Critical Feedback across the Racial Divide," *Personality and Social Psychology Bulletin* 25, no. 10 (1999): 1302–1318. To learn more about stereotype threat and how to reduce it, see http://reducingstereotypethreat.org (accessed December 31, 2008).

33. As mentioned earlier, Derek Bruff is more than just an occasional user of clickers; he has interviewed faculty across the country about their innovative use of clickers for his book *Teaching with Classroom Response Systems: Creating an Active Learning Environment* (San Francisco, Calif.: Jossey-Bass, 2009).

7. Getting Better

1. This chapter does *not* address decisions about graded assessments of students' learning—I don't know whether it's better to give exams or papers, individual or group projects when you're teaching outside of your expertise. Those decisions are driven more by the big questions that you developed in Chapter 3 and by what you're hoping students will be able to do at the end of the course than by the fact that you're teaching content that's unfamiliar. If you're looking for advice on how to pick the right kind of graded assignment based on your learning objectives and your teaching methods, try Grant Wiggins and Jay McTighe, *Understanding by Design* (Upper Saddle River, N.J.: Prentice-Hall, 2001). See also Dee Fink, *Creating Significant Learning Experiences* (San Francisco, Calif.: Jossey-Bass, 2003).

2. National Research Council, *How People Learn: Brain, Mind, Experience and School* (Washington, D.C.: National Academy of Sciences, 2000).

3. Karin J. Spencer and Liora Pedhazur Schmelkin, "Student Perspectives on Teaching and Its Evaluation," *Assessment and Evaluation in Higher Education* 27 (2002): 397–409. Research shows that students have little confidence that faculty and administrators pay attention to the feedback they provide on the final course evaluations, so it may be enlightening for students when an instructor responds to their written feedback.

4. Thomas A. Angelo and K. Patricia Cross, *Classroom Assessment Techniques: A Handbook for College Teachers,* 2nd ed. (San Francisco, Calif.: Jossey-Bass, 1993).

5. Chester E. Finn, "Popular Myths about 'No Child Left Behind,'" *Washington Post,* March 30, 2008, p. B-03.

6. For data on the impact of midterm evaluations, see Jesse Overall and Herbert W. Marsh, "Midterm Feedback from Students: Its Relationship to Instructional Improvement and Students' Cognitive and Affective Outcomes," *Journal of Educational Psychology* 71 (1979): 856–865. For data ranking different factors and their correlations with end-of-course evaluations, see Kenneth A. Feldman, "Identifying Exemplary Teachers and Teaching: Evidence from Student Ratings," in Raymond P. Perry and John C. Smart, eds., *Effective Teaching in Higher Education: Research and Practice* (Bronx, N.Y.: Agathon Press, 1997), pp. 368–395.

7. As a neuroscientist, I cringe at the title of the book I'm about to recommend, but if you're looking for some practical advice to give students about strategic and efficient reading strategies, a good source is Tony Buzan's *Use Both Sides of Your Brain* (New York: Plume, 1991). He has a chapter titled "Reading Faster and More Efficiently." Buzan is not writing for an academic audience, and his is not the kind of advice you'd want to give students in a literature or poetry class where you might want them to linger on each word. But if you're teaching in the sciences or social sciences and you find that students are not getting through the readings, you might find some good suggestions to share with your class. And please be reassured that yes, you do use both sides of your brain on most tasks, without any added effort on your part.

8. Advice for Administrators

1. I've changed the professor's identifying information to protect people involved in his difficult situation.

2. Laura L. B. Barnes et al., "Effects of Job-Related Stress on Faculty Intention to Leave Academia," *Research in Higher Education* 39, no. 4 (1998): 457–469.

3. Ibid., quote p. 462. Their survey sample was impressive: they surveyed over 3,000 faculty across 306 schools, spanning institutions in all nine Carnegie classifications (from two-year colleges to Research 1 universities), so their findings generalize to a wide variety of institutions. All the faculty were on the tenure-track, however, so we cannot use these findings to make claims about why adjunct or contract faculty leave their institutions.

4. Susan A. Ambrose et al., "A Qualitative Method for Assessing Faculty Satisfaction," *Research in Higher Education* 46, no. 7 (2005): 803–830. For more on the importance of the department chair in retaining faculty, see R. W. Neinhuis, "Satisfied Faculty and Involved Chairpersons: Keys to Faculty Retention." Paper presented at the Nineteenth Annual Meeting of the Association for the Study of Higher Education, November 10–13, 1994, Tuscon, Ariz.

5. See Ambrose et al., "A Qualitative Method"; and Barnes et al., "Effects of Job-Related Stress." Many studies show that lack of collegiality spurs faculty to leave, and that the presence of collegiality can mitigate other frustrations, such as being overworked or underpaid. To see how junior faculty are particularly sensitive to the presence or absence of collegiality, see James L. Turner and Robert Boice, "Starting at the Beginning: The Concerns and Needs of New Faculty," in J. Kurfiss et al., eds., *To Improve the Academy*, vol. 6: *Resources for Faculty, Instructional, and Organizational Development* (Stillwater, Okla.: New Forums Press, 1987), pp. 41–47.

6. Henry L. Allen, "Faculty Workload and Productivity in the 1990's: Preliminary Findings," *The NEA 1996 Almanac of Higher Education:* 21–34. For research on changes in state policies, see J. S. Fairweather and A. L. Beach, "Variations in Faculty Work at Research

Universities: Implications for State and Institutional Policy," *Review of Higher Education* 26, no. 1 (2002): 97–115. For information on how faculty workload relates to faculty satisfaction, see Barnes et al., "Effects of Job-Related Stress"; and C. L. Comm and D. F. X. Mathaisel, "A Case Study of the Implications of Faculty Workload and Compensation for Improving Academic Quality," *International Journal of Educational Management* 17, no. 5 (2003): 200–210.

7. Christine Stanley, ed., *Faculty of Color Teaching in Predominantly White Colleges and Universities* (Bolton, Mass.: Anker Publishing, 2006).

8. I was surprised to find that many schools, even large research institutions, indicate that factors such as class size should be taken into account when a committee reviews a tenure candidate's teaching effectiveness. A quick web search revealed that institutions such as University of Florida, University of Washington, Wichita State, and University of South Carolina all have specific language in their criteria for promotion and tenure indicating that class size should be taken into account when evaluating the individual's contribution to teaching.

9. Therese A. Huston et al., "Expanding the Discussion of Faculty Vitality to Include Productive but Disengaged Senior Faculty," *Journal of Higher Education* 78, no. 5 (2007): 493–522.

10. The Beloit College "Mindset List" is updated each fall for each new freshman class. The most recent version can be found on the school's website: http://www.beloit.edu/mindset/ (accessed July 21, 2008).

11. Milton Cox, the director of the Center for the Enhancement of Learning and Teaching at Miami University, has a well-organized and resource-laden website for developing faculty learning communities: http://www.units.muohio.edu (accessed August 24, 2008).

Acknowledgments

Although I'm not sure how I'll be remembered, I secretly hope it might be for once helping people I'd never met. Most of the folks I'm about to thank are people who know me well, but some know me only by email. A patient few know me best through my clunky use of a digital recorder. Total strangers have encouraged me, given me great ideas, or simply repeated my words back to me. I'm humbled by how much people can give, even people who don't know if I take coffee or tea.

There's a fabulous team of people at Harvard University Press who write much better than I do. Elizabeth Knoll was my acquisitions editor, which means that she slogged through the early, uncut chapters and saw beyond what I had written to what I could potentially write. I don't know how she developed that talent, but I'm so glad she did. She asked hard questions, lots of them, but the one that inspired me most was, "How will readers know a real person wrote this book?" Christine Thorsteinsson was my manuscript editor, and I now believe there is a special place in heaven for editors. She answered every question patiently, told me my instincts were good when I was heading in the right direction, and quietly rewrote something when I wasn't. Sheila Barrett-Smith, Michael Higgins, and Rose Ann Miller have been turning the publicity crank, finding clever ways to make what I have to say topical and available in a bookstore near you.

If this book reflects some part of your classroom experience, you can thank all the people who sat down and revealed what it's like to teach outside of their expertise. These faculty and administrators offered insightful answers and nudged me toward better questions: John Bean, Michael Bérubé, Derek Bruff, Erin Buzuvis, Maria Ferreyra, Mike Flynn, Eugene Fram, Linda Gabriel, Allan Greer, Sylvia Hurtado, Ron Krabill, Junlei Li, Eric Mazur, Lydia McAllister, Andrew Mills, Kevin Otos, Parker Palmer, Melissa Pasquinelli, Codrina Popescu, Jill Ramsfield, Dan Simons, Mary Deane Sorcinelli, Christine Stanley, Myra Strober, Beverly Daniel Tatum, and Barb Tewksbury. I also want to thank the people whose stories are told but whose real names aren't complicating things. They are simply captured here as Zach, Andy, Susan, Cheryl, Penelope, and Akira. I'm especially grateful for Akira's willingness to share that bleak first year. I hope it saves a career or two.

Many friends and colleagues closer to home helped me as well. Sven Arvidson advised me on how to woo a publisher and write a proposal. David Green generously read early drafts and asked me, almost daily, how the book was coming along. I'm lucky that Julie Stein did some brilliant copy-editing and that Bryce Hughes diligently transcribed a dozen interviews. Janelle Choi also transcribed her fair share, but more important, she asked me questions as if I were a real writer. Anna Suessbrick listened to all the ups and downs as the book came together. I'm indebted to Jacquelyn Miller for giving me time to write and for modeling work-life balance, something few of us in the academy achieve. Peter Felten, bless his heart, said, "Hey, let me introduce you to a publisher," and was the first to invite me to campus to give a talk.

Although we write alone at the keyboard, we're fueled or depleted by our communities. Luckily, I was fueled by my women's leadership group and by my clearness committee. These two groups have been bookends to the writing process, one encouraging me at the very beginning and the other holding me steady at the very end.

My friends have kept me going. I thank Mary-Antoinette Smith, whose eyes glisten when I talk about writing, and Pascal Sahuc, who asks the exciting questions about royalties and book tours. Meghan and Chad Lyle made me countless dinners. I hold dear the Li family—Junlei for that car ride to the Strip District, when he told me all the reasons teachers need this book, and Karen, who makes me feel like the world's most cherished guest. I thank Maria Farmer, who meets me at Trader Joe's and steers me back onto the path of sanity and bakes me cookies. And fortunately, there's Linda Selig, my friend of twenty-six years (and counting), who remembers what's important and listens to the rest anyway.

I am intensely aware of how my family shaped this book and my ability to write it. I am thankful for my dad, Robert Huston, who died abruptly and so unfairly while I was writing Chapter 4. He had always wanted to be a published writer himself. I hope he's in a better place and that he's smiling for me. My sister, Jamie Adaway, shares my every writing success with her ninth-grade English class. She's the true teacher in our family, and she has faith and courage where most of us kick around self-pity and doubt. And then there's my mom, who cheered me on every time I considered a new major in college. She taught me to love vacation, share what I'm eating, and sit next to the lonely person on the bus. She thought I'd become a college president someday, but I hope she'll settle for a writer instead.

Most of all, I want to thank Jonathan Foster, my husband and dream come true. He created time and space for writing in our little home; he learned to make fabulous lasagna and watch movies with headphones. If he could have any three wishes, and I mean any three lantern-rubbed wishes, one would probably be that I do more yoga. And as he will tell you, the right answer is tea.

Index